KB047268

영어 회화의
결정적
구동사들

Luke Kim 김상혁

UCLA Economics 학사
Oxford Seminars TESOL

(현) 룩룩잉글리쉬 대표 ┃ (현) 강남 파고다 어학원 청취/스피킹 강사

저서 〈영어 회화의 결정적 패턴들〉〈영어 회화의 결정적 상황들〉(사람in), 〈매일 쓰는 미국 영어 회화 100〉(넥서스), 〈비즈니스 영어 실수 고침 사전〉(길벗이지톡), 〈중학독서평설(2023〜) 월간지〉(지학사)

원어민 검수 **Sahara Meyer**

Bachelor of Science, Missouri State University
Juris Doctorate, Saint Louis University

(현) 룩룩잉글리쉬 자문위원 ┃ (현) Traill International School 원어민교사
(전) Cambridge University Press 에디터

영어 회화의 결정적 구동사들

지은이 룩룩잉글리쉬
초판 1쇄 발행 2023년 5월 10일
초판 3쇄 발행 2024년 1월 17일

발행인 박효상   **편집장** 김현   **기획 · 편집** 장경희, 김효정, 권순범   **디자인** 임정현
마케팅 이태호, 이전희   **관리** 김태옥

기획 · 편집 진행 김현
교정 · 교열 전명희
본문 · 표지디자인 고희선

종이 월드페이퍼   **인쇄 · 제본** 예림인쇄 · 바인딩

출판등록 제10-1835호   **발행처** 사람in   **주소** 04034 서울시 마포구 양화로 11길 14-10 (서교동) 3F
전화 02) 338-3555(代)   **팩스** 02) 338-3545   **E-mail** saramin@netsgo.com
Website www.saramin.com

책값은 뒤표지에 있습니다.
파본은 바꾸어 드립니다.

ISBN
978-89-6049-807-5 14740
978-89-6049-783-2 세트

우아한 지적만보, 기민한 실사구시 사람in

영어 회화의
결정적
구동사들

POUR DOWN

(비가) 마구 쏟아지다, 퍼붓다

BEND
DOWN

VEG OUT

느긋하게 쉬다

Top
off

가득 찰 때까지 추가하다

이미지로 익히는 구동사! 돌아서도 잊지 않는다!

영어 회화에서 절대 안 빠지고 영어 문장에서 반드시 나오는 최고의 학습 가성비, 영어 구동사

룩룩잉글리쉬 저
Sahara Meyer 감수

사람in

돌아서면 잊어 버리는 구동사도
룩룩잉글리쉬와 함께하면 오래 갑니다!

영어 팝송을 한번 들어 보세요. 미드를 한번 보세요.
그리고 좋아하는 영어 유튜브 영상들을 보세요. 상황이 된다면
원어민 친구와 대화를 해 보세요. 원어민이 얼마나 구동사를
즐겨 사용하는지 바로 확인 가능할 겁니다.
사실 이 책을 보는 분들의 목적은 영어를 자유롭게 듣고,
말하고자 하는 것일 거예요. 영어교육과 관련된 일들을 20년 가까이
해 오면서, 이디엄, 슬랭 관련 표현, 발음, 패턴, 어법 등 여러 다양한
영어책을 봐 왔지만, 신기한 것은 원어민들이 가장 즐겨 쓰는
구동사 관련 책들은 정작 따분하게 전치사/부사 중심으로 확장하고,
그것과 관련한 예문 중심으로 설명된 것들이 대부분입니다.
문제는 이렇게 공부하면 실제 상황에 응용하는 것이 쉽지가 않고,
금방 질리기 마련이라는 것입니다. 그래서 '질리지 않고, 재미있게
공부할 수 있고, 동시에 오랫동안 기억에 남으면서, 실제 생활에
사용하고, 원어민과 대화를 해도 굉장히 자연스러운 그런
구동사 책을 만들면 되겠다'라는 생각이 들었습니다.
제게는 항상 지키는 철칙이 있습니다. 영어를 잘하려면,
영어를 공부하려 하지 말고, 콘텐츠를 접하면서 그걸 영어로 한다,
그리고 그 콘텐츠는 정말 실제 원어민들이 보고, 듣고, 말하는 것이고,
즐길 수 있고, 배웠을 때 뿌듯한 것이어야 한다입니다.
이번 책도 그 원칙을 철저하게 지켰고요. 다른 구동사 책과 차별되는
부분이라고 자신 있게 말씀드리는 부분은 다음과 같습니다.

① 모든 대화가 주제별로, 상황별로 구성되어 있습니다.

② 현실적인 대화를 중심으로 제가 직접 선별한 영어 원어민과 작업했습니다.

③ 대화의 상황을 상상하면서 읽고, 말하고, 따라 하다 보면 자연스럽게 원어민들이 가장 많이 사용하는 구동사를 익힐 수 있습니다.

④ 시중에 있는 거의 대부분의 구동사 책들과 온라인에 있는 구동사 관련 콘텐츠들을 분석해서, 많은 원어민과 빈도를 확인하는 과정을 거쳤습니다.

⑤ 저와 원어민이 계속 관련 콘텐츠를 제작해서 공부할 수 있게 도와드리겠습니다.

가장 자연스럽고 현실적인 대화를 만들기 위해서 몇 번을 수정하면서 나온 책입니다. 애착이 가는 책인 만큼 독자분들이 즐겁게 보면서, 정말 자연스러운 영어를 듣고 말하는 데 큰 도움이 되길 바랍니다. 적어도 원어민들이 많이 사용하는 구동사 99%를 커버했다고 자부하니, 믿고 따라 오면 될 것 같아요.
또 구동사 동영상도 작업하고 있으니 아래 QR코드를 찍으면 동영상 강의를 볼 수가 있습니다.

 궁금한 점을 제가 운영하는 블로그, 유튜브 등으로 알려 주시면 언제든지 친절하게 답변 드리겠습니다. 여러분의 건투를 빕니다.

블로그   blog.naver.com/koreangenie
유튜브   youtube.com/looklookenglish
카톡 ID talk2canadians
Email   looklookenglish@gmail.com

룩룩 잉글리쉬

Luke

Phrasal verbs are so commonly used by native English speakers, that without learning them, students will be completely lost in a real conversation.
I have spent over half a decade teaching English to students from all across the globe, and, I have to say, the English language can be a challenge. As a language learner myself, I can relate to my readers on just how difficult it can be to understand the nuances of another language.
Learning phrasal verbs is no exception. Phrasal verbs can be complicated and confusing, but they are absolutely necessary to know. With my help, readers will learn the ways in which phrasal verbs are used correctly and, in turn, will be more confident and natural-sounding when they use them in English conversations.

구동사는 원어민들이 정말 밥 먹듯이 사용하기에, 제대로 모르면 소통하는 데 큰 문제가 생길 수밖에 없습니다. 저는 전 세계 학생들에게 영어를 가르치면서 5년 넘는 시간을 보냈습니다. 저도 인정하지만 영어는 어려운 문제이자 도전이 될 수 있습니다. 저 역시 언어 학습자로서, 다른 언어의 뉘앙스를 이해하는 것이 얼마나 어려운지 공감합니다. 구동사를 배우는 것도 예외는 아니죠. 구동사는 복잡하고 혼란스러울 수 있지만 반드시 알아야 합니다. 이 책을 통해서, 여러분들은 구동사를 올바르게 쓰는 법과 그 결과, 앞으로 실제 원어민과의 대화에서 자연스럽고, 자신 있게 대화하게 될 거예요.

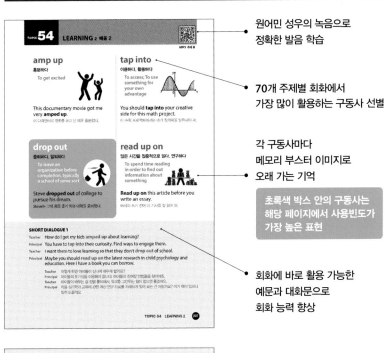

원어민 성우의 녹음으로
정확한 발음 학습

70개 주제별 회화에서
가장 많이 활용하는 구동사 선별

각 구동사마다
메모리 부스터 이미지로
오래 가는 기억

> 초록색 박스 안의 구동사는
> 해당 페이지에서 사용빈도가
> 가장 높은 표현

회화에 바로 활용 가능한
예문과 대화문으로
회화 능력 향상

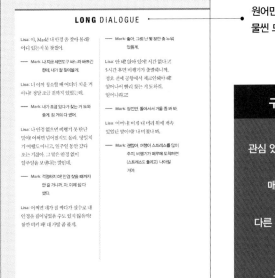

원어민의 감정과 뉘앙스가
물씬 드러나는 long dialogue

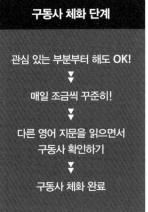

구동사 체화 단계

관심 있는 부분부터 해도 OK!

매일 조금씩 꾸준히!

다른 영어 지문을 읽으면서
구동사 확인하기

구동사 체화 완료

CHAPTER 4

CHAPTER 5

CHAPTER 6

CHAPTER 7

CHAPTER 8

CHAPTER

1

PHRASAL VERBS

look at
~을 보다

To move eyes to see someone or something

I **looked at** the flowers.
난 꽃을 보았다.

look for
~을 찾다

To search

Can you help me **look for** my coat?
내 코트 찾는 것 좀 도와줄수 있어?

listen up
잘 듣다

To listen for something

Listen up for the oven timer, okay?
오븐 타이머 소리 잘 들어. 알았지?

see through
~을 꿰뚫어 보다

To gaze past or through something

We couldn't **see through** the fog.
우리는 안개 너머를 볼 수가 없었다.

SHORT DIALOGUE 1

Max   Can you help me **look for** my dog, Sarah? He chased a cat, and I can't find him.
Sarah Where did you see him last? Wait, **listen up!** I think I hear him barking.
Max   I hear him, too. **Look at** those trees over there! He is right behind the trees.
Sarah Yeah, I can **see through** the trees. He's coming.

Max   Sarah, 내 강아지 찾는 것 도와줄 수 있어? 고양이를 쫓아갔는데, 못 찾겠어.
Sarah 마지막으로 어디서 봤어? 잠깐, 잘 들어 봐! 지금 짖고 있는 것 같은데.
Max   나도 들려. 저기 나무들 좀 봐! 나무 바로 뒤에 있네.
Sarah 응, 저기 나무들 사이로 보여. 저기 오네.

look around

둘러서 찾아 보다

To search an area

Can you **look around** for my watch?
내 시계 좀 찾아줄래?

die down

(소리 등이) 약해지다,
잦아들다

To gradually
become less
strong;
To gradually become weak

When is the thunder going to **die down**?
언제 천둥소리가 잦아들까?

look over

~을 살펴보다, 검토하다

To read or study
something,
especially documents

Look over this contract before you
sign it.
서명하기 전에 이 계약서를 잘 살펴봐.

shut out

(소리를) 차단하다

To ignore a sound
or noise

These walls are thick enough to
shut out outside sounds.
이 벽들은 밖의 소음이 안 들릴 정도로 두껍다.

SHORT DIALOGUE 2

Keira   Oh my god! There are so many people in this cafe. **Look around** for an open table.

John   It's so loud in here. I hope that all this noise will **die down** soon.

Keira   I wanted to show you my new song, but we'll wait. Can you **look over** the lyrics?

John   I want to hear it. Play me the song, and I'll try to **shut out** the noise.

Keira   아… 정말! 카페에 사람들 진짜 많네. 빈자리가 있는지 한번 둘러봐.

John   여기 너무 시끄럽다. 좀 조용해지면 좋겠어.

Keira   너한테 내가 작곡한 새로운 곡을 들려 주려고 했는데, 기다려야겠다. 가사 좀 볼래?

John   나 듣고 싶어. 노래 좀 틀어 봐. 집중해서 들어 볼게. (* 주변 소리를 차단하고 듣는 상황)

look out for

~을 조심히 살피다

To pay attention to
what is happening
around you so that you
will notice a particular
person or thing

You should **look out for** pickpockets
here.

여기서는 소매치기 조심해야 해.

listen in (on)

엿듣다

To secretly listen to;
To overhear

How do you know where I was? Did
you **listen in on** my phone calls?

너 내가 어디 있었는지 어떻게 알아? 내 전화 통화
엿들은 거야?

hear out

말을 끝까지 듣다

To listen to what
someone has to say

Hear out what your parents have to
say.

부모님이 말씀하시는 것 끝까지 잘 들어.

hear about

~에 관해서 (소식을) 듣다

To get to know some
information

Did you **hear about** the new
manager we are getting on
Monday?

월요일에 오는 새 매니저에 대해 들었어?

SHORT DIALOGUE 3

Sophia　　Hey, Elijah. **Look out for** Kate. She said that she wanted to talk to you.

Elijah　　I know. I was **listening in on** your conversation with her. I know that she's mad
at me.

Sophia　　Then you should talk to her. She's your friend. You should try to **hear** her **out**.

Elijah　　She's always mad at me about something stupid. Honestly, I don't want to **hear
about** it.

　　　Sophia　　Elijah! Kate 조심해! 걔가 너랑 이야기하고 싶댔어.
　　　Elijah　　알고 있어. 네가 Kate랑 대화하는 거 엿들었거든. 나도 걔가 나한테 화난 거 알아.
　　　Sophia　　그럼 Kate한테 가서 말해 봐. 네 친구잖아. 그 애가 무슨 말을 하는지 끝까지 들어 봐야지.
　　　Elijah　　걘 항상 별것 아닌 일로 나한테 화낸단 말야. 솔직히 걔가 하려는 말 별로 듣고 싶지도 않아.

TOPIC 2 — BODY ACTION AND MOVEMENT
신체 동작과 움직임

MP3 **002**

sit up
똑바로 앉다

To move from a lying or slouching to a sitting position

Amy **sat up** and yawned.
Amy는 똑바로 앉아서 하품을 했다.

pick up
집다, 들어 올리다

To take hold of and lift or move someone or something

I dropped my phone. Can you **pick it up** for me?
내 전화기를 떨어뜨렸네. 그것 좀 주워 줄래?

fall over
넘어지다

To lose balance and collapse to the ground

I tripped on a branch and **fell over**.
난 나뭇가지에 걸려서 넘어졌다.

put away
치우다(제자리에 갖다 놓다)

To place something where it belongs

Put away the dishes after dinner.
저녁 먹고 나서 그릇 치워.

SHORT DIALOGUE 1

Mom   Jeremy! Can you **sit up**, please? I want to talk to you about your room.

Jeremy What now?

Mom   I asked you yesterday to **pick up** all your toys off the floor. I can't even walk through your room without **falling over**.

Jeremy Fine. I'll **put away** my toys, but then can I have a snack?

> Mom   Jeremy! 좀 똑바로 앉을래? 네 방에 대해서 얘기 좀 하자.
> Jeremy 또 뭔데요?
> Mom   내가 어제 방바닥에 있는 장난감 다 집어서 치우라고 했지. 넘어지지 않고는 도대체 네 방을 걸어 다닐 수가 없잖아.
> Jeremy 알았어요. 장난감 치울게요. 그런데 그럼 간식 먹을 수 있는 거죠?

clean up

정리하다, 치우다

To tidy up;
To organize

Clean up your room before your parents come in!

너희 부모님 오시기 전에 네 방 치워!

lie down

눕다

To move one's body into a flat position

Lie down on the bed if your head hurts.

머리가 아프면 침대에 누워 있어.

move over

(자리를 만들기 위해) 몸을 움직이다

To make room for someone or something

Move over, and let me sit down on this bench.

나도 이 벤치에 앉게 옆으로 좀 가 봐.

get up

일어나다

To leave a resting position or stand up

Get up, and go to work!

일어나, 일 나가야지!

SHORT DIALOGUE 2

Kurt   Wow! Our house looks great! I'm glad we spent the day **cleaning up**.

Amy   Yeah! I'm exhausted! Do you want to **lie down** on the couch with me?

Kurt   I would love to! **Move over** a little so I have some room.

Amy   I think I might sleep here. I don't want to **get up**.

Kurt   왜! 우리 집 정말 훤해 보이는데! 하루 종일 청소한 보람이 있네.

Amy   그러게! 나 완전 피곤해! 자기도 나랑 같이 소파에 누울래?

Kurt   그래, 좋지! 나도 좀 눕게 옆으로 좀 가 봐.

Amy   나 그냥 여기서 잘까 봐. 일어나기 싫다.

turn around

(몸을) 돌리다, 돌다

To rotate 180 degrees
or rotate one's body to
face behind
oneself

Turn around and look at that
mirror.

돌아서서 거울을 보세요.

mess up

망치다

To make a mess of;
To ruin; To destroy

I'm sorry I **messed up** your drawing.

네 그림을 망쳐서 미안해.

bend down

몸을 굽히다

To curve downward

I **bent down** to pick up the cat.

난 고양이를 들어올리려고 허리를 굽혔다.

stand up

서다

To rise to one's feet

The crowd **stood up** and clapped.

사람들은 일어서서 박수를 쳤다

SHORT DIALOGUE 3

Greg   Are you crying? **Turn around** and let me see your face.

Emma   Yes, I was. My back really hurts. I think I **messed** it **up**.

Greg   It's probably from sitting all day. Here, **bend down** and touch your toes, wait
three seconds then **stand up**. It'll help.

Emma   That does help! Thanks!

> Greg   너 우니? 돌아봐 봐. 얼굴 좀 보게.
> Emma   응. 울었어. 허리가 너무 아파. 아무래도 허리를 완전히 망가뜨렸나 봐.
> Greg   아마 하루 종일 앉아 있어서 그럴 거야. 자, 허리를 굽혀서 손을 발끝에 대고, 3초 기다렸다가 일어나
> 봐 . 도움이 될 거야.
> Emma   오. 괜찮은데! 고마워!

pack up

(여행 가게) 짐을 싸다

To fill a bag or suitcase, especially for a trip

Pack up your bags and leave!

가방 싸서 떠나!

check in

(호텔·공항에) 체크인하다

To register at a hotel or airport

We need to **check in** to the hotel.

우리 호텔에 체크인해야 해.

check out

(호텔에서) 체크아웃하다

To finalize a stay at a hotel and leave

It's already 11. We have to **check out** of the hotel immediately.

벌써 11시야. 우리 빨리 호텔 체크아웃 해야 해.

take off

이륙하다, 뜨다

To take a flight

When the plane **takes off**, I'm gonna take a nap.

비행기가 이륙하면, 난 낮잠 잘 거야.

SHORT DIALOGUE 1

Tom   **Pack up** your bag quickly! We need to leave soon!

Nelle   Don't rush me! We can **check in** to the hotel any time before midnight tonight.

Tom   Our flight **takes off** at 9 AM tomorrow! We need a full night's sleep.

Nelle   How early do we have to leave? What time do we need to **check out** of the hotel in the morning?

Tom   가방 좀 빨리 싸! 우리 곧 출발해야 해!

Nelle   재촉 좀 하지 마! 오늘 밤 자정 전에만 호텔 체크인 하면 된다니까.

Tom   비행기가 내일 아침 9시에 이륙해. 그러니 (일찍 체크인해서) 푹 자야 한다고.

Nelle   얼마나 빨리 떠나야 하는데? 아침 몇 시에 호텔에서 체크아웃해야 하는 거야?

touch down

(비행기가) 착륙하다

To land at
a destination,
especially
regarding planes

Text me when the plane **touches down** in LA.

비행기가 LA에 착륙하면 나에게 문자 줘.

get away

휴가 가다

To take
a vacation

I'm so stressed at work. I need to **get away**.

직장에서 엄청 스트레스 받아. 난 휴가가 필요해.

get in

도착하다

To arrive at a
destination

The train **got in** late.

기차가 연착됐다.

get off

(교통수단에서) 내리다

To leave a bus,
plane, or train

Let's **get off** at the next station.

다음 정거장에서 내리자.

SHORT DIALOGUE 2

Tim   When does our flight **touch down** in Cincinnati tomorrow? I want to **get off** that plane and get home as fast as possible.

Susan   It lands at four. It has been nice to **get away** from work, but I miss our bed.

Tim   What? We're **getting in** that late?!

Susan   Yeah. Even though we leave Denver at 10:00, we have a layover in Atlanta.

> **Tim**   우리 비행기가 신시내티에 내일 언제 도착하지? 비행기 내려서 최대한 빨리 집에 가고 싶어.
> **Susan**   4시에 도착해. 일 안 하고 휴가 가는 것도 좋았는데, 우리 침대가 그립다.
> **Tim**   뭐라고? 그렇게 늦게 도착한다고?!
> **Susan**   응. 덴버에서 10시에 출발하기는 하는데, 애틀랜타를 경유하거든.

drop off

(~을 장소에) 내려 주다

To stop and let
somebody get
out of a car

Drop me **off** at the bus station,
please.
버스 정류장에서 저 내려 주세요.

get on

(교통수단에) 타다

To go onto
a bus, train,
aircraft, or
boat

I **got on** the plane to LA to visit my
friend.
난 친구를 만나러 LA로 가는 비행기를 탔다.

head out

떠나다

To leave
or depart

Come on, it's time we **head out** if
we want to make our flight.
서둘러! 비행기 타려면 지금 우리 떠나야 해.

see off

배웅하다

To accompany
someone to a train
platform, airport, or
dock

I'll **see** you **off** to the train station.
기차역까지 내가 너 배웅해 줄게.

SHORT DIALOGUE 3

Chloe   I'll be out of town for a week starting tomorrow. Can you **drop** me **off** at the
airport on the way to work?

Michael   No problem. When are you **getting on** the plane?

Chloe   The departure time is 11:30 AM.

Michael   Then let's **head out** around 8:15. Actually, I'm off tomorrow so I can **see** you **off**
at the airport.

Chloe   나 내일부터 일주일 동안 출장이야. 출근하는 길에 나 좀 공항에 내려 줄래?
Michael   물론이지. 언제 비행기 타는데?
Chloe   출발 시간이 오전 11시 30분이야.
Michael   그럼 8시 15분쯤 출발하자. 실은 나 내일 휴무라서 공항에서 너 배웅할 수 있어.

LOOK **A**T

LOOK FOR

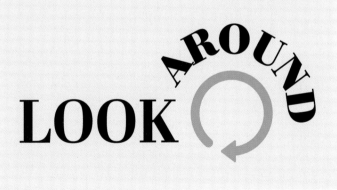

LOOK AROUND

LONG DIALOGUE

Lisa: 야, Mark! 내 안경 좀 찾아 볼래? 어디 있는지 못 찾겠어.

— Mark: 나 지금 세면도구 싸느라 바쁘긴 한데, 내가 잘 찾아볼게.

Lisa: 너 아까 청소할 때 어디다 치운 거 아냐? 정말 조금 전까지 있었는데.

— Mark: 내가 조금 있다가 찾는 거 도와 줄게. 짐 거의 다 썼어.

Lisa: 나 안경 없으면 비행기 못 탄단 말야! 어쩌면 넘어질지도 몰라. 당일치 기 여행도 아니고, 일주일 동안 갔다 오는 거잖아. 그 말은 안경 없이 일주일을 보낸다는 말인데.

— Mark: 걱정하지 매! 안경 찾을 때까지 안 갈 거니까. 자, 이제 짐 다 썼다.

Lisa: 어쩌면 네가 짐 싸다가 실수로 내 안경을 집어넣었을 수도 있지 않을까? 잠깐 비켜 봐! 네 가방 좀 볼게.

— Mark: 좋아. 그럼 난 몇 분만 좀 누워 있을게.

Lisa: 안 돼! 앉아 있어! 시간 없다고! 5시간 후면 비행기가 출발하니까, 정오 전에 공항에서 체크인해야 해! 일어나서 빨리 찾는 거 도와줘. 일어나라고!

— Mark: 잠깐만. 돌아서서 거울 좀 봐 봐.

Lisa: 어머나! 이게 내 머리 위에 계속 있었단 말이야? 나 미쳤나 봐.

— Mark: 괜찮아. 여행이 스트레스를 많이 주지. 비행기가 페루에 도착하면 (스트레스도 풀리고) 나아질 거야.

Lisa: Hey Mark! Can you **look around** for my glasses? I can't find them.

— **Mark:** I'm busy **packing up** my toiletries right now, but I'll **look out for** them.

Lisa: Did you **put** them **away** somewhere when you were **cleaning up** earlier? I swear I had them recently.

— **Mark:** I'll help you **look for** them in a little while. I'm almost done packing.

Lisa: I can't **get on** the plane without my glasses! Without them, I might **fall over**. This isn't a day trip. We're **getting away** for a whole week. That means a week without my glasses.

— **Mark:** Don't worry! We won't **head out** until we find them... Okay, I'm all packed.

Lisa: Maybe you accidentally **picked** them **up** while you were packing. **Move over**! Let me look in your bag.

— **Mark:** Fine, I'll just **lie down** for a few minutes then.

Lisa: No! **Sit up**! There's no time! Our flight **takes off** in five hours, and we have to **check in** at the airport before noon! **Get up** and help me **look for** them. **Stand up**!

— **Mark:** Wait. **Turn around** and look at the mirror.

Lisa: Oh my god, they were on top of my head this whole time. I'm going crazy.

— **Mark:** It's alright. Traveling is stressful. You'll feel better when our plane **touches down** in Peru.

pull into

차를 대다

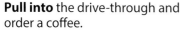

To move a
vehicle to a particular
place

Pull into the drive-through and
order a coffee.

드라이브스루에 차 대고, 커피 주문해.

back up

후진하다

To reverse

Back up a bit. You are blocking the
crosswalk.

차 좀 뒤로 빼 봐. 네가 횡단보도를 막고 있잖아.

pick up

속도를 내다

To accelerate

We need to **pick up** speed to get
there in time.

우리가 거기 제시간에 도착하려면 속도를 내야 해.

rev up

(정지 상태에서) 엔진 속도를 올리다

To press the
accelerator with your
foot when the vehicle
is not moving

Rev up the engine! This guy wants
to race you.

엔진 회전 속도 올려! 이 친구가 너랑 경주하고 싶나
보네.

SHORT DIALOGUE 1

Dan   Okay, Patricia, **pull into** my driveway, here.

Patricia   It's too steep. I can't drive up. I need to **back up** and try again.

Dan   Yes, try again, but you don't need to **rev up** your engine first. You just need to
pick up speed a little.

Patricia   Okay... and... there we go. Thanks. I'll park behind your car, yeah?

> Dan   오케이, Patricia. 여기 우리 집 진입로에 차 대.
> Patricia   경사가 너무 가파른데. 위로 못 올라가겠어. 후진해서 다시 한 번 해 볼게.
> Dan   그래, 다시 해 봐. 그런데 먼저 정지 상태에서 막 밟지는 마. 그냥 속도를 약간만 올리면 돼.
> Patricia   알았어… 아! 됐다. 고마워. 네 차 뒤에 주차할게. 그러면 되지?

pull up

차를 대다

To drive a car
next to or up to
something or
someone

Pull up to the curb and drop me off.
길가에 차 대고 나 좀 내려 줘.

fill up

기름을 가득 채우다

To replenish
a tank of gas

Fill up the gas tank before we head
out.
출발하기 전에 기름 가득 채워.

slow down

속도를 낮추다

To decelerate

Slow down before you take this
turn.
커브 돌기 전에 속도를 줄여.

pull out

차를 빼다, 도로로 진입하다

To move away from
the side of a road;
To drive a car into
a road or intersection
from another road or a parking spot

Don't **pull out** yet. There's a car
coming.
아직 차 빼지 마. 차가 오고 있어.

SHORT DIALOGUE 2

Stephanie	**Pull up** to that gas station, right there. The tank is almost empty.
Rob	Oh yeah, I almost forgot that we need to **fill up**.
Stephanie	Woah, **SLOW DOWN**! Wow. We almost hit that guy!
Rob	It's not my fault! That idiot **pulled out** right in front of me!

Stephanie	바로 저기, 저 주유소에다 차 대. 기름이 거의 다 떨어졌어.
Rob	응, 알았어. 하마터면 기름 채우는 걸 깜빡할 뻔했네.
Stephanie	야, 천천히! 와, 우리 하마터면 저 사람 칠 뻔했잖아!
Rob	내 잘못 아니야! 저 바보가 바로 내 앞에서 차를 뺀 거라고!

speed up

속도를 내다

To accelerate

Speed up to pass this car in front of you.
속도 내서 네 앞에 가는 차 추월해.

run into

부딪치다, 들이박다

To hit something or someone

Don't **run into** the car behind you while parking.
주차하다가 네 뒤에 있는 차 박지 마.

pull over

(도로 가장자리에) 차를 대다

To stop on the side of the road

Pull over your car when you see a firetruck coming behind you.
뒤에 소방차가 오는 것을 보면 차를 세우세요.

cut in

끼어들다

To pull into the space directly in front of another vehicle

Cut in front of that BMW in the next lane.
옆 차선에 있는 저 BMW 앞에 끼어들어.

SHORT DIALOGUE 3

Kelly   Woah! Why are you **speeding up**?

Milo   I had to because the light was turning red. And if that moron hadn't **cut in** front of me, it would have been green.

Kelly   You're going to **run into** someone and cause an accident!

Milo   Look! If you don't like my driving, I can **pull over** and you can drive. Is that what you want?

     Kelly   오! 왜 속도를 내는 거야?

     Milo   그래야 했어. 빨간불로 막 바뀌는 중이었거든. 그 멍청한 놈만 내 앞에 안 끼어들었으면, 녹색불이었을 거야.

     Kelly   너 그런 식으로 운전하다가 누구 하나 치고 사고 내겠다.

     Milo   야! 내가 운전하는 게 맘에 안 들면, 차 댈 테니까 네가 운전해. 그렇게 하고 싶어?

MP3 006

pull off

(도로를) 벗어나다

To take an exit on a highway or stop on the side of the road

Pull off at this exit and park somewhere.

이 출구로 나가서 아무데나 주차해.

blow out

(타이어가) 터지다

To pop a tire

All of a sudden, the left side of my front tire **blew out**.

갑자기 전방 좌측 타이어가 터졌다.

flag down

(손을 흔들며) 정지하라고 하다

To signal someone to stop by waving

I **flagged down** a cab and hopped into the front seat.

나는 택시를 잡아서 앞 좌석에 탔다.

run over

(차로) 치다

To drive a car over something or someone

Stop before you **run over** that woman!

저 여자 치기 전에 차 세워!

SHORT DIALOGUE 1

Keaton What was that sound? I'm going to **pull off** this road and have a look.

Jennie It sounds like your tire **blew out**... yep, this tire is completely flat.

Keaton Darn. I don't have the tools to fix it. I'll **flag** someone **down** for help.

Jennie This is strange. Maybe you **ran over** something that popped it.

> Keaton 무슨 소리지? 도로 밖으로 빠져 나가서 한번 봐야겠어.
> Jennie 타이어가 터진 거 같은데… 그러네. 이 타이어가 완전히 펑크가 났네.
> Keaton 이런. 고칠 연장도 없는데. 지나가는 차 세워서 도와달라고 해야겠다.
> Jennie 이상하네. 뭔가 타이어를 터트릴 만한 것 위를 치고 갔었나 봐.

block in

(차를 가까이 주차해서)
~가 빠져나가지 못하게
하다

To put something in front of
someone or something so that
person or thing cannot move freely

I was **blocked in** by a delivery truck
that parked behind my car.

내 뒤에 주차한 배달 트럭 때문에 난 빠져나가지
못했다.

ease off

가속페달에서 조금씩 발을 떼다, 브레이크를
살짝 밟다

To remove a foot from
the gas pedal or break
slowly

Ease off the gas. You're going too
fast.

가속페달에서 발을 조금씩 떼. 너 너무 빨리 달린다.

turn on

(헤드라이트 등을) 켜다

To start the flow of
electricity, gas, water
by moving a switch
or pressing a button

Make sure to **turn on** the headlights
so you get a clear view.

시야가 잘 보이게 헤드라이트를 꼭 켜세요.

step on

(가속페달을) 밟다

To place or press
the foot on

Step on the gas. We're going to be
late!

밟아. 우리 늦겠어!

SHORT DIALOGUE 2

Mandy	Okay, I **turned on** the engine, now what?
Driving Instructor	You know what to do. **Ease off** the break and **step on** the gas, slowly.
Mandy	I'm doing it! I'm driving! Where to? This way?
Driving Instructor	No! See the posts? We're **blocked in**, so you can't drive that way.

Mandy	네, 시동 켰어요. 이제 뭘 하죠?
Driving Instructor	어떻게 하는지 알잖아요. 브레이크에서 발을 살짝 떼면서, 가속페달을 천천히 밟아요.
Mandy	지금 하고 있어요! 제가 운전을 하네요! 어디로 가죠? 이쪽으로요?
Driving Instructor	아뇨! 저기 기둥 보이죠? 그쪽은 막혀서, 가면 안 돼요.

knock over

부딪쳐 쓰러뜨리다

To hit something in
such a way that it
falls over

Don't **knock over** those cones
when turning left.

좌회전할 때 트래픽 콘 쓰러뜨리지 마.

let out

(교통수단에서) 내려 주다

To allow someone
or something to
exit from some
place

Can you **let** me **out** at the next
intersection?

다음 교차로에서 내려 줄래?

get in

(차에) 타다

To enter, sit down in
(a car)

It's time to leave; **get in** the car
please.

출발할 시간이에요. 차에 타세요.

get out

(차에서) 내리다

To exit;
To leave (a car)

I'm **getting out** of the taxi now.

나 지금 택시에서 내려.

SHORT DIALOGUE 3

Ella Kevin! You just hit a stop sign! Why did I **get in** the car with you, you're such a
bad driver.

Kevin It's not a big deal. I barely hit it.

Ella You **knocked** it **over**! That's it. I'm **getting out**.

Kevin Fine, if that's how you feel, then I'll just **let** you **out** right here on the side of the
road.

Ella Kevin! 너 방금 정지 표지판 박았어! 왜 내가 네 차를 탔나 몰라. 넌 정말 운전 못 하는구나.
Kevin 별거 아니야. 거의 건들지도 않았어.
Ella 그거 넘어뜨렸잖아! 됐어. 나 내릴 거야.
Kevin 좋아. 그렇게 하고 싶으면, 여기 길가에 바로 내려 줄게.

get out

(밖으로) 나가다

To go to different places and spend time enjoying yourself

It is so nice to **get out** and enjoy the day!

밖에 나가 즐거운 하루를 보낼 수 있어서 정말 좋다!

take back

반품하다

To return an item

I need to **take back** these shoes that don't fit.

나, 맞지 않는 이 신발 반품해야 해.

try on

입어 보다

To put on clothes to see if they fit

Try on this suit. I think it'd look good on you.

이 정장 입어 봐. 너한테 잘 어울릴 것 같아.

shop around

여러 가게를 돌아다니다

To visit different stores in search of an item

I want to get a new TV. I'll **shop around** the area for one.

나 TV 새로 사고 싶어. 여기저기 둘러볼 거야.

SHORT DIALOGUE 1

Jen   Thanks so much for **getting** me **out** of the house today!

Lily   No problem! Do you mind if we stop at this shop? I need to **take back** a dress that didn't fit and look for a new one for a wedding next Saturday.

Jen   Sure! While you **try on** some new dresses, I'll look around for a cute purse.

Lily   Great! And if we don't find what we need here, we can **shop around**. There are other boutiques in the area.

Jen   오늘 방구석에서 시간 보내지 않게 해 줘서 정말 고마워!

Lily   에이 고맙기는! 이 가게 좀 들를래? 원피스가 안 맞아서 반품하고, 다음 주 토요일 결혼식에 입을 원피스 좀 보려고.

Jen   그래! 니가 원피스 새로 입어 볼 동안에, 난 이쁜 지갑이나 있나 봐야겠다.

Lily   좋아! 여기서 우리가 사야 하는 게 없으면, 여기저기 둘러보자. 여기 다른 양품점들도 있으니까.

knock down

가격을 낮추다

To reduce the price of something by a certain amount

This discount **knocks down** the price to about twenty dollars.

이 할인을 적용하면 가격이 약 20달러 정도로 떨어져.

come down

가격을 내리다

To become lower

Housing prices have **come down** a lot recently.

최근에 집값이 많이 하락했다.

rip off

바가지 씌우다

To charge someone too much money

We got totally **ripped off**.

우리 완전히 바가지 썼어.

take off

(표시된 금액 등에서) 빼다, 깎다

To remove a portion of the total price

I'll **take off** 20% from your total.

총 금액에서 20% 빼 드릴게요.

SHORT DIALOGUE 2

Gloria	Excuse me, sir? How much does today's sale **knock down** the price of these?
Shop assistant	It's 20% off all shoes, so the price **comes down** to 80 dollars.
Gloria	You must be **ripping** me **off**! 80 dollars for these slippers?!
Shop assistant	I'll see with my manager if we can **take off** 15% more.

Gloria	저기요? 오늘 이거 원래 가격에서 얼마나 할인해요?
Shop assistant	모든 신발을 20% 할인합니다. 그 신발 가격은 20% 할인해서 80달러예요.
Gloria	이거 정말 바가진데요! 이 슬리퍼가 80달러라고요?!
Shop assistant	매니저님께 15% 추가 할인이 가능한지 확인해 볼게요.

wrap up

포장하다

> To box or package
> an item decoratively

They **wrapped up** these gloves at
the store.

가게에서 이 장갑을 포장해 줬어요.

sell out

다 팔리다, 매진되다

> To sell the entire
> stock of an item

BTS's Busan concert **sold out** in
15 minutes.

BTS 부산 콘서트가 15분 만에 매진되었다.

stock up (on)

(한꺼번에) 많이 사서 비축하다

> To buy a large
> quantity of an item

I **stocked up on** food in case the
war broke out.

혹시나 전쟁이 일어날까 싶어 식량을 비축했다.

check out

계산하다

> To complete a
> transaction and pay

Grab some cereal and then we can
go to the front and **check out**.

시리얼 가지고 앞에 가서 계산하자.

SHORT DIALOGUE 3

Retail worker   Would you like me to **wrap up** this scarf for you, ma'am?

Tina   That's all right. By the way, are you **sold out** of this shirt in a small size?

Retail worker   Yes, unfortunately, but we'll **stock up on** more next week. Would that be all?

Tina   Yes, I'll just get this scarf. I'm ready to **check out**. Here's my card.

> Retail worker   고객님, 이 스카프 포장해 드릴까요?
> Tina   괜찮아요. 그런데 혹시 이 셔츠 작은 사이즈는 다 나갔나요?
> Retail worker   예, 아쉽게도 다 나갔어요. 그렇지만 다음 주에 더 들어올 거예요. 이렇게 드릴까요?
> Tina   네, 이 스카프만 살게요. 계산할게요. 여기 카드요.

RUN INTO
RUN OVER

KNOCK
OVER

LONG DIALOGUE

James: 안녕하세요. 최근에 고속도로에서 타이어가 펑크 나서 바꾸려고요.

— Sales clerk: 당연히 바꾸셔야죠! 그런데 도로에서 뭘 밟고 지나가신 거예요?

James: 그런 것 같지 않은데, 고속도로 빠져 나와서 보니까 펑크가 나 있더라고요.

— Sales clerk: 차 대시고 나서, 타이어에 뭐가 있는지 보셨나요?

James: 아니요. 앞에 있는 차를 추월하려고 속도를 냈는데, 큰 소리가 났어요. 속도를 줄였을 때, 차가 흔들리기 시작했고, 타이어가 펑크 났다는 걸 알았죠.

— Sales clerk: 아, 네. 혹시 그 타이어 가지고 계세요?

James: 네, 있어요. 전화했을 때 가지고 오라고 하셔서요.

— Sales clerk: 걱정하지 마세요. 무료로 교환해 드릴게요. 직원 불러서 새 타이어 찾으실 수 있게 도와드릴게요.

James: 실은 같은 타이어 재고가 없다고 알고 있는데, 혹시 괜찮다면 다른 데도 좀 돌아봐도 될까요?

— Sales clerk: 사계절 타이어는 저희가 재고로 항상 가지고 있어야 합니다. 혹시 다른 것을 찾으신다면, 원래 구입하신 타이어 가격에서 빼 드릴게요.

James: 새 타이어를 한번 끼워 봐도 될까요?

— Sales clerk: 그럼요! 정비사 한 분이 도와드릴 거예요.

James: Hello. My tire recently **blew out** on the highway. I'm looking to replace it.

— **Sales clerk:** Of course! Now, did you **run over** anything on the road?

James: I don't think so. I **pulled off** the highway after, and I saw I had a flat tire.

— **Sales clerk:** After you **pulled over**, did you see anything in the tire?

James: Nope. I was just **picking up** speed to pass a car, and I heard a loud noise. When I **slowed down**, the car started shaking, and I realized that the tire had popped.

— **Sales clerk:** Okay, sir. Do you have the tire with you?

James: Yes, I was told to **take** it **back** here when I called.

— **Sales clerk:** Well, don't worry, we can exchange it at no cost. I'll **flag down** one of my employees to help you find a new tire.

James: I actually saw that you were **sold out** of the same tire, so I'll **shop around** for another one if that's alright with you.

— **Sales clerk:** We do have to **stock up on** the all-season tires. If you find another one, we'll just **take off** the price of the original tire.

James: Could I **try on** the new tire?

— **Sales clerk:** Of course! One of our mechanics can help with that.

CHAPTER

2

PHRASAL VERBS

put on

~을 입다, 걸치다

To place an item of clothing or accessory on the body

I'm going to throw out the trash after I **put on** some clothes.

나 옷 좀 걸치고 쓰레기 버릴게.

pull off

(옷, 장신구 등을) 잘 소화하다

To wear a piece of clothing in a way that looks good

Katie **pulls off** that dress very nicely.

Katie는 그 원피스를 정말 멋지게 소화한다.

go with

어울리다

To match something in style or color

That tie **goes with** your shirts.

그 넥타이가 네가 입은 셔츠하고 잘 어울린다.

zip up

지퍼를 잠그다

To fasten the zipper on a piece of clothing or accessory

Can you help me **zip up** my dress?

내 원피스 지퍼 올리는 것 좀 도와줄래?

SHORT DIALOGUE 1

Keith   **Put on** this dress. I think you'd look very good in it.

Jody   It's lovely, but it might be a little too bold for me to **pull off**.

Keith   I disagree. Plus, I think that color **goes with** your skin tone.

Jody   Okay, I'll try it on. Here. Could you **zip** it **up** for me?

> Keith   이 원피스 입어 봐. 네가 입으면 정말 어울릴 것 같아.
> Jody   예쁘다. 그런데 내가 소화하기엔 좀 너무 화려한 것 같기도 하고.
> Keith   아닌데. 게다가 옷 색깔이 네 피부색이랑도 정말 잘 어울릴 것 같아.
> Jody   알았어. 한번 입어 볼게. 여기. 지퍼 좀 올려 줄래?

MP3 009

dress up
차려입다

To wear fancy or nice clothing

Do we have to **dress up** for the party tonight?
오늘 밤 파티에 차려입고 가야 해?

have on
입다 (입은 상태)

To wear

Erin always **has on** something nice whenever I meet her.
Erin은 만날 때마다 늘 좋은 옷을 입고 있어.

tie together
(보통 나비 모양으로) 옷을 끈으로 묶다

To fasten together two pieces of string or other long, thin material

I like how this dress **ties together** in the back.
난 이 드레스 뒤로 끈을 묶은 게 참 마음에 든다.

bundle up
옷을 (따뜻하게) 챙겨 입다

To wear warm clothing

It's snowing outside. You need to **bundle up**.
밖에 눈이 오네. 따뜻하게 챙겨 입어.

SHORT DIALOGUE 2

Mike   What are you wearing to the event tonight? Do we need to **dress up**?

Kim   No, just **have on** something nice. Not too fancy.

Mike   I like that cardigan. It's really cute how it **ties together** in the front.

Kim   Thank you! You should bring a jacket, too. It's a bit chilly. You may have to **bundle up**.

Mike   오늘 밤 행사에 뭐 입을 거야? 차려입고 가야 하나?
Kim   아니, 그냥 괜찮아 보이는 거 입어. 너무 화려한 거 말고
Mike   난 저 카디건이 마음에 들어. 앞에서 끈으로 묶으니까 정말 예쁘더라.
Kim   고마워! 재킷도 가지고 와. 약간 쌀쌀해서 옷을 껴입어야 할 수도 있어.

get ready

(챙겨 입고) 준비하다

To prepare for an event, typically in terms of putting on clothes and makeup

I need to **get ready** to go to work.
나 출근 준비해야 해.

take off

(옷 등을) 벗다, (화장을) 지우다

To remove clothing, accessories, or makeup

Take off your dirty clothes and put on new ones.
지저분한 옷 벗고 새옷으로 갈아입어.

change into

~로 갈아입다

To take off an outfit or article and replace it with another

I usually **change into** something more comfortable before I go on a walk.
나는 산책 가기 전에 보통 편한 옷으로 갈아입는다.

dress down

편하게 입다

To wear something more casual or comfortable

I always **dress down** for long flights.
난 장거리 비행할 때는 항상 편안한 복장을 한다.

SHORT DIALOGUE 3

Jill   What are you wearing to the party tonight?

Simon   I haven't decided yet, but I think I'll **dress down** and wear something comfortable.

Jill   That's a good idea. Don't forget to **take off** your work clothes first. **Get ready** fast.

Simon   Yeah, okay. I'll take a quick shower, and then **change into** something nice. Give me five minutes.

> Jill   오늘 밤 파티에 뭐 입고 갈 거야?
> Simon   아직까지 결정 못 했는데, 간편하고 편안한 옷 입으려고.
> Jill   좋은 생각이야. 먼저 근무복 벗는 거 잊지 말고, 빨리 준비해.
> Simon   그래. 알았어. 빨리 샤워하고 괜찮은 옷으로 갈아입을게. 5분만 줘.

MP3 **010**

fling off
빨리 벗어버리다

To take off an item or items of clothing quickly

I can't wait to get home and **fling off** these uncomfortable clothes.
빨리 집에 가서 이 불편한 옷 좀 벗어버리고 싶어.

slip into
후딱 입다

To put on another outfit or item of clothing, typically one that is more comfortable

Use the changing room if you need to **slip into** your bathing suit.
수영복으로 후딱 갈아입으려면 탈의실을 이용해.

hang up
(빨래 등을) 걸다

To place on a hook or hanger designed for the purpose

Hang up your wet socks in the laundry room so that they can dry.
젖은 양말이 마르게 세탁실에 걸어 놔.

fit into
(옷 등이) ~에 꼭 들어맞다

To have clothing that is the right size

I lost some weight and need new pants that I can **fit into**.
살이 빠져서 나한테 맞는 새 바지가 필요해.

SHORT DIALOGUE 1

Rachel When I get home, I'm going to **fling off** these dirty clothes and change into something comfortable.

Ashley Yeah, I had a fun day, but I'm ready to **slip into** my pajamas and sleep.

Rachel I **hung up** my pajamas this morning. I hope they're dry.

Ashley If they're not dry, I probably have a few pairs you'd **fit into**. So not to worry.

Rachel 집에 가면, 이 지저분한 옷 좀 훌러덩 벗어버리고, 편안한 옷으로 갈아입어야지.
Ashley 그래, 재미있었지만 후딱 잠옷 입고 자야지.
Rachel 오늘 아침에 잠옷 걸어 뒀는데, 다 말랐으면 좋겠다.
Ashley 안 말랐어도, 아마 나한테 너에게 맞는 잠옷이 몇 벌 있을 테니, 걱정하지 마.

doll up

차려입다, 치장하다

To make oneself look pretty or attractive

I love **dolling** myself **up** before going out for a date.
난 데이트 나가기 전에 꾸미는 것을 참 좋아해.

put up

머리를 높이 묶다

To fasten hair, typically in a braid, bun, or ponytail

Put up your hair before bed.
잠자기 전에 머리를 높이 묶어.

tie up

머리를 묶다

To keep hair away from your neck, shoulders, and back

Tie up your hair if you're going to go on a run.
달리기하러 나가려면 머리 묶어!

let down

머리를 풀다, 머리를 내리다

To wear hair without fastening it;
To unfasten hair

You look prettier when you **let down** your hair.
너는 머리 풀면 더 예뻐 보여.

SHORT DIALOGUE 2

Greg What are you **dolling** yourself **up** for, Marie?

Marie I'm going to a party tonight. Can you help me **put up** my hair?

Greg Sure, I could **tie** it **up** for you, but I think you look better with it down.

Marie That may be true, but I'll be dancing. I can't **let** my hair **down**, or it'll get messed up!

Greg 뭐 때문에 그렇게 치장하는 거야, Marie?
Marie 오늘 밤에 파티에 가거든. 머리 묶는 거 좀 도와줄래?
Greg 그래. 머리 묶어 줄게. 그런데 머리를 내리는 게 더 나아 보일 것 같아.
Marie 그럴 수도 있는데, 춤출 거라서 머리 내리면 안 돼. 그럼 완전 엉망이 될걸!

wear out

낡아 떨어지다, 닳아 없어지다

To damage or
ruin an item of
clothing through
overuse

I've finally **worn out** my favorite
shoes after 5 years.
내가 가장 좋아하는 신발이 5년 만에 다 닳았다.

get rid of

~을 제거하다, 처리하다

To throw away;
To dispose of

I **got rid of** some of my old clothes
by donating them.
나는 헌옷들을 기부해서 전부 치워 버렸다.

grow out of

(옷 등이) 너무 작아지다

To become too large for
something

My son's **grown out of** all his clothes
from last year.
우리 아들이 작년에 입었던 옷이 다 너무 작아졌다.

stretch out

늘어나다

To widen or expand
something to a larger
size

Don't put on my shirt. You'll **stretch
it out**.
내 셔츠 입지 마. 네가 입으면 늘어난다고.

SHORT DIALOGUE 3

Becky   Mike, take off that shirt! You've worn it so much; you've **worn** it **out**!

Mike   It's my most comfortable shirt. I can't **get rid of** it!

Becky   You **grew out of** it five years ago. It's time to say goodbye.

Mike   I guess it has **stretched out** a bit. I'll donate it. Can you help me find a new one?

Becky   Mike, 그 셔츠 좀 벗어! 너무 많이 입었었잖아. 다 낡아 떨어졌네!
Mike   이게 가장 편안한 셔츠야. 못 없앤다고!
Becky   이미 5년 전부터 작았거든. 이제 그만 작별할 시간이야.
Mike   좀 늘어난 것 같기는 한데, 기부나 해야겠다. 새 옷 좀 찾는 것 좀 도와줄래?

wind down

긴장을 풀다, 휴식을 취하다

To relax, especially after a long day

It's important to **wind down** after a long day at work.

직장에서 힘든 하루를 마치고 휴식을 취하는 것은 중요하다.

tire out

피곤하게 하다

To make someone very tired

This long meeting really **tired** me **out**.

이 회의가 길어서 난 정말 피곤했다.

loosen up

긴장을 풀다, (뭉친) 근육을 풀다

To relax; To relax one's muscles

I got a massage to **loosen up**.

난 뭉친 근육을 풀기 위해서 마사지를 받았다.

lie around

빈둥대며 쉬다

To spend time lying down and doing very little

My kids just **lie around** all day watching TV on the weekend.

우리 애들은 주말에 TV만 보면서 온종일 빈둥거린다.

SHORT DIALOGUE 1

Jodie Aren't you glad we could get to the beach today? It's so nice to **wind down** after this stressful week!

Eric Not really, I don't like the beach. The sun **tires** me **out**.

Jodie Stop complaining and **loosen up**! Learn to relax a little bit.

Eric I don't understand why people spend time and money **lying around** the beach all day. What a waste!

Jodie 오늘 이렇게 해변에 오니까 좋지 않아? 힘든 한 주 후에 이렇게 쉬니까 정말 좋다!

Eric 아니 별로… 나 해변 안 좋아해. 햇빛 쐬면 난 피곤해.

Jodie 불평 그만하고 긴장 풀어! 쉬는 것도 좀 배워라.

Eric 난 왜 사람들이 해변에서 하루 종일 빈둥거리면서 시간과 돈을 쓰는지 이해가 안 돼. 이 무슨 낭비야!

wipe out
정말 피곤하게 하다

To exhaust completely

After working for twelve hours, I'm completely **wiped out**.

12시간 동안 일하고 나면 난 완전히 녹초가 돼.

turn in
잠자리에 들다

To go to bed

I'm so tired. I'm gonna **turn in** early tonight.

나 너무 피곤해. 오늘 밤에는 일찍 잘 거야.

sleep in
(평소보다) 늦게까지 자다

To wake up later than usual

I don't work tomorrow, so I can **sleep in**.

나 내일 일하지 않아서 늦게까지 잘 수 있어.

nod off
잠깐 졸다

To fall asleep for a short time

I was **nodding off** in history class. It was so boring.

나 역사 수업 시간에 잠깐 졸았어. 정말 지루했거든.

SHORT DIALOGUE 2

Danny I had a long day at work. I'm completely **wiped out**.
Carol Are you sleepy? Maybe you can **turn in** early.
Danny I think I will. And I don't work tomorrow, so I can **sleep in** till 10.
Carol Well then, you should go to bed. You're already **nodding off**.

Danny 오늘 회사에서 엄청 힘들었어. 완전히 피곤하다.
Carol 졸려? 일찍 자는 건 어때?
Danny 그러려고. 그리고 내일 일 안 하니까, 10시까지 늦잠 잘 수 있어.
Carol 그래, 그럼 어서 가서 자. 벌써 고개가 끄덕끄덕 한다.

chill out

편안히 쉬다

To relax; To spend time doing relaxing things

Watching TV is a good way to **chill out** after a long day.

힘든 하루를 마치고 TV 보는 게 편안히 쉬는 좋은 방법이긴 하지.

hang around

기다리다, 서성거리다

To wait or spend time somewhere, usually for no particular reason

I'll just **hang around** here until you get here.

네가 올 때까지 나 그냥 여기서 기다릴게.

veg out

느긋하게 쉬다

To relax completely; To be lazy

I just **vegged out** all weekend because I didn't have to do anything.

특별하게 할 일이 없어서 난 주말 내내 느긋하게 쉬었다.

stay in

바깥에 나가지 않고 집에 있다

To do nothing; To not leave home

My wife and I **stayed in** for our wedding anniversary.

아내와 나는 결혼기념일에 아무데도 나가지 않고 집에서 있었다.

SHORT DIALOGUE 3

Erin   Hey, Shawn. Do you want to **chill out** at my place tonight?

Shawn   I'm pretty tired. Last night I went to a concert and **hung around** after the show to meet the band. I didn't get to bed until three in the morning.

Erin   We don't have to do anything crazy. Let's just **veg out** and watch TV.

Shawn   I don't know. I think I'll **stay in** tonight. Maybe some other time.

Erin   야, Shawn. 오늘 밤에 우리 집에 와서 놀래?

Shawn   나 좀 많이 피곤해. 어젯밤에 콘서트 가서 밴드 만나려고 콘서트 끝나고서도 기다렸거든. 새벽 3시가 돼서야 잤어.

Erin   뭐 대단한 거 할 필요도 없어. 그냥 쉬면서 TV나 보자는 거지.

Shawn   모르겠어. 오늘 밤에는 그냥 아무데도 안 가고 집에 있을래. 다음에 하자.

DRESS UP

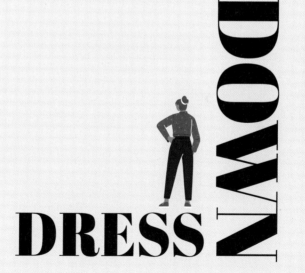

DRESS DOWN

LONG DIALOGUE

Samantha: 지금 빈둥대면서 뭐 하는 거야? 준비해야지. 2시간 후면 파티 시작해.

— Charles: 자기야. 마음 좀 편안히 가져! 그리고 나 정말 피곤하다고. 일주일 내내 일하고 오늘 하루 쉬는데, 내가 이 파티에 꼭 가야 하는 거야? 진짜, 그냥 오늘 밤에는 느긋하게 쉬고 싶다고.

Samantha: 같이 간다고 일주일 전에 말했잖아! 자기, 집에 못 있어. 게다가 내 친구들이랑은 거의 시간을 안 보내잖아. 나한테 이 파티가 정말 중요하다고.

— Charles: 그렇게 잘 알지도 못하는 사람들하고 같이 있는 거 피곤해. 에라, 모르겠다. 오늘 일찍 잠자리에 들 수 있다고 약속하면 같이 갈게. 나 이거 입으면 되는 거야?

Samantha: 안 돼! 티셔츠 입지 마. 자기 바지하고도 안 어울려. 내가 어제 차려 입고 가야 한다고 했잖아. 좀 괜찮은 걸로 입어 봐. 예전 양복은 어때? 정말 오랫동안 그 옷 입는 거 못 봤는데.

— Charles: 아직도 나한테 맞나 한번 봐야겠다. 살이 좀 쪘거든. 옷이 늘어날 수도 있겠는데.

Samantha: 그거 입으면 자기 정말 근사할 거야. 나 화장 마무리하고 머리 올릴게. 내가 돌아오면, 자기는 갈 준비가 돼 있어야 해!

— Charles: 알았어, 알았다고. 가서 빨리 꾸미고 와. 바로 준비할게.

Samantha: What're you doing **lying around**? You need to **get ready**. The party is in two hours.

— **Charles:** Hey, **chill out**! I'm really **wiped out**. I worked all week, and on my one day off, I have to go to this party? Honestly, I just wanted to **veg out** tonight.

Samantha: You told me you would come with me a week ago! You can't **stay in**. Besides you hardly ever spend time with my friends. This is really important for me.

— **Charles:** Being around people I don't know that well **wears** me **out**. Whatever. I'll go with you if you promise that we can **turn in** early. Can I wear this?

Samantha: No! You can't wear a t-shirt! It doesn't even **go with** your pants. I told you yesterday that we had to **dress up**. **Put on** something nice. What about your old suit? I haven't seen you wear that thing in forever.

— **Charles:** I'll see if I still **fit into** it. I've put on some weight. I might **stretch** it **out**.

Samantha: I think you'll look great in it. I'm going to finish my makeup and **put** my hair **up**. When I come back, you should be ready!

— **Charles:** Yeah, yeah. You go get **dolled up**. I'll be ready soon.

call off

(회의, 행사 등을) 취소하다

To cancel something
such as an event,
a meeting

I'm too sick to work. I have no choice
but to **call off** the meeting.

몸이 너무 안 좋아서 일 못하겠어. 회의를 취소할 수
밖에 없겠어.

catch up

(일·공부를) 따라잡다

To make progress on
a project after
a period of inactivity

I'm staying late at work to **catch up**
on some work.

몇 가지 일들을 처리하느라 야근하는 중이야.

bog down

얽매이다, 진전이 없다

To prevent
somebody from
making progress in
an activity

Let's not get **bogged down** with
the details. See the big picture first.

세세한 것에 얽매이지 말자. 먼저 큰 그림을 봐.

put off

(일을) 미루다

To procrastinate
a task

I've **put off** doing my assignment
and now I have to stay up all night.

업무를 미뤄 놔서 나 오늘 밤새워야 해.

SHORT DIALOGUE 1

Tony   What's up, Brenda! I **called off** work today. Are you busy?

Brenda   I'm afraid so. I have to **catch up** with some work. I have a deadline soon.

Tony   That's too bad. Work has been **bogging** you **down** lately.

Brenda   Yeah. I **put off** this project for too long. Now I have no free time!

Tony   Brenda, 잘 지내? 나 오늘 일 취소했어. 바쁘니?

Brenda   (아쉽게도) 응. 해야 할 일들이 있어서. 곧 마감이거든.

Tony   아이고 어쩌냐. 요즘 일에 얽매여 있구나.

Brenda   어. 이 프로젝트를 너무 오래 미뤄 뒀어. 이제 나한테 자유 시간은 없어!

write back

(이메일 등에) 답장을 하다

To respond to an email or letter

I sent an email to Jayden, but he never **wrote** me **back**.

Jayden에게 이메일 보냈는데, 나한테 답장을 안 보냈어.

pile up

(업무·책임 등이) 쌓이다

To grow in size, normally in terms of responsibility or work load

When I miss a day of work, the papers on my desk just **pile up**.

하루만 일을 못해도, 내 책상에 처리할 서류들이 쌓인다.

set up

준비하다

To prepare something; To put something together

Can you **set up** the conference room for a meeting?

회의할 수 있게 회의실 좀 준비해 주겠어요?

walk through

차근차근 단계를 알려 주어 도와주다

To help someone do something by going through its steps slowly

I'd like you to **walk through** how to use the program for our new employees.

우리 신입 직원들에게 프로그램 사용법을 차근차근 설명해 주세요.

SHORT DIALOGUE 2

Dana   You didn't **write back** about that new project we're working on.

Ken   Sorry. I've been busy. My emails have been **piling up**, and I didn't get to them.

Dana   Well, we have to **set up** for an event this weekend. Can you do that?

Ken   Yes, I can. I'll read your email, or you can **walk** me **through** it if you have time right now.

Dana   우리가 하고 있는 새 프로젝트에 관해서 네가 답변을 안 줬더라고.
Ken   미안. 바빴어. 이메일은 계속 쌓이는데, 메일 확인할 여유가 없었어.
Dana   저기, 우리 이번 주말에 행사 준비해야 하는데, 할 수 있겠어?
Ken   그럼, 할 수 있지. 이메일 읽어 볼게. 아니면 너 지금 시간 있으면 나한테 차근차근 알려 줘도 되고.

slave away

노예처럼 일하다

To work intensely

I'm **slaving away** to get this report done, but it seems no closer to being done.

나는 이 보고서를 끝내려고 뼈 빠지게 일하고 있지만, 끝내려면 아직 먼 것 같다.

invest in

투자하다

To devote time or money to something

Invest in my company and you won't regret it.

저희 회사에 투자해 주세요. 그러면 절대 후회하지 않을 겁니다.

go under

망하다

To become bankrupt

The company will **go under** unless their profit increases.

그 회사는 수익이 늘지 않으면 망할 거예요.

keep up

(행동을) 유지하다

To continue a course of action

Well done. **Keep up** the good work!

잘했어요. 앞으로도 계속 잘해 줘요!

SHORT DIALOGUE 3

Bobby Hey Jessie! How's it going? Have you been able to **keep up** with work during busy season so far?

Jessie Yeah. I feel like I've been **slaving away** for the past two months at the tour company. I'm glad summer is almost over. How about you?

Bobby I recently **invested in** this new biotech startup. They are growing so fast.

Jessie Be careful! 50% of startups **go under** within five years.

Bobby 안녕, Jessie! 잘 지냈어? 성수기에 일은 밀리지 않고 잘하고 있는 거야?
Jessie 응. 지난 2개월 동안 여행사에서 완전 뼈 빠지게 일했어. 여름이 거의 끝나서 정말 기쁘다. 넌 어때?
Bobby 최근에 이 새로운 바이오테크 스타트업에 투자했거든. 이 회사가 굉장히 빨리 성장하고 있어.
Jessie 조심해! 스타트업 회사 중 50%는 5년도 안 돼서 망한다고.

close down
사업을 접다, 문 닫다, 영업을 종료하다

To cease business or operation, especially permanently

I finally decided to **close down** my business.
난 결국 사업을 접기로 결정했다.

deal with
~을 다루다, 처리하다

To work through; To assume the burden of

My manager asked me to **deal with** training the new employees.
매니저가 나에게 새로 들어온 직원들의 교육을 맡겼다.

tie up
매우 바쁘다

To occupy someone to the exclusion of any other activity

Sorry I couldn't make it last night. I got **tied up** at work.
어젯밤에 못 가서 죄송해요. 일이 너무 바빴어요.

climb up
올라가다, 승진하다

To go up or ascend

You are promoted.

I'm not so interested in **climbing up** the corporate ladder.
난 회사에서 승진하는 것에는 별로 관심이 없다.

SHORT DIALOGUE 1

Interviewer So Paula, have you ever had to **deal with** stress in the workplace?

Paula Oh yes. My last job was very stressful before the business **closed down**. But I don't let it distract me. I work well under pressure.

Interviewer That's good to hear. With that attitude, you will be **climbing up** the corporate ladder in no time. So, if you worked here, how would you handle a slow day?

Paula Oh, there is always something that needs to be done. I would just find something to **tie** myself **up** with.

Interviewer 그럼 Paula 씨, 직장에서 스트레스를 해결해야 했던 적이 있나요?

Paula 그럼요. 지난번 직장은 회사가 망하기 전에 정말 스트레스가 심했어요. 하지만 전 스트레스가 일을 방해하게 두지 않습니다. 전 압박을 받는 상황에서도 일을 잘 합니다.

Interviewer 다행이네요. 그런 태도라면, 승진도 금세 하겠네요. 그럼, 만약 여기서 일하는데, 업무가 많지 않다면 어떻게 하시겠어요?

Paula 아, 분명 뭔가 해야 할 일은 항상 있기 마련이죠. 제 스스로를 바쁘게 할 무언가를 찾을 겁니다.

move up

승진하다

To be promoted or find higher success in a career

Nick **moved up** in his company very quickly because of his hard work.

Nick은 열심히 일해서 회사에서 매우 빠르게 승진했다.

take over

대신하다, 인수하다

To assume the responsibilities of another position or person

Julia is going to **take over** your job after you leave the company.

네가 회사를 떠난 후에는 Julia가 네 업무를 맡을 거야.

take on

(일·책임을) 떠맡다

To assume; To take responsibility for

I'm going to **take on** more classes as of next month.

전 다음 달부터 더 많은 수업을 맡게 됩니다.

let down

실망시키다

To disappoint

I'm sorry to **let** you **down**.

실망시켜서 죄송해요.

SHORT DIALOGUE 2

Manager I've got some good news, Alex. You're **moving up** in the company.

Alex I got the promotion? Thank you. I assume I'll be **taking over** Jennifer's role since she quit?

Manager Yes. But that also means you'll be **taking on** more responsibility. Can you handle that?

Alex Yes, I can. I won't **let** you **down**! Thank you for this opportunity!

Manager 좋은 소식이 있네, Alex. 자네가 회사에서 승진을 한다네.
Alex 제가 승진을요? 감사합니다. Jennifer가 그만두었으니 제가 Jennifer가 하던 일을 하겠네요.
Manager 그렇지. 그런데 그건 책임이 무거워진다는 것이기도 하지. 할 수 있겠나?
Alex 네, 실망시키지 않겠습니다! 기회를 주셔서 감사합니다!

step down

물러나다, 사퇴하다

To resign from an
important job or
position

He **stepped down** when his
criminal record was revealed.
범죄 기록이 밝혀지고 나자 그는 자리에서 물러났다.

lay off

자르다, 해고하다

To fire;
To terminate
someone's position

Many companies have had to **lay
off** their employees because the
economy is so bad.
경기가 너무 안 좋아서 많은 회사들이 직원들을
내보내야 했다.

shut down

문을 닫다, 전원을 끄다

To close; To turn
something off

Many businesses **shut down** due to
the pandemic.
팬데믹 때문에 많은 사업장들이 문을 닫았다.

be cut out for

~에 적합하다, 소질이 있다

To have the qualities
and abilities needed for
something

I'm not **cut out for** this job.
난 이 일에 소질이 없다.

SHORT DIALOGUE 3

Supervisor   We have to talk. I need to ask you to **step down**.

Luke   What? Are you **laying** me **off**? But I've worked here for years!

Supervisor   It just doesn't seem like you**'re cut out for** the workload. We almost had to
shut down one of the factories because of your mistakes.

Luke   But that wasn't my fault! This is so unfair!

    Supervisor   우리 얘기 좀 하지. 자네가 그 자리에서 내려왔으면 하네.
    Luke   뭐라고요? 절 해고하시는 겁니까? 제가 여기서 일한 세월이 얼만데요!
    Supervisor   자네가 업무량을 제대로 처리하지 못하는 것 같네. 자네가 한 실수들로 인해 공장 하나가 문
        닫을 뻔했어.
    Luke   하지만 그건 제 잘못이 아니었어요! 이건 정말 부당합니다!

back up

(증거, 주장 등을) 뒷받침하다

To support; To provide evidence

Stacy **backed up** Angela's claim that her car was stolen.

Stacy는 차를 도난당했다는 Angela의 주장을 거들었다.

agree with

~에 동의하다

To approve of

It's hard to **agree with** someone that you don't like.

좋아하지 않는 사람의 의견에 동의하기는 어렵다.

stick by

지지하다, 지켜 주다

To support someone or something, typically in spite of criticism

My mother **stuck by** my side even after I lost all of my friends.

내가 친구들을 다 잃었을 때조차도 엄마는 내 곁에서 날 지켜 줬다.

side with

~의 편을 들다

To approve of someone's opinion, typically in spite of another point of view

I **sided with** Julia when Jayden yelled at her for being rude.

Jayden이 Julia에게 무례하다고 소리 질렀을 때 난 Julia 편을 들었다.

SHORT DIALOGUE 1

Cole   Kathy thinks I'm partying too much. Can you talk to her? You'll **back** me **up**, right?

Pete   I don't know, man. You have been going pretty crazy. I think I **agree with** Kathy.

Cole   What? You're my best friend?! Aren't you supposed to **stick by** me? You're just like her.

Pete   I'm sorry, but I'm not really **siding with** Kathy. She's just right about this.

Cole   Kathy는 내가 파티를 너무 많이 한다고 생각하더라. 걔한테 말 좀 해 줄래? 옆에서 거들어 줄 거지?
Pete   잘 모르겠어. 네가 정말 좀 지나치긴 했지. 나도 Kathy랑 비슷한 생각이야.
Cole   뭐? 넌 내 절친이잖아?! 날 지지해 줘야 하는 거 아냐? 너도 걔하고 똑같아.
Pete   미안한데, 내가 Kathy 편 드는 건 아니거든. 그런데 이건 걔 말이 맞아.

speak out
자기 의사를 확실히 말하다

To make one's
opinion heard

When I saw Emily steal the money,
I had to **speak out** against her.
Emily가 돈을 훔치는 것을 보았을때, 난 그녀에게
그러면 안 된다고 단호하게 말해야 했다.

object to
~에 반대하다

To disagree or take
issue with someone or
something

I **object to** war or violence of any
kind.
난 어떠한 전쟁이나 폭력에도 반대한다.

back down
(잘못을) 인정하다

To admit that you are
wrong

He made a big mistake. But he
didn't **back down**.
그는 큰 실수를 저질렀지만, 인정하지 않았다.

take care of
~을 하다, 처리하다

To make sure of doing
something

Don't worry, I'll **take care of** dinner
tonight since you're busy.
걱정하지 마. 너 바쁘니까 오늘 밤에는 내가 저녁을
할게.

SHORT DIALOGUE 2

Bryan　Paul has gone too far. I've had enough. Someone has to **speak out** against him.

Natalie　After what he did to Will, I can't **object to** that. What should we do?

Bryan　Let me **take care of** this. I'm going to make this right for sure.

Natalie　Okay. But he won't **back down** easily.

Bryan　Paul이 너무했지. 나도 참을 만큼 참았어. 누군가 걔한테 그러면 안 된다고 확실히 말해 줘야 해.
Natalie　걔가 Will한테 한 짓을 보니까, 나도 네 말에 반대 못 하겠다. 어떻게 해야 하지?
Bryan　이건 나한테 맡겨. 이번에 확실히 바로잡을 거야.
Natalie　알았어. 근데 걔가 쉽게 잘못을 인정하진 않을 거야.

compare to

~와 비교하다

To consider the similarities and differences of things or people

How does the new BMW **compare to** the older models?

새 BMW가 기존 모델들하고 어떤 차이가 있어?

tell apart

구별하다

To differentiate between two or more things

They are identical twins. People can't **tell** them **apart**.

그들은 일란성 쌍둥이예요. 사람들은 누가 누군지 구별을 못해요.

figure out

해결하다, 이해하다

To find the answer to a question; To solve a problem

I can't **figure out** the answer to this problem.

난 이 문제의 답을 잘 모르겠어.

go with

선택하다, 받아들이다

To choose or accept something

I'm glad that you decided to **go with** the first option.

네가 첫 번째 선택지를 골라서 기뻐.

SHORT DIALOGUE 1

Jack   How does Karate **compare to** Taekwondo? I want to learn a martial art.

Robin   They're easy to **tell apart** because Taekwondo puts more focus on kicking than Karate.

Jack   I know this sounds stupid, but I still can't **figure out** the difference.

Robin   Then just **go with** both of them for now, and decide later which one you like better.

     Jack   태권도와 비교해서 가라테는 어때? 나 무술 배우고 싶거든.
     Robin   구분하기 쉬워. 태권도가 가라테보다 발차기에 더 중점을 두니까.
     Jack   바보같이 들리겠지만, 난 아직도 차이를 잘 모르겠어.
     Robin   그러면 일단 그 둘을 다 해 보고, 어느 것이 더 좋은지 나중에 결정해.

weigh out

따져 보다, 저울질하다

To compare;
To consider options

You have to **weigh out** all of the options before you decide.

결정하기 전에 모든 선택지를 따져 봐야 해.

stand out

눈에 띄다

To be clear;
To be noticeable

Jay **stood out** in that meeting. He is funny, energetic, and even smart.

Jay는 그 회의에서 눈에 띄었어. 그는 재미있고, 에너지가 넘치고, 똑똑하기까지 해.

choose from

~에서 선택하다

To select something from many options

I can't **choose from** all of the options on this menu. It's too big!

메뉴가 너무 많아서 선택할 수가 없어.

match up

일치하다, 맞아 떨어지다

To compare two things to see if they are the same or similar

The price of this laptop doesn't **match up** with its quality.

이 노트북의 가격이 품질과 일치하지 않는다.

SHORT DIALOGUE 2

Maria   I'm having trouble deciding which car to buy.

Ben   Have you **weighed out** the pros and cons of each option?

Maria   Hmm. It's tough trying to **choose from** those options. They all look good!

Ben   Maybe you should test drive them and see which one **matches up** with your driving style. One might **stand out** as the best choice once you've tried them all.

Maria   어떤 차를 살지 정말 결정하기 힘드네.

Ben   각각의 장단점은 잘 따져 봤어?

Maria   음, 선택하기가 쉽지 않아. 다 좋아 보인단 말이야!

Ben   한번 시운전해 보고, 어떤 게 네 운전 스타일에 맞는지 확인해 보지 그래. 직접 시운전해 보면 최고의 차가 딱 들어올 거야.

LONG DIALOGUE

Ryan: 나 정말 일해야 하는데. 네가 보기에 내가 뭘 잘할 것 같아? 생각해 놓은 건 몇 개 있는데, 여전히 어떤 것을 선택할지 고민이야.

— Joan: 바텐더 하는 건 생각해 봤어? 일이 정말 많고, 승진할 기회는 별로 없지만, 돈은 많이 벌 수 있잖아.

Ryan: 음. 재밌겠지만, 너무 스트레스 받는 일은 하고 싶지 않아. 내 생각엔 음식점이나 큰 가게에서 일하고 싶은지 파악하는 게 먼저인 것 같아.

— Joan: 백화점에 비해서, 음식점에서 일하는 건 수월해. 웨이터는 싫어?

Ryan: 아니야. 오히려 좋아 보이는데. 그러면 늦게까지 일 안 해도 될 테고. 술집은 문을 너무 늦게 닫잖아.

— Joan: 하긴 그래. 내가 바텐더로 꽤 오래 일했거든. 매일 밤 끝날 때 2시간 동안 뼈 빠지게 일해야 했다니까.

Ryan: 난 감당할 수 없을 거 같아.

— Joan: 내가 너라면 웨이터를 선택 하겠어.

Ryan: 오늘 돌아가면 일단 근처 음식점에서 구인하는 곳이 있나 알아 봐야겠어. 큰 식당에서는 일하고 싶지 않거든.

— Joan: 많은 음식점들이 지금 사람을 구하고 있어. 빠르면 내일이라도 인터뷰 잡을 수 있을 거야. 이력서 준비하는 게 좋겠다.

Ryan: 도와줘서 고마워, Joan!

Ryan: I really need a job. What do you think I'd be good at? I have a few ideas, but I'm still **weighing out** my options.

— Joan: Have you thought about bartending? The workload is intense, and there isn't much opportunity to **move up**, but you can make a lot of money.

Ryan: Hmm. It sounds fun, but I don't want to **take on** something too stressful. I guess the first step is to **figure out** whether I want to work in a restaurant or a big store.

— Joan: **Compared to** working in a department store, working in restaurants is easy. Would you **object to** being a waiter?

Ryan: Not really. Actually, it sounds great. Then I wouldn't have to work so late. **Closing down** a bar takes forever.

— Joan: I **agree with** you. You know, I was a bartender for years. I had to **slave away** for two hours at the end of every night.

Ryan: I don't think I could **deal with** that.

— Joan: I would **go with** being a waiter if I were you.

Ryan: I'll see if there are any local restaurants hiring nearby when I get back today. I don't want to work for a big restaurant.

— Joan: A lot of restaurants need workers right now. You can probably **set up** an interview as early as tomorrow. You'd better start preparing your résumé.

Ryan: Thanks for the help, Joan!

CHAPTER

3

PHRASAL VERBS

talk about

~에 대해 말하다, 이야기하다

To discuss a certain topic or person in particular

I wish that Steve would stop **talking about** me.

Steve가 내 얘기 좀 그만하면 좋겠어.

drone on

오래 질질 끌며 말하다

To speak in a boring way, usually for a long time

The speaker **droned on** about the topic for an hour.

발표자가 한 시간 동안 그 주제에 대해서 질질 끌며 말했다.

explain away

해명하다

To try to escape being blamed for something bad, usually by making it seem unimportant

Paul **explained away** what he meant by his rude comments the day before.

Paul은 전날에 했던 무례한 말에 대해서 무슨 의미인지 해명했다.

shut up

입을 다물다, 닥치다

To stop speaking abruptly

Sometimes I wish that my colleagues would **shut up** about politics.

가끔은 내 동료들이 정치에 대해서 입 닥치고 말 안 했으면 좋겠다.

SHORT DIALOGUE 1

Sandra   How was the lecture? What was Professor Hugh **talking about**?

Neil   It was so boring. He was **droning on** about the economy and the stock market. I was glad when he finally **shut up**. I hate this class.

Sandra   Well, we all have to attend the class anyways. What else can we do? Skip?

Neil   Maybe I will. I'm sure I could easily **explain away** my absence.

Sandra   강의는 어땠어? Hugh 교수님이 무슨 얘기한 거야?
Neil   정말 지루했어. 교수님이 경제하고 주식 시장에 대해서 질질 끌며 말씀하셨어. 교수님이 입 닫으니까 좋더라. 난 이 수업 정말 싫어.
Sandra   음, 어쨌든 우리 다 그 수업에 들어가야 하잖아. 우리가 뭘 할 수 있겠어? 수업 빠지는 거?
Neil   난 그럴지도 몰라. 내가 왜 결석했는지 쉽게 해명할 수 있을 것 같아.

freeze up

(긴장되어서) 얼다

To suddenly
be unable to speak
or act normally

The moment he got on stage, he
froze up and could not speak.

무대에 올라가자마자, 그는 긴장이 돼 얼어서 말을
못했다.

come up with

(말할 것을) 생각해 내다

To formulate

I need to **come up with** something
to say during my speech tonight.

오늘 밤 연설에서 무슨 말을 해야 할지 생각해 내야 해.

let out

(감정을) 표출하다

To express, often in a way that
releases emotion

Sometimes you should **let** your
feelings **out**. It is good for your
health.

가끔은 숨기지 말고 감정을 표출해야 해. 그게
네 건강에 좋아.

chatter away

오랫동안 떠들다

To speak for
a long time

Once my daughter starts speaking,
she just **chatters away** all day long.

내 딸은 일단 말하기 시작하면, 하루 종일 떠든다.

SHORT DIALOGUE 2

Jessica You totally **froze up** on stage. What happened?

Leo When I saw all of those people, I got nervous and couldn't **come up with**
anything to say.

Jessica You need to find a way to relax. Next time, just take a breath and **let it out**.

Leo I know. I can normally just **chatter away**, but public speaking scares me.

Jessica 너 무대 위에서 완전히 얼었는데, 어떻게 된 거야?
Leo 그 많은 사람들을 보니까, 긴장돼서 무슨 말을 해야 할지 생각이 안 났어.
Jessica 긴장을 푸는 방법을 찾아야겠다. 다음 번에는 호흡을 깊게 하고 내쉬어 봐.
Leo 알았어. 평소에는 잘도 떠드는데, 사람들 앞에서 말하는 건 정말 무서워.

open up

마음을 터놓고 말하다

To share true feelings
or emotions

It's time for me to **open up** to my
wife about how I really feel.

내가 내 심경이 어떤지 아내와 마음을 터놓고 솔직한
대화를 나눌 때인 것 같아.

prattle on

~에 대해서 계속 수다를 떨다

To speak for a long
time, longer than
necessary

You've been **prattling on** about the
same thing for hours.

넌 같은 이야기를 몇 시간째 계속 하고 있어.

talk down to

~에게 (얕보는 듯한 투로) 말하다

To talk to someone
as if they are less
intelligent than you

Don't **talk down to** me like that. I'm
not an idiot.

나한테 그렇게 깔보는 투로 말하지 마! 내가 바본 줄
알아?

cut in

(말·대화에) 끼어들다

To interrupt someone
while they are
speaking

I'm sorry, but I need to **cut in** here;
you're wrong.

미안한데, 내가 여기서 좀 끼어들어야겠어.
네가 틀렸어.

SHORT DIALOGUE 3

Beth And then my boss came into my office and started **talking down to** me. And
then the photocopier stopped working, and…

Jerry I hate to **cut in**, Beth. But you've been talking about work for an hour. Do you
remember my question?

Beth I'm so sorry! I've just been **prattling on** and on. What did you ask?

Jerry It's okay. I'm glad that you feel comfortable **opening up** to me. I just asked if you
wanted to go get some ice cream. Maybe after your bad day, you'll feel better.

Beth 그러고 나서 보스가 사무실에 들어오더니 나를 깔보는 투로 말하기 시작했어. 그리고 복사기가
작동이 안 되는 거야. 그리고….

Jerry Beth, 끼어들고 싶지 않은데, 너 한 시간 내내 일 이야기만 하고 있어. 너 내가 물어본 건 기억해?

Beth 정말 미안해! 계속 내 이야기만 했지. 네가 뭐 물어봤더라?

Jerry 괜찮아. 네가 편안하게 느껴서 나한테 솔직하게 터놓고 말해 줘서 기뻐. 아이스크림 먹으러 갈지 물어
봤어. 재수 없는 날에는 (아이스크림 먹으면) 기분이 좋아질 거야.

let in on

(비밀을) 알리다

To trust someone or
share a secret with
someone

I **let** Gail **in on** our secret, okay?

내가 Gail에게 우리 비밀을 알렸는데, 괜찮지?

talk to

~와 대화하다, 말하다

To speak with

You got a minute? I need to **talk to you.**

시간 좀 있어? 너한테 할 얘기가 있어.

go off on

버럭 화를 내다,
소리를 지르다

To rant or yell
at someone

When Jane told me she hated my
husband, I **went off on** her.

Jane이 내 남편이 싫다고 말했을 때, 난 버럭 화를
냈다.

have (it) out

논쟁하다, 결판을 짓다

To have an
argument

Sometimes the only way to solve
a disagreement is to **have** it **out**
with that person.

때때로 의견 차이를 해결하는 유일한 방법은
그 사람과 결판을 짓게 이야기하는 것이다.

SHORT DIALOGUE 1

Thomas   Can I **let** you **in on** a secret?

Kimberly   Of course. You know you can always **talk to** me.

Thomas   I overheard Samantha **going off on** your little sister yesterday. I thought you
should know.

Kimberly   I'll **have** it **out** with her when I see her tomorrow.

Thomas   내가 비밀 하나 알려 줄까?
Kimberly   그래. 나한테는 뭐든 항상 말해도 돼.
Thomas   어제 Samantha가 네 여동생한테 막 뭐라고 하는 거 우연히 들었어. 너도 알아야 할 것 같아서.
Kimberly   내일 걔 보면 제대로 한번 결판을 지어야겠어.

speak up

목소리를 내다, 크게 말하다

To say something
or speak louder

Speak up about your own issues
and encourage others the same.

자신의 문제에 대해 목소리를 내고 다른 사람들도
똑같이 그렇게 하도록 격려하세요.

carry on

계속 같은 이야기를 하다

To speak about the
same topic without
end

The retired actress kept **carrying
on** about how she could have been
famous.

그 은퇴한 여배우는 어떻게 자신이 유명해질 수
있었는지 계속해서 말했다.

let on

비밀을 말하다, 털어놓다

To reveal or divulge
information to
someone

Please don't **let on** to anyone that
I won the lottery.

내가 복권 당첨된 건 아무에게도 말하지 말아 줘.

let go

(감정, 기억 등을) 내려놓다

To release something
that is held back or
to forget about
something bothersome

I know you and Mary got into a
fight, but it's time to **let go** of the
anger you have about her.

너랑 Mary가 다툰 거 아는데, 이제 그만 Mary한테
화 풀어.

SHORT DIALOGUE 2

Lauren	I need to **speak up** about something.
Wade	Fine, but don't **carry on**. I don't have all day.
Lauren	Taylor **let on** that you've been talking about me. What did you say about me?
Wade	Oh, **let** it **go**, Lauren. You're so sensitive.

Lauren	나 뭐 좀 말해야겠는데.
Wade	좋아. 그런데 길게 하지는 마. 나 시간이 별로 없거든.
Lauren	Taylor가 네가 나에 대해서 말하고 다닌다고 털어놓았어. 나에 대해서 뭐라고 한 거니?
Wade	그냥 잊어. Lauren. 너 너무 예민하다.

PHONES AND PHONE CALLS
전화와 전화 통화

MP3 **020**

call up

~에게 전화를 걸다

To make a phone call to someone in particular

You can **call** me **up** anytime if you need my help.
내 도움이 필요하면 언제든지 전화해.

hang up (on)

전화를 끊다

To end a phone call

Don't **hang up on** your mother without saying "I love you."
사랑한다는 말도 없이 어머니의 전화를 끊지 마세요.

text back

문자 회신하다

To return a text

Sometimes I forget to **text back** my friends.
가끔 나는 친구들에게 문자 회신하는 것을 잊는다.

call back

(전화를 했던 사람에게)
다시 전화하다

To return a call

I'm still waiting for my lawyer to **call** me **back**.
저는 아직 제 변호사의 회신 전화를 기다리고 있어요.

SHORT DIALOGUE 1

Maxine   I'm sorry to **call** you **up** so late.

Kayla   I really don't want to **hang up on** you, but I can't talk right now. Everyone is in bed.

Maxine   I missed your call earlier. I just thought I would call instead of just **texting** you **back**.

Kayla   Thanks for that. I'll **call** you **back** first thing in the morning. Good night!

Maxine   너무 늦게 전화해서 미안.
Kayla   전화 끊기는 싫은데, 지금은 통화 못 해. 다들 자고 있어서.
Maxine   부재중 전화가 와 있어서. 문자 보낼까 하다가 전화한 거야.
Kayla   고마워. 내가 내일 아침에 일어나서 바로 전화할게. 잘 자!

check out

살펴보다, 확인(조사)하다

To evaluate someone
or something

I just got a new phone, and I can't
wait to **check out** all of its cool
features!

나 전화기 새로 샀는데, 그 죽여주는 기능들을 얼른
확인하고 싶어 죽겠어!

zoom in

줌 렌즈로 클로즈업해서 잡다, 확대하다

To adjust the lense of
a camera or perspective
of a photograph so that
objects seem bigger
or closer

You can **zoom in** on this photo to
see all of the tiny details.

네가 세세한 것까지 다 보려면 이 사진을 확대하면 돼.

zoom out

(줌 렌즈를 써서 피사체를) 축소하다

To adjust the lense of
a camera or perspective
of a photograph so that
objects seem smaller
or more distant

Zoom out on the map so
that I can see where we are.

여기가 어딘지 알 수 있게 지도를 축소해 봐.

pick up

전화를 받다

To answer a phone

The last three times I called you, you
didn't even **pick up**!

내가 마지막으로 세 번이나 전화했는데도 네가 전화
안 받았잖아!

SHORT DIALOGUE 2

Lana   **Check out** my new phone! See how close you can **zoom in** on the camera?

Robert   Even when **zoomed out**, the quality is amazing!

Lana   You're right. And the speakers are great as well.

Robert   Call Jessie. I want to hear the sound quality. I hope she **picks up**.

> Lana   내 새 전화기 좀 봐 봐! 카메라로 얼마나 가까이 확대할 수 있는지 봐 보라니까.
> Robert   줌 아웃했을 때도, 화질이 장난 아니네!
> Lana   맞아. 스피커도 너무 좋아.
> Robert   Jessie한테 전화해 봐. 통화 음질은 어떤지 듣고 싶다. Jessie가 전화 받으면 좋겠는데.

call around

여기저기 전화하다 (보통 정보를 얻기 위해 여러 사람들에게 전화하다)

To call different people or businesses with a request or question

It would be good to **call around** and see if any local restaurants are hiring.

여기저기 전화해서 동네 식당에서 사람을 구하고 있는지 알아보면 좋을 것 같아.

hang on

(전화를 끊지 않고) 기다리다

To pause; To wait

Hmm

Hang on while I get my brother to come to the phone.

오빠가 전화 받을 때까지 끊지 말고 기다려 주세요.

put on

전화를 바꿔 주다

To hand the phone to someone

Can you **put** Luke **on** the phone?

Luke 좀 바꿔 줄래?

transfer to

전화를 연결해 주다
(다른 사람이나 번호로 전화를 연결하다)

To put a call through; To direct a call to another person or number

Thank you for your call. Allow me to **transfer** you **to** our sales department.

전화 주셔서 감사합니다. 영업부로 연결해 드리겠습니다.

SHORT DIALOGUE 3

Jay
Hello. Is this Corner Bookshop? I'm **calling around** to find a place to sell my used books.

Employee
You have the right place! **Hang on** while I get a pen and paper.

Jay
Actually, could you just **put on** your manager for me?

Employee
Sure! She's in the office, but I can **transfer** you **to** her.

Jay
여보세요. Corner 서점이죠? 제 중고책들을 팔 수 있는 곳에 전화를 하고 있는데요.

Employee
전화 잘하셨어요! 펜하고 종이 가져올 동안 잠시 기다려 주세요.

Jay
저 실은, 매니저님 좀 바꿔 주시겠어요?

Employee
알겠습니다. 지금 사무실에 계시는데, 전화 연결해 드릴게요.

LONG DIALOGUE

Lyla: Trevor! 어제 전화 못 받아서 미안해. 정말 바빴거든. 아, 좋은 소식 있어. 이곳저곳 전화를 돌렸는데, 우리가 공연할 수 있는 장소를 찾았어!

— Trevor: 그래서 전화 바로 못했구나? 어디에 있는데?

Lyla: Uncle Sam's Bar and Grill이라는 곳이야. 매니저하고 통화했는데, 나를 사장한테 연결해 줬어. 사장이 무슨 요일에 연주할 수 있는지 내일 전화 준다고 했어.

— Trevor: 좋았어! 이번이 우리 첫 라이브 콘서트가 되겠네. 긴장하지 않고 잘하면 좋겠다. 또 다른 곳에도 연락해 봤어?

Lyla: 다른 곳들도 연락해 봤는데, 별로 였어. 대부분은 그냥 바로 전화를 끊었고, 한 남자는 진짜 좀 이상했어.

— Trevor: 왜?

Lyla: 자기가 어떻게 록 음악을 싫어하게 되었는지 계속 말하더라고. 그냥 다 말하게 됐어.

— Trevor: 도대체 록 음악을 누가 싫어 해? 완전 구닥다리네.

Lyla: 음, 마침내 그 사람이 입을 다물었을 때, 어쨌든 그 사람 바에서 우리 음악을 연주하기는 힘들 것 같다고 말했어.

— Trevor: 그 사람 그냥 아니라고 말했으면 될 텐데 참. 굳이 그렇게 계속 말할 필요가 없었잖아.

Lyla: 그런 식으로 나한테 막 말하는 거 별로였어. 앞으로 다시는 그 누구도 나한테 깔보듯 말하지 못 하게 할 거야.

— Trevor: 잠깐만! 우리 곧 콘서트가 있잖아. 그럼 연습해야지! 오늘 밤에 우리 집에 모여서 리허설 하자고.

Lyla: Trevor! Sorry. I didn't **pick up** your call yesterday. I was super busy. Well, I've got some good news. I **called around** and found a venue where we could perform!

— **Trevor:** That's why you didn't **call** me **back**, huh? Where is this place?

Lyla: It's called Uncle Sam's Bar and Grill. I **talked to** the manager, and she **transferred** me **to** the owner himself. He said he would **call** me **up** tomorrow and tell me what days we could play.

— **Trevor:** Amazing! This will be our first live concert. I hope we don't **freeze up**. Did you call anywhere else?

Lyla: I **called up** a few other places, but they didn't seem right. Most of them **hung up on** me. One guy was really weird.

— **Trevor:** What makes you say that?

Lyla: He kept **prattling on** about how he hated rock music. I allowed him to **let** it all **out** before I said anything.

— **Trevor:** Who doesn't like rock music? He's so old school.

Lyla: Well, when he finally **shut up**, I told him that he probably couldn't handle our music, anyway.

— **Trevor:** He could have just said "no." He didn't need to **carry on** like that.

Lyla: I didn't appreciate him **going off on** me. I will never let anyone **talk down to** me like that again.

— **Trevor:** **Hang on**! We have a concert soon. Then, I think we have to practice! Let's meet at my place tonight to rehearse.

print out
(프린터로) 출력하다

To produce a physical copy of something with a printer

I need to **print out** our tickets for the flight.
난 우리 비행기 표를 출력해야 해.

log on
단말기나 계정에 접속하다

To access an account or device, typically with a username and password

Log on to your computer so that I can use it.
내가 네 컴퓨터를 사용할 수 있게 네가 접속해 줘.

scroll down
스크롤 바를 내리다

To move the page on a screen down

You need to **scroll down** to see the price of the tickets on this website.
이 웹사이트에서 티켓 가격을 보려면 스크롤 바를 내려야 해.

switch on
(전등 따위의) 스위치를 켜다

To activate or start a device with a switch or button

Switch on the fan over there for me. The room is very hot.
저기 저 선풍기 전원 좀 켜 줘. 방이 너무 더워.

SHORT DIALOGUE 1

Steve I need to **print out** an assignment. Can you do that for me?

Nelle Sure. I just need to **log on**. Can you email it to me with your phone?

Steve I already did. Go to your inbox and **scroll down**. You will be able to find it.

Nelle Here it is. Let me **switch on** the printer. I hope this works. My printer is very old.

Steve 나 과제물 프린트해야 하는데, 네가 좀 해 줄래?
Nelle 그래. 나 로그온 좀 하고, 네 폰으로 나한테 메일 보내 줘.
Steve 이미 보냈어. 메일함에 들어가서 스크롤 바를 내려 봐. 찾을 수 있을 거야.
Nelle 여기 있네. 프린터 켤게. 프린터가 작동을 하면 좋겠다. 내 프린터가 정말 오래됐거든.

MP3 022

tune in

(라디오·텔레비전 프로를) 청취[시청]하다

To choose a radio station; To listen to a broadcast

Paul **tuned in** to the weather station to hear about the storm.

Paul은 폭풍과 관련해 들으려고 날씨 채널을 들었다.

rig up

(뭐든 있는 재료를 가지고) ~을 급히 만들다, 설치하다

To create or put together equipment, typically in a sudden and improvised fashion

It was too dark out, so I had to **rig up** some lighting for the photoshoot.

밖이 너무 어두워서, 나는 사진 촬영을 위해 급히 조명을 설치해야 했다.

pull up

접속하다

To access a page, document, or application on a device

Let me **pull up** the spreadsheet that shows our sales last year.

작년 저희 매출액을 보여 주는 엑셀 자료를 열어서 보여 드릴게요.

drown out

(소음이) ~을 들리지 않게 하다

To overpower or block one sound with another

The sound of the crowd **drowned out** my voice.

사람들 소리에 내 목소리가 묻혀 버렸다.

SHORT DIALOGUE 2

Travis You are doing your live podcast tonight, right? I wanted to **tune in** live, but I might have to work late.

Jenny I hope I can do it live, but the problem is I just **rigged up** a good camera for live streaming, but my microphone isn't working.

Travis I have a microphone you can use. It's good because it will **drown out** the background noise.

Jenny Thanks, man. And, don't worry if you can't watch the live stream. You can just **pull up** the recording on the website later.

Travis 오늘 밤에 너 팟캐스트 라이브 방송하지, 그렇지? 라이브로 듣고 싶었는데, 야근할 수도 있어서.
Jenny 라이브로 하면 좋겠는데, 문제는 라이브 하려고 좋은 카메라는 연결했는데, 마이크가 작동하지 않네.
Travis 나한테 네가 쓸 만한 마이크가 있거든. 이거 괜찮아. 주변 소리를 잘 잡아 줄 거야.
Jenny 고마워. 그리고 라이브로 못 봐도 걱정 마. 나중에 웹사이트 접속해서 녹화한 거 보면 되니까.

plug in

~의 플러그를 꽂다[전원을 연결하다],
~을 …에 연결하다

To connect a device
to a power source or
another device with
a cable

I'll need to **plug in** my phone
because it's almost dead.
내 전화기 배터리가 거의 없어서 플러그 꽂고
충전해야겠다.

load up

프로그램을 돌리다, 작동시키다

To run a program

Load up the software that you use
to edit pictures.
사진을 편집하는 데 사용하는 소프트웨어를 작동시켜
주세요.

tune up

정비하다, (악기를) 조율하다

To repair or perform
maintenance on a device
or instrument;
To adjust the strings
of an instrument till it is
in the correct key

Julia **tuned up** her violin before she
walked on to the stage.
Julia는 무대에 올라가기 전에 바이올린을 조율했다.

play back

(음악·비디오를) 틀어[들려/보여] 주다

To play a sound,
song, or video that
has recently been
captured

Play back the song we just
recorded.
우리가 방금 녹음한 노래를 틀어 줘.

SHORT DIALOGUE 3

Grayson   I can't wait to **plug in** this new guitar and get some recording done.

Sophia   I **loaded up** a new program that'll make editing our music a lot easier. Are you
ready?

Grayson   Let me just **tune up** my guitar. Alright, sounds good. Start recording.

Sophia   Wow! Sounds great. I'll **play** it **back** for you so you can hear it.

Grayson   새로 산 이 기타에 전원 연결해서 녹음 좀 빨리 끝내고 싶어.
Sophia   내가 음악 편집을 훨씬 쉽게 해 주는 새 프로그램도 작동시켜 놨어. 준비됐어?
Grayson   기타 음 좀 맞추고. 됐어. 소리 좋네. 녹음 시작해.
Sophia   와! 소리 정말 좋은데. 네가 들어 보게 틀어 줄게.

MP3 **023**

turn off
(전기·가스·수도 등을) 끄다

To stop the operation or flow of something by means of a tap, switch, or button

Remember to **turn off** the gas.
가스 불 끄는 것 잊지 마.

charge up
(배터리 등을) 충전하다

To give power to the battery of a device

I have to **charge up** my laptop before I go on vacation.
휴가 가기 전에 내 노트북을 충전해야 한다.

hook up
연결하다

To plug in

You have to **hook up** your phone to the computer.
네 전화기를 컴퓨터에 연결해야 해.

start up
~을 시작하다, 시동을 걸다

To cause a machine or device to begin operating or being used

You will have to wait for a few seconds after you **start** it **up**.
시동을 걸고 나서 몇 초 기다려야 해.

SHORT DIALOGUE 1

Susie Hello, my phone keeps **turning off**. Can you help me out?

Service Provider Is the battery low? Maybe you need to **charge** it **up**.

Susie That's not it. I've had it **hooked up** to the charger all day.

Service Provider Let me try to reset it. If it doesn't **start up** after that, I may need to keep it here for a few hours while our technicians look at it.

Susie 제 전화기가 계속 꺼져요. 좀 도와주시겠어요?
Service Provider 배터리가 거의 없는 거 아니에요? 충전을 하셔야 할 것 같은데요.
Susie 그게 아니에요. 충전기에 하루 종일 연결해 놨어요.
Service Provider 제가 한번 초기화해 볼게요. 그래도 시작이 안 되면, 저희 기술자가 보는 동안에 몇 시간 정도 전화기를 맡기셔야 할 수도 있습니다.

open up

(앱이나 문서 등을) 열다

To access a page, document, or application

Open up the document on my computer.
내 컴퓨터에 그 문서를 열어 놔.

hack into

해킹하다

To gain access to something through hacking

Someone **hacked into** my computer and stole all of my photos.

누군가가 내 컴퓨터를 해킹해서 내 사진을 전부 다 훔쳐 갔어.

set up

(소프트웨어를) 설치하다, 설정하다

To assemble something or to install software

Can you help me **set up** my email account?
내 이메일 계정 설정하는 것 좀 도와줄 수 있어?

log off

단말기 작동을 끝내다, 로그오프[로그아웃]하다

To exit an account on a computer or program

I forgot to **log off** of my bank account.
내 은행 계좌에서 로그아웃하는 걸 깜박했어.

SHORT DIALOGUE 2

Andrew　My email account got **hacked into**! Someone is using my email address to send strange messages.

Jena　I would just delete that account and **set up** a new one if I were you.

Andrew　I can't. I got **logged off**, and someone changed my password.

Jena　Oh, no! How did this happen? Did you **open up** a suspicious email or something?

Andrew　내 이메일 계정이 해킹당했어! 누군가 내 이메일 주소를 사용해서 이상한 메시지를 보내고 있어.
Jena　내가 너라면 계정 삭제하고, 새 계정을 만들겠다.
Andrew　그렇게 못해. 내가 로그오프됐고, 누군가 내 비번을 바꿔 놨어.
Jena　이런! 어떻게 이런 일이 일어났지? 너 수상한 이메일 같은 거 열었니?

MP3 **024**

let in

~을 들어오게 하다, 통하게 하다

To allow entry or access to

My mother's here. Can you **let** her **in**?

저희 엄마가 여기 계시는데요. 엄마 들어가시게 해 주세요.

fit in

~이 들어갈 공간을 만들다

To find room or have sufficient space for someone or something

I don't think those things will **fit in** here.

그것들이 여기에 안 들어갈 것 같아요.

turn away

(입장이나 접근을) 거부하다

To deny access or entry to

I was **turned away** from the club.

나는 클럽에서 입장 거부당했어.

roll up

도착하다, 모습을 드러내다

To arrive

Can we get some food before we **roll up** to Amy's house?

Amy의 집에 도착하기 전에 음식 좀 살까?

SHORT DIALOGUE 1

Dennis   Molly! Jane is here. I know that you two aren't friends anymore. Should I **let** her **in**?

Molly   I'm not sure. I don't know how many more people I can **fit in** my apartment.

Dennis   I'll just go downstairs and **turn** her **away**. Don't worry about it.

Molly   Thanks. I can't believe she's here. How could she **roll up** to my party after what she said about me?

Dennis   Molly! Jane이 왔어. 너네 이제는 친구 아닌 거 아는데, 들어오라고 해?
Molly   글쎄. 사람들이 얼마나 더 우리 집에 들어올 수 있을지도 모르겠고.
Dennis   내가 내려가서 돌려보낼게. 걱정하지 마.
Molly   고마워. 걔가 여기 왔다는 게 안 믿겨. 어떻게 나에 대해 그렇게 말하고 나서 내 파티에 올 수 있지?

come out

나오다, 참석하다

To go to a social event

Is Paul gonna **come out** to the party?

Paul이 파티에 오나요?

join in

참여하다

To participate

I want to come over and **join in** the fun.

나는 들러서 재미있는 시간 같이 보내고 싶다.

show up

(예정된 곳에) 나타나다, 도착하다, 오다

To arrive to an event or location

We need to be ready when the guests **show up** to the party.

손님들이 파티에 올 때 우리는 맞을 준비가 돼 있어야 한다.

miss out

~을 놓치다

To fail to or be unable to experience something

I recorded the concert for you so that you don't **miss out**.

네가 놓치지 않게 내가 콘서트를 녹화했어.

SHORT DIALOGUE 2

Amber   Where were you last night? Why didn't you **come out** with us?

Joe   I was already asleep when you texted me. I'm sorry I couldn't **join in**.

Amber   It's okay. Not many people **showed up**, so you didn't miss much.

Joe   I still feel like I **missed out**. I'll join you for the next one, though.

Amber   어젯밤에 어디 있었어? 왜 우리랑 안 간거야?
Joe   네가 문자 보냈을 때 난 이미 자고 있었어. 같이 가지 못해서 미안해.
Amber   괜찮아. 그렇게 많이 오지도 않았어. 그래서 별로 놓친 것도 없고.
Joe   그래도 뭔가 기회를 날린 기분이 드네. 그렇지만 다음에는 참석할게.

turn up

(공식적인 장소에) 나타나다, 도착하다

To make an
appearance;
To arrive

I'm tired and probably won't **turn up** tonight.

내가 피곤해서 오늘 밤에는 참석 못 할 것 같아.

pour in

쏟아져 들어가다[들어오다]

To enter an area or building in overwhelming numbers

People started **pouring in** to get the best seats for the concert.

사람들이 콘서트에서 가장 좋은 자리를 잡기 위해 몰려 들어오기 시작했다.

jam out

열정적으로 음악에 맞추어 춤을 추다, 열정적으로 연주하다

To dance or move to the music with enthusiasm

I often **jam out** in my car.

난 종종 내 차 안에서 음악에 맞춰 몸을 흔든다.

invite back

답례로 초대하다, ~를 다시[재차] 초대하다

To be asked to return at a later date, typically after making a good impresssion

Because I played so well, the band **invited** me **back** to play with them.

내가 연주를 정말 잘해서, 그 밴드가 같이 연주하자고 나를 다시 초대했다.

SHORT DIALOGUE 3

Nicole   How many people do you think will **turn up** to our concert?

Harry   I invited a lot of people. Hopefully, people will be **pouring in** the doors.

Nicole   I hope so, too. We're going to be **jamming out** till midnight. I hope it's busy.

Harry   If we bring a lot of people in, then they'll probably **invite** us **back** to perform again.

Nicole   우리 콘서트에 사람들이 얼마나 올 것 같아?

Harry   내가 사람들 많이 초대했거든. 정말로 많이 몰려 오면 좋겠다.

Nicole   나도 그러면 좋겠어. 우리 자정까지 열심히 공연할 거잖아. (사람들이 정말 많이 와서) 북적거리면 좋겠다.

Harry   우리가 사람들을 많이 끌어들이면, 거기서 다시 공연해 달라고 우리를 또 초대할 거야.

LONG DIALOGUE

Tommy: 일단 먼저, 여기에 몇 명이나 들어갈 수 있는지 확인해 봐야 해. 큰 행사라서 말이야. 사람들이 많이 올 거라고 생각해?

—— Erica: 토요일 밤이니까 사람들이 많이 올 것 같은데.

Tommy: 그래. 우리가 5,000명 규모의 공연을 준비하되, 혹시 모르니까 안전하게 7,000석을 준비하는 게 어떨까 해. 그렇게 하면, 더 많은 사람들이 참여해서 즐겨도 걱정 없잖아.

—— Erica: 좋아. 내가 무대 옆에 스피커 설치할게. 스피커는 어디다 꽂지?

Tommy: 저쪽 벽에 콘센트 있어. 그럼 내가 스피커를 여기 내 컴퓨터에 연결할게.

—— Erica: 비번이 뭐야? 혹시나 내가 로그인해야 할 수도 있으니까.

Tommy: 비번은 sunglasses야. 사실 네가 컴퓨터가 있는 음향 조정실에 가 있으면 하는데. 행사 끝난 후에 컴퓨터 로그오프하고, 조명도 좀 꺼 줘.

—— Erica: 우왜! 나 음향 조정실에 한 번도 가 본 적 없는데. 내가 사람들이 밴드가 열정적으로 공연하는 소리, 밤새 잘 들을 수 있게 확실히 책임질게.

Tommy: Okay so first, we need to get an idea of how many people will **fit in** here. It's a big event. Do you think a lot of folks will **show up**?

— **Erica:** It's a Saturday night, so I think a lot of people will **come out**.

Tommy: Yeah. I'd say we should prepare for about 5,000 people **turning out** but **set up** for 7,000 seats to be safe. Then we don't have to worry in case more people **join in** the fun.

— **Erica:** Okay. I'll **rig up** the speakers by the stage. Where can I **plug** them **in**?

Tommy: On the wall over there, and I'll **hook** them **up** to my computer over here.

— **Erica:** What's the password in case I have to **log in**?

Tommy: The password is "sunglasses." I'll actually want you in the sound booth with the computer. Just make sure you **log off** and **turn off** the lights after the event.

— **Erica:** Oh wow! I've never been in the sound booth before. I'll make sure everyone will hear the band **jamming out** all night.

CHAPTER

4

PHRASAL VERBS

cook up

빠르게 음식 준비를 하다

To prepare an ingredient or meal especially quickly

Can you **cook up** something nice for my parents when they come over?

우리 부모님이 오시면 맛있는 것 좀 만들어 줄 수 있어?

dig in

(어서) 먹다

To start eating food that is in front of you

Food is ready. Go ahead. **Dig in**!

밥 다 됐다. 어서 먹어라!

order in

(전화로) 음식을 배달시키다

To order food to be delivered

I'm tired and don't want to cook, so we should **order in** tonight.

피곤해서 요리하기 싫어. 오늘 밤에는 배달시켜 먹자.

eat out

외식하다

To eat at a restaurant

We're going to **eat out** at a nice restaurant on my birthday.

내 생일에 우리는 근사한 식당에서 외식할 거야.

SHORT DIALOGUE 1

Don   Dinner is served! I made some lemon chicken and **cooked up** some asparagus on the side.

Megan   This looks delicious! Thanks, Don. I'm happy we didn't **order in** tonight.

Don   Let's **dig in**! Because I don't cook that often. This is a rare occasion.

Megan   I wish we cooked more often. We'd save so much money if we didn't **eat out** so much… Mmm! This is delicious!

Don   저녁 준비됐어! 레몬 치킨하고, 사이드로 아스파라거스 준비했어.
Megan   맛있어 보인다! 고마워, Don. 오늘 저녁엔 배달 안 시켜서 좋다.
Don   먹자! 나 요리 자주 안 하니까. 이건 좀처럼 없는 기회라고.
Megan   더 자주 요리하면 좋겠다. 외식 많이 안 하면 돈도 많이 절약할 텐데. 음… 이거 정말 맛있네!

fry up

(보통 기름을 사용해서) 굽다, 볶다, 튀기다

To prepare something
in a deep fryer or
a frying pan

Let's **fry up** some fish for dinner
tonight.
오늘 밤에는 저녁으로 생선 구워 먹자.

nibble on

~을 조금씩 먹다

To eat slowly or
a small portion

I just need something small to
nibble on before we eat dinner.
저녁 먹기 전에 나 군것질 좀 하고 싶어.

warm up

데우다

To heat something up,
typically leftovers
or as opposed to
cooking from scratch

I'm just going to **warm up** some
leftovers for dinner tonight.
오늘 밤에는 저녁으로 그냥 남은 음식 좀 데울게.

wash down

(음식이나 약을 먹고) ~을 마시다

To take a drink after
consuming food or
medicine

Can I get some more water so I can
wash down these pills?
이 약 먹고 마시게 물 좀 더 주세요.

SHORT DIALOGUE 2

Kelly   Hey, sweetie. What do you want for dinner? Would you like me to **fry up** the last of our dumplings?

Ralph   I'm not too hungry. I'll just find something small to **nibble on**.

Kelly   In that case, I'll **warm up** some leftover pizza instead. I'm not that hungry, either.

Ralph   Here, I'll pour you a coke to **wash** it **down**.

     Kelly   자기야! 저녁 뭐 먹고 싶어? 만두 마지막으로 남은 거 튀겨 줄까?
     Ralph   나 별로 배 안 고픈데. 그냥 가볍게 먹을 수 있는 거 찾아볼게.
     Kelly   그러면, 피자 남은 거 데울게. 나도 그렇게 배고프지 않거든.
     Ralph   여기. 난 피자랑 마실 콜라 따라 줄게.

thaw out

녹이다, 해동하다

To let a frozen item or ingredient come to room temperature

Take the chicken out of the freezer so it will **thaw out** for dinner.

저녁으로 먹게 냉동실에서 닭고기 좀 꺼내서 해동시켜.

whip up

(식사·요리를) 잽싸게 만들어 내다

To cook something quickly

I have to **whip up** a quick lunch before we go to the movies.

우리 영화 보러 가기 전에, 내가 빨리 점심을 만들어야 해.

top off

가득 찰 때까지 추가하다

To add to something until it is full

Do you want me to **top off** your glass?

잔을 가득 채워 드릴까요?

boil over

끓어 넘치다

To heat a liquid to the point that it spills over the top of its container

When boiling water, watch the pot so that it doesn't **boil over**.

물을 끓일 때는 냄비가 넘치지 않도록 잘 봐.

SHORT DIALOGUE 3

Manager   Can I talk to you? You didn't let the steak **thaw out** completely, and now we can't serve it to the customers.

Cook   Sorry. If you'd like, I can **whip up** something to replace it. Maybe pork?

Manager   Not necessary. We **topped off** their wine for free as an apology.

Cook   I won't let it happen again. Oh, I have to return to the stove before my pot **boils over**.

Manager   얘기 좀 할 수 있어? 스테이크를 충분히 해동하지 않아서, 손님들에게 나갈 수 없어.
Cook   죄송합니다. 괜찮으시면, 대신 다른 음식을 빨리 만들 수 있어요. 음, 돼지고기는 어떨까요?
Manager   그럴 필요 없어. 우리가 사과의 표시로 와인을 가득 채워서 따라 드렸어.
Cook   다시는 이런 일 안 일어나게 하겠습니다. 아, 냄비 끓어 넘치기 전에 가 봐야겠어요.

MP3 **027**

shake up

(칵테일을) 흔들어 섞다

To mix something
quickly, typically
cocktails

I'll **shake up** a few cocktails after
dinner.
저녁 식사 후에 내가 칵테일 만들어 줄게.

go with

어울리다

To pair with

Does this wine **go with** the cheese
you picked out?
이 와인은 당신이 고른 치즈와 잘 어울리나요?

drink up

(빨리) 마시다, 들이키다

To drink quickly or at an
accelerated rate

Drink up before the bar closes.
술집 문 닫기 전에 얼른 마시자.

water down

~에 물을 타서 희석시키다

To dilute something

too much
water

This lemonade is too **watered
down**!
이 레모네이드는 물을 너무 많이 탔네!

SHORT DIALOGUE 1

Bettie   I've **shaken up** some cocktails for you while you wait. Here you go.

Brad   What kind of cocktail is it? Will it **go with** the meal that we're having?

Bettie   It's a Black Manhattan, and yes, of course it will. Give it a try. **Drink up**!

Brad   Hmm… Ew! You **watered** it **down** too much. You used too much ice!

> Bettie   네가 기다리는 동안 칵테일 좀 만들었어. 자! 여기.
> Brad   이건 무슨 칵테일이야? 우리가 먹는 식사랑 어울리는 거야?
> Bettie   이거 Black Manhattan이야. 식사하고 잘 어울리지 한번 마셔 봐! 쭉 들이켜!
> Brad   음… 웩! 물을 너무 많이 넣었다. 얼음을 너무 많이 넣었잖아!

chop up

잘게 썰다

To cut into smaller pieces

Chop up the onions for the stew I'm making.
지금 만드는 스튜에 넣을 양파를 잘게 썰어 줘.

take out

가지고[데리고] 가다/오다, 꺼내다

To take something somewhere; To move something from the place that held, enclosed, or hid it

I'm going to **take out** some beers for the party tonight.
오늘 밤 있을 파티에 맥주 가지고 갈 거야.

pig out

게걸스럽게 먹다, 과식하다

To eat quickly and excessively

Are you ready to **pig out** today?
오늘 많이 먹을 준비 됐지?

balance out

조화롭게 하다, 다른 재료를 넣어 덜 자극적이거나 진하게 만들다

To make a flavor or ingredient less powerful or intense by adding another flavor or ingredient

The basil really **balances out** the tomato in your pasta sauce.
바질이 파스타 소스의 토마토 맛을 균형 있게 잡아 주네.

SHORT DIALOGUE 2

Wayne　I'll finish **chopping up** these onions, then it'll be time to boil the spaghetti.
Krystal　Cool. Just tell me when I should **take out** the garlic bread. It's in the oven now.
Wayne　Do we really need the garlic bread? We're really **pigging out** tonight.
Krystal　Of course, it's necessary! It'll help **balance out** the spiciness of the pasta sauce.

Wayne　이 양파 잘게 썰고 나서, 스파게티 삶을 거야.
Krystal　좋아. 언제 마늘빵 꺼내야 하는지 말해 줘. 지금 오븐에 굽고 있어.
Wayne　우리 마늘빵이 필요한가? 오늘 밤에 정말 돼지같이 먹겠는걸.
Krystal　당연하지. 마늘빵은 필수야! 파스타 소스의 매운 맛을 잡아 줄 테니까.

MP3 **028**

run into

뛰어들어 가다, ~와 우연히 만나다

To move into in a sudden way; To meet by chance

I **ran into** my old boss at the grocery store.
난 식료품점에서 예전 상사를 우연히 마주쳤다.

ask out

~에게 데이트를 신청하다

To ask someone to go on a date

How do I **ask** her **out**?
어떻게 그녀에게 데이트 신청을 하죠?

ask after

~에 대해 (안부를) 묻다

To ask for news regarding someone who is not present

My mother **asked after** you when I spoke with her on the phone.
어머니와 통화했을 때 어머니가 네 안부를 물었어.

pass by

~ 옆을 지나가다

To walk past

I **passed by** my old school yesterday.
나는 어제 내 모교를 지나갔다.

SHORT DIALOGUE 1

Dana   I was **passing by** the shops on Main Street yesterday, and do you know who I **ran into**? Glenda! You remember her?

Shane   Yeah. She was that girl I **asked out** a few months ago. How is she?

Dana   She seemed good. She **asked after** you, too. I told her you were doing well.

Shane   That's sweet.

> **Dana**   어제 Main Street 상점가를 지나가는데, 내가 누구랑 마주쳤는지 알아? Glenda 만났어! 걔 기억해?
> **Shane**   응. 내가 몇 달 전에 데이트 신청했던 애잖아. 어떻게 지내?
> **Dana**   좋아 보이던데. 걔도 네 안부 묻더라. 그래서 잘 지낸다고 했지.
> **Shane**   그래, 잘했어.

stumble upon

~을 우연히 발견하다

To discover or find something spontaneously and without planning

I **stumbled upon** this great dating site on the way back home.

난 집에 오다가 정말로 멋진 이 데이트 장소를 우연히 발견했어.

try out

시도해 보다, 시험해 보다

To do something for the first time for the sake of testing its quality

We should **try out** a Korean restaurant sometime.

우리 언제 한국 식당에 가서 식사를 해 보자.

pencil in

(나중에 바뀔지도 모르지만)
일단은 ~을 예정해 놓다

To make time for someone or something in a schedule

We've **pencilled in** a meeting for Monday morning.

우리가 월요일 아침에 회의를 하는 것으로 일단 잡아 놓았다.

round up

(사람들을) 모으다

To gather

Can you **round up** the employees for a meeting in the break room?

휴게실에서 회의하게 직원들을 불러 모아 줄래요?

SHORT DIALOGUE 2

Ethan   I **stumbled upon** a cool bar yesterday. We should go there sometime.

Tonya   Hmm. I've been looking for a new spot to **try out**. When are you free?

Ethan   I have a busy week, but maybe I can **pencil** you **in** on Thursday or Friday night.

Tonya   That works. And I'll **round up** some more people to go with us!

Ethan   내가 어제 우연히 끝내주는 술집을 발견했어. 언제 한번 거기 가 보자.
Tonya   음. 새로운 곳을 찾고는 있었는데. 넌 언제 시간 돼?
Ethan   이번 주는 좀 바쁘긴 한데, 목요일이나 금요일 저녁에 일단 시간 낼 수 있을 것 같아.
Tonya   나도 그때 괜찮아. 같이 갈 사람들을 더 모아 볼게!

pop into
~을 잠깐 방문하다

To visit a place spontaneously and typically without staying long

Have you ever **popped into** that new bar on the corner?
혹시 모퉁이에 새로 생긴 술집에 가 봤어?

meet up (with)
만나다

To join someone or to socialize with someone

Have you **met up with** Jason since he got back from vacation?
Jason이 휴가에서 돌아온 후에 만난 적 있어?

have around
(친구나 물건) 가까이에 있다

To be in the presence of someone or something

You're a good friend to **have around** when I'm sad.
넌 내가 슬플 때 곁에 있어 주는 좋은 친구야.

lead on
(특히 거짓말로) ~를 유혹하다

To flirt without the intention of doing anything romantic

I want you to stop **leading on** my best friend!
너 내 가장 친한 친구 유혹하는 것 그만둬!

SHORT DIALOGUE 3

Anna   You'll never guess who **popped into** my cafe today. Jeff!

Mary   Jeff? You mean that cute guy you **met up with** a few months ago?

Anna   The same one, yeah. I guess I really missed **having** him **around**.

Mary   Anna! Don't contact him if you're just going to **lead** him **on**.

Anna   오늘 우리 카페에 누가 들렀는지 너 상상도 못 할걸. Jeff가 왔어!
Mary   Jeff? 몇 달 전에 네가 만났던 그 매력적인 애 말하는 거야?
Anna   응, 바로 그 애. 내가 걔랑 함께했던 시간이 정말 그리웠나 봐.
Mary   Anna! 너 또 그 사람이랑 제대로 사귈 맘도 없으면서 그럴 거면 연락하지 매!

go out
사귀다

> To go on a date;
> To be dating

Is it weird if I **go out** with my coworker?
내가 직장 동료하고 사귀면 이상한가?

take out
데리고 나가다

> To invite someone on or plan a date

You have to plan the date if you want to **take** me **out**.
날 데리고 나가려면 네가 데이트 계획을 세워야 해.

wait around
(상대가 준비될 때까지) 기다리다

> To wait for someone or something to be ready

I'm not going to **wait around** for you to get here.
난 네가 여기 올 때까지 안 기다릴 거야.

go for
~을 먹으러[마시러] 가다

> To go get food, a meal, or drinks with someone

You want to **go** out **for** a drink?
술 한잔하러 갈래?

SHORT DIALOGUE 1

Matt   I really like Liz. But she'd never **go out** with a guy like me.

Frank   The first step is to **take** her **out** as friends. That way, you can see if you have anything in common.

Matt   You're right. I keep **waiting around** for the right opportunity. I should just do it.

Frank   Yeah! Just ask her to **go for** a drink with you. And be yourself. Don't take it too seriously.

Matt   나 Liz가 정말 좋아. 그런데 걔는 나 같은 사람하고는 데이트 안 하겠지.

Frank   먼저 데리고 나가서 친구처럼 가볍게 만나 봐. 그러다 보면, 뭔가 통하는 게 있는지 알 수 있잖아.

Matt   네 말이 맞아. 나는 계속 좋은 기회만 오기를 기다리는데, 그냥 해 봐야겠어.

Frank   그래! 그냥 술 한잔하자고 해 봐. 평소 네 모습대로 해. 너무 진지하게 생각하지 말고.

hook up

같이 자다, 성관계를 맺다

To engage in sexual activities

I **hooked up** with my crush last night.

난 첫눈에 사랑에 빠진 그녀와 어젯밤에 같이 잤다.

put off

~을 싫어하게 만들다

To cause someone to dislike someone or something

I was very **put off** by the way my date treated the waiter.

내 데이트 상대가 웨이터를 대하는 걸 보고 정말 싫어져 버렸다.

turn on

(성적으로) 흥분시키다

To sexually arouse

Seeing Jim lifting weights really **turns** me **on**.

Jim이 역기를 드는 모습을 보면 난 흥분이 돼.

give in

굴복하다, 항복하다

To surrender

Jack kept asking me on a date until I finally **gave in**.

Jack은 내가 결국 오케이 할 때까지 계속해서 데이트 신청을 했어.

SHORT DIALOGUE 2

Katherine You'll never believe it, Ellie. I went out with Vince last night and we **hooked up**!

Ellie What?! Last time we spoke, you were pretty **put off** by him constantly asking you out. What made you **give in**?

Katherine Well, we hung out yesterday, and he was sweet and thoughtful, nothing like how he acts at work. And then later he was really **turning** me **on**…

Ellie Okay, okay, I get it. So, do you think it will be awkward when you see him in the office tomorrow?

Katherine Ellie, 너 이거 절대 안 믿을걸. 나 어젯밤에 Vince랑 데이트하고 같이 잤어.

Ellie 뭐?! 지난번에는 너한테 계속 데이트하자고 해서 정말 싫다고 하지 않았어? 왜 넘어간 거야?

Katherine 그게, 어제 함께 시간을 보냈는데, 정말 다정하고 사려 깊더라. 직장에서 행동하는 것과는 전혀 달랐어. 그리고 나중에는 걔가 날 흥분시키더라고.

Ellie 알았어. 이해해. 그래서 내일 사무실에서 그 사람 보면 어색할 거라는 생각은 안 해?

LONG DIALOGUE

Devin: 그래서 어젯밤에 뭐 했어?

—— **Kristy:** 너 Hank 알지? 지난달에
나한테 데이트 신청한 애.

Devin: Hank… 아! 이제 기억난다.

—— **Kristy:** 어쨌거나, 목요일에 봤는데,
또 다시 데이트하자고 해서,
어젯밤에 결국 그러자고 했어.

Devin: 어땠어?

—— **Kristy:** 정말 좋았어! Main Street의
이탈리아 식당에 날 데리고
갔어. 일 년 동안 거길
지나다녔지만, 안에는 한 번도
들어간 적이 없거든.

Devin: 와! 나도 그 식당 가 보고
싶었는데. 어땠어?

—— **Kristy:** 음식이 정말 끝내줬어. Hank가
애피타이저로 조금 먹기 딱
좋은 아란치니 볼을 골랐어.
그리고 우리가 마신 와인이
파스타와 너무 잘 어울리더라.

Devin: 아란치니 볼이 뭐야?

—— **Kristy:** 아, 빵가루를 묻혀서 튀긴
리소토 볼이야. 찍어 먹을 수
있게 마리나라 소스를 주는데,
정말 맛있어.

Devin: 맛있겠다.

—— **Kristy:** 유일하게 맘에 안 들었던 건
서비스였어. 주문하는 데 너무
오래 기다려야 했던 것 같아.

Devin: 데이트하면서 또 뭐 했어?

—— **Kristy:** 저녁 먹은 후에 우연히 발견한
작은 빵집에 들러서 Hank가
같이 먹을 브라우니를 사 줬어.
그리고 커피 한잔 같이 마시고
싶은지 물어봤어.

Devin: 와… 그래서 너희들 같이
잔 거야?

—— **Kristy:** 아니야, 당연히 아니지! 첫 번째
데이트였다니까!

Devin: So what did you do last night?

— Kristy: You know that guy, Hank? He's the one who **asked** me **out** last month…

Devin: Hank… Oh yeah! I remember now.

— Kristy: Anyways, I saw him on Thursday, and he asked me to **go out** with him again. So last night I finally **gave in**.

Devin: How was it?

— Kristy: It was great! He **took** me **out** to that Italian restaurant on Main Street. You know, I've been **passing by** it for a year, but I'd never been inside.

Devin: Oh! I've been wanting to **try** that place **out** too. How was it?

— Kristy: The food was great. Hank picked out the perfect appetizer, these arancini balls, to **nibble on**. And the wine we had **went** great **with** my pasta.

Devin: What are arancini balls?

— Kristy: Oh, they are these risotto balls that are breaded and **fried up**. They serve them with marinara sauce to dip them in. They are so good.

Devin: Sounds delicious.

— Kristy: The only problem was the service. I felt like we had to **wait around** a long time to order.

Devin: Did you guys do anything else on your date?

— Kristy: We **popped into** this little bakery that we **stumbled upon** after dinner and Hank bought us a brownie to share. And then he asked if I wanted to **go for** some coffee.

Devin: That great... So, did you guys **hook up**?

— Kristy: No, of course not! It was the first date!

die for

~을 너무 사랑하다

To love intensely

I would **die for** my children.

난 우리 아이들을 위해서라면 죽을 수도 있을 만큼 사랑해.

warm up to

~을 좋아하게 되다, 가까워지다

To become familiar with something or someone; To grow to enjoy something

It takes a bit for me to **warm up to** new people.

난 새로운 사람들과 가까워지기까지는 시간이 좀 걸린다.

grow on

~이 (시간이 갈수록) 점점 좋아지다, 마음에 들다

To like someone or something more over time

This book is really **growing on** me.

이 책이 시간이 갈수록 점점 내 마음에 든다.

do without

~ 없이 지내다, 해내다

To live or work without having someone or something

I can't **do without** my family.

난 가족 없이는 살 수가 없어.

SHORT DIALOGUE 1

Paco   I would **die for** my dog, Dolly. I love her so much!

Salena   I have to admit, I didn't like her at first, but now I'm **warming up to** her.

Paco   Yeah! She tends to **grow on** people if you give her enough time.

Salena   You're right. I could **do without** most dogs, but Dolly is special.

Paco   난 우리 개 Dolly를 위해서라면 죽을 수도 있을 만큼 사랑해. 정말 너무 사랑한다니깐!

Salena   솔직히, 처음에는 Dolly가 별로였는데, 지금은 좋아지고 있어.

Paco   그래! Dolly하고 충분한 시간을 보내면, 사람들이 보통 Dolly를 점점 좋아하더라고.

Salena   맞아. 대부분의 개들은 없어도 살겠는데, Dolly는 특별해.

care for

좋아하다

To be fond of;
To love

I really do **care for** my nieces and nephews.
나는 조카들을 정말 좋아한다.

feel for

~를 불쌍히 여기다, 동정하다

To feel sympathy towards someone

I **feel for** my friend who lost her job.
난 직장을 잃은 내 친구가 불쌍하다.

catch on

(~을) 이해하다, 알게 되다

To understand;
To become aware of something

Have you **caught on** that my father doesn't like you?
우리 아빠가 너를 마음에 안 들어하는 거 알았어?

be interested in

이성으로 감정을 가지다

To have feelings for someone

Do you know that Blake **is interested in** you?
Blake가 너에게 관심이 있다는 것 알고 있어?

SHORT DIALOGUE 2

Justin   I do **care for** Mariana, but I don't love her like she loves me.

Lilly   I **feel for** you, dude. That's a tough situation to be in for both of you.

Justin   Do you think I have to talk to her, or will she **catch on** that I just want to be friends?

Lilly   You have to talk to her. She deserves to know that you**'re not interested in** her.

Justin   난 Mariana가 좋긴 좋아. 그런데 Mariana가 날 사랑하는 것만큼은 아니야.

Lilly   이해해. 이런 상황이 두 사람한테 다 힘들지.

Justin   Mariana한테 말해야 한다고 생각해? 아니면, 내가 그냥 친구로 남기 원한다는 것을 Mariana가 눈치챌까?

Lilly   Mariana에게 직접 말해야지. 네가 걔한테 (이성으로) 관심이 없다는 걸 Mariana도 마땅히 알아야지.

stay over

(남의 집에서 하룻밤) 자다

To spend the night (at another person's house)

Would you like to **stay over** at my house tonight?

너 오늘 밤에 우리 집에서 자고 갈래?

get together

함께 만나다, 모이다

To meet socially

My friends and I are going to **get together** at a bar.

친구들과 나는 술집에서 모임을 가질 것이다.

come over

(누구의 집에) 들르다

To go to someone's house

I hope you don't mind that Kate is **coming over**.

Kate가 오는 것을 개의치 않으면 좋겠어요.

pick up after

정리하다, 치우다, 뒤처리하다

To clean someone else's mess

I'm tired of having to **pick up after** my son.

난 우리 아들 뒤치다꺼리 하는 것에 지쳤어.

SHORT DIALOGUE 1

Phillip Mom! Can Caiden **stay over** at our house tonight?

Mom I'm not sure if tonight is a good night for a sleepover. You two can **get together** some other time.

Phillip But Mom! I cleaned up the living room and my bedroom so he could **come over**.

Mom Fine! Since you cleaned your room, he can come. Just **pick up after** yourselves, okay?

Phillip 엄마! 오늘 밤에 Caiden이 우리 집에서 자고 가도 돼요?
Mom 오늘 밤은 자고 가기 좀 그런데. 둘이 다음에 만나면 되잖니.
Phillip 하지만 엄마! Caiden이 놀러 올 수 있게 거실이랑 제 방을 다 치웠는데요.
Mom 좋아! 네 방을 치웠다고 하니, Caiden이 와도 좋아. 너희들이 어지럽힌 것은 스스로 치워라, 알았지?

count on

의지하다, 기대하다

To put trust in;
To depend
upon
someone

You can **count on** me if you ever need help.

도움이 필요하면 언제든지 저에게 의지하세요.

look after

~을 돌보다

To ensure the safety
of someone or
something

Can you come over and **look after** my children?

네가 우리 집에 와서 우리 아이들 좀 봐 줄 수 있니?

revolve around

~을 중심으로 돌아가다

To center upon;
To be at the core
of something

My life **revolves around** spending time with my family.

제 삶은 가족과 시간 보내는 걸 중심으로 돌아갑니다.

rely on

~을 믿다, 의지하다

To trust in someone
or something

You can **rely on** me to fix your car.

제가 당신 차를 고칠 거라고 믿으셔도 돼요.

SHORT DIALOGUE 2

Dad No, Cate! You can't go over to Shannon's house! I was **counting on** you to watch your little brother.

Cate I'm always **looking after** my brother on the weekends. I never get out anymore.

Dad The world doesn't **revolve around** you! You have a responsibility for your brother.

Cate Fine. But don't **rely on** me to take care of you when you get too old to live alone.

> **Dad** 안 돼, Cate! 너 Shannon 집에 못 가! 네가 동생 볼 거라고 믿고 있었는데.
>
> **Cate** 주말에 늘 제가 동생 보잖아요. 저 밖에도 안 나가고요.
>
> **Dad** 세상은 네 중심으로 돌아가지 않아! (세상은 네가 원하는 대로 되는 게 아냐) 넌 동생에 대한 책임이 있는 거야.
>
> **Cate** 좋아요. 그런데 나중에 나이 들어 혼자 살기 힘들 때 저한테 돌봐 달라고 의지하지 마세요.

fall out

(~와) 사이가 틀어지다

To conflict with someone to the point of ending a relationship

My girlfriend and I **fell out** after she cheated on me.
내 여자 친구가 바람을 피운 이후 나와 사이가 틀어졌다.

confide in

~에게 비밀을 털어놓다

To trust someone with vital or personal information

I **confided in** my best friend that I was in love with her.
나는 가장 친한 친구에게 그녀를 사랑하고 있다고 털어놓았다.

boss around

~에게 자꾸 이래라저래라 하다

To tell someone what to do

I hate it when my mother **bosses** me **around**.
나는 엄마가 나에게 이래라저래라 명령하는 게 정말 싫다.

pick on

(반복해서) 놀리다, 괴롭히다

To make fun of someone repeatedly

Stop **picking on** your brother because of his height.
키 가지고 네 동생 좀 그만 괴롭혀.

SHORT DIALOGUE 3

Austin	Hey, Pam. Teddy and I **fell out** a bit. We had a huge fight.
Pam	Woah. What happened? You can **confide in** me. I won't tell anyone.
Austin	I was tired of him always **bossing** me **around**, so I yelled at him.
Pam	I noticed he would always **pick on** you. I think you did the right thing.

Austin	야, Pam. Teddy하고 내가 사이가 좀 틀어졌어. 우리 크게 싸웠거든.
Pam	워, 무슨 일이야? 나한테는 솔직하게 다 털어놔도 돼. 아무한테도 말 안 할게.
Austin	나한테 매번 이래라저래라 하는 것에 진절머리가 나서 걔한테 소리를 빽 질렀어.
Pam	나도 걔가 항상 너 괴롭히는 걸 봤는데. 잘했어.

FRIENDS AND FAMILY 2 친구와 가족 2

MP3 **033**

bring out
(특성이나 자질 등을) 끌어내다

To cause something to
become available or to
come out

I know how to **bring out** the best in
students.
난 학생들의 최고 기량을 이끌어내는 법을 알아요.

depend on
~을 믿다, ~에 의존하다

To have need
of someone or
something; To trust
in someone

In times of crisis, my family always
depend on each other for support.
어려운 시기에, 우리 가족은 언제나 항상 서로
의지합니다.

come to
참석하다, 오다

To attend something

Is Robin **coming to** my birthday
next Saturday?
Robin이 다음 주 토요일 내 생일에 오니?

hang out
쉬다, 놀다, 즐거운 시간을 보내다

To spend time
relaxing or
socializing informally

Do you want to come to my house
and **hang out** with me?
우리 집에 와서 나랑 놀래?

SHORT DIALOGUE 1

Frances I love **hanging out** with you, Robby! You **bring out** the best in me.

Robby Same goes for you. I feel like I can **depend on** you to be there for me.

Frances Of course! That's what friends are for. You can always **come to** me for help.

Robby Well, now that you mention it, I have been having some issues with Ian. Can I
talk to you about it?

Frances 너랑 같이 다니는 게 너무 좋아, Robby! 넌 내가 최고로 잘할 수 있도록 이끌어 주니까.
Robby 너도 그래. 네가 항상 내 곁에 있어 줄 거라고 믿을 수 있을 것 같아.
Frances 당연하지! 그게 친구잖아. 도움이 필요하면 언제든 나한테 와도 돼.
Robby 음, 그래서 말인데, 내가 Ian하고 좀 문제가 있거든. 그것에 대해서 얘기 좀 할 수 있을까?

turn against

~에게 등을 돌리다

To grow suddenly
hostile against
someone;
To betray

My business partner **turned against**
me and took over the company.
내 동업자가 나에게 등을 돌리고서는 그 회사를
인수했다.

start in on

비난하다

To grow critical;
To nag

Don't **start in on** me about my
weight!
내 몸무게에 대해서 비난하듯 뭐라고 하지 마!

go easy on

~을 관대하게 대하다

To be lenient;
To treat without
harshness

Go easy on Jacob because he just
started this job.
Jacob이 이 일을 시작한 지 얼마 안 됐으니 관대하게
대해 주세요.

turn to

~에 의지하다, 기대다

To go to someone or
something for help
or guidance

After he lost his mother, Jeremy
turned to religion for comfort.
어머니를 떠나보낸 후, Jeremy는 마음의 위안을
얻기 위해 종교에 의지했다.

SHORT DIALOGUE 2

Jason   Did you hear that Andy **turned against** Doug?

Naomi   Yeah, I heard about that. Apparently, Andy just **started in on** him out of
nowhere!

Jason   If you ask me, he was **going easy on** Doug. He's a huge jerk!

Naomi   That's why he has no one else to **turn to**. Andy was his only friend.

Jason   Andy가 Doug랑 손절했다는 거 들었어?
Naomi   응, 들었어. 딱 보니까, Andy가 갑자기 Doug를 비난한 것 같아.
Jason   내 생각에, Andy는 Doug한테 아량 있게 대해 줬거든. Doug가 정말 나쁜 놈이야!
Naomi   그러니까 Doug한테는 의지할 사람이 아무도 없는 거지. Andy가 유일한 친구였는데 말이야.

MP3 **034**

stay away

(정서적·물리적으로) 떨어지다, 멀어지다

To keep at
a distance;
To avoid

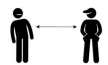

Stay away from that guy. He has
a knife.

저 사람한테서 떨어져. 칼을 가지고 있다고.

come between

끼어들다, 이간질하다

To interfere;
To create tension

I'm under finanical stress, but I won't
let this **come between** us.

난 경제적으로 힘들지만, 이것 때문에 우리 사이가
갈라지게 하지는 않을 거야.

hit on

들이대다, 작업 걸다

To flirt with; To make
sexual advances

You shouldn't **hit on** your
coworkers.

동료한테 작업 걸면 안 돼.

patch up

(관계를) 회복하다

To fix

I've been a lot happier since
I **patched up** my relationship with
my wife.

아내와 관계를 회복한 후 난 훨씬 더 행복해졌어.

SHORT DIALOGUE 1

Isabella | Hey, Katy. I need you to **stay away** from Jerome. I don't like the way you talk to him.

Katy | What is this about? You know I would never do anything to **come between** you two.

Isabella | I know that you've been **hitting on** Jerome in class. He's my boyfriend, not yours.

Katy | I'm not the issue. You are. **Patch up** your relationship and don't blame your problems on me!

Isabella | 야, Katy. Jerome한테서 떨어져 줄래? 네가 걔한테 말하는 태도, 나 별로 맘에 안 들거든.
Katy | 뭐 때문에 그러는 거야? 내가 너희 둘 사이에 절대 안 끼어들 거라는 거 너도 알잖아.
Isabella | 네가 수업 시간에 Jerome한테 들이대는 거 알아. 걔 네 남친 아니고 내 남친이거든!
Katy | 문제는 내가 아니라 너야. 너희 둘 관계나 잘 회복해 괜히 엄한 사람한테 책임 떠넘기지 말고!

break up

(관계가) 깨지다, 헤어지다

To end a relationship;
To stop dating
someone

I think I need to **break up** with my girlfriend.

나 아무래도 여자 친구랑 헤어져야 할 것 같아.

move on

(어려운 상황을 극복하고) 나아가다

To heal from something;
To make peace with
a difficult situation

I've stopped missing my ex-girlfriend so it's time to **move on**.

전 여친이 더 이상 보고 싶지 않아. 이제 나도 내 삶을 살아야지.

cut out

연락을 끊다, 관계를 끊어 버리다

To cease contact with
someone

He was my best friend till I **cut him out** of my life.

내가 그 친구를 손절하기 전까지 걔는 나의 베프였어.

drift apart

(시간이 지나면서) 사이가 멀어지다

To lose your
connection to
someone over time

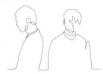

It is natural for friends to **drift apart**.

시간이 지나면서 친구들이 멀어지는 것은 자연스러운 일이야.

SHORT DIALOGUE 2

Alejandro Tina! Can I talk to you? Hillary and I just **broke up**. I don't know what to do.

Tina I heard about that. It may take a while to **move on**.

Alejandro How could she just **cut** me **out** from her life like that? We've been dating for five years.

Tina Sometimes people **drift apart**. Maybe it's difficult for her right now, too.

Alejandro Tina! 얘기 좀 할 수 있어? 나 Hillary랑 깨졌어. 뭘 어떻게 해야 할지 모르겠다.
Tina 나도 들었어. 잊어버리고 네 인생 살려면 시간 좀 걸리겠다.
Alejandro 어떻게 걔는 날 자기 인생에서 그렇게 딱 잘라 낼 수가 있지? 5년이나 사귀었는데 말이야.
Tina 때때로 사람들은 그냥 사이가 멀어지기도 해. 걔도 너처럼 지금 힘들어할지도 몰라.

settle down

정착하다, (가족을 이루고) 안정된 삶을 살다

To find stability in
life, especially in
terms of marriage

Amy **settled down** with Blake and
they started a family.

Amy는 Blake와 정착하여 가정을 이루었다.

fuss over

호들갑 떨다, (쓸데없이) 지나치게 관심을 갖다

To give a person
or animal too
much attention

Let's not **fuss over** just a little
problem.

사소한 문제 가지고 너무 호들갑 떨지 말자.

flirt with

작업 걸다, 집적대다

To attempt to attract
someone

He was **flirting with** pretty much
every girl in the room.

그는 그 방에 있는 거의 모든 여자들에게 작업을 걸었다.

suck up to

아부하다, 비위 맞추다

To be overly flattering
or attentive, especially
in hopes of gaining
something

Sarah is just **sucking up to** the
teacher to get a good grade.

Sarah는 좋은 성적을 받으려고 선생님께 아부한다.

SHORT DIALOGUE 3

Bradley   I'm glad I found a beautiful woman like you to **settle down** with. I love you.

Elizabeth   Oh, stop! We're already married. You don't need to **fuss over** me.

Bradley   What? Yeah. We get married, and suddenly I'm not allowed to **flirt with** you?

Elizabeth   Hmmm. Now that I think about it, it's nice when you **suck up to** me.

> Bradley   나와 평생 함께할 당신 같은 아름다운 여성을 찾게 돼서 기뻐. 사랑해.
> Elizabeth   그만 좀 해! 우리 이미 결혼했잖아. 그렇게 법석 안 떨어도 된다고.
> Bradley   뭐? 그래. 우리 결혼했지. 그렇다고 갑자기 당신한테 작업 거는 멘트도 하면 안 된다는 거야?
> Elizabeth   음… 생각해 보니, 당신이 나한테 비위 맞춰 주고 하는 것도 괜찮은데.

LONG DIALOGUE

Mom: 네가 관심 있다는 이 새로운 여자애는 누구야? 똑똑해? 믿을 만하니? 너한테 관심은 많이 보여?

— **Joy**: 엄마! 그렇게 진지한 사이 아니에요. 누가 그래요? 왜 그런 이야기를 해요?

Mom: 네 동생이 네가 이 여자애하고 시시덕거리는 거 봤다고 하던데. Erica? 그애 이름이 Erica 맞지? 정말 잘됐다.

— **Joy**: 별거 아니에요! 우리 겨우 두 번밖에 안 만났어요.

Mom: 너 Merryl하고 거의 1년 전에 헤어졌잖아. 이제 다른 사람 만날 때도 됐어.

— **Joy**: 아, 제 연애사에 대해서 뭐라고 좀 하지 마세요! 동생이 말했다니 정말…. 걔한테 믿고 털어놨는데.

Mom: 우린 가족이잖아! 걱정하지 마. 엄마가 그냥 너 챙겨 주는 것뿐이야. 그래 이 Erica라는 애는 예쁘니? 언제 우리 집에 와서 내가 만나 볼 수 있는 거야?

— **Joy**: 엄마가 그 사람한테 살살 하겠다고 하면 오라고 초대할게요. 너무 많이 질문하지 마시고요.

Mom: 그 사람, 직업이 뭐니?

— **Joy**: 아동병원 레지던트예요.

Mom: 오, 벌써부터 마음에 들기 시작 하는걸!

— **Joy**: 이번 주말에 초대할게요. 함께 모여서 저녁을 먹거나 해요. 제발, 그 사람한테 잘해 주세요!

Mom: So who is this new girl you**'re interested in**? Is she smart? Can you **rely on** her? Does she **fuss over** you enough?

— **Joy:** Mom! It's not that serious. Who told you? Why do you bring it up?

Mom: Your younger brother told me he saw you **flirting with** this new girl. Erica? That's her name, right? I'm happy for you.

— **Joy:** It's not a big deal! We've only **hung out** twice.

Mom: You **broke up** with Merryl almost a year ago. It's time that you **move on** to someone else.

— **Joy:** Oh, don't **start in on** me about my dating life. I can't believe my bro told you. I **confided in** her.

Mom: We're family! Don't worry. I'm just **looking after** you. So, this "Erica," is she cute? When is she going to **come over** so that I can meet her?

— **Joy:** I will invite her over if you promise to **go easy on** her. Don't ask her too many questions.

Mom: What does she do for a living?

— **Joy:** She's a resident at the children's hospital.

Mom: Oh, she's **growing on** me already!

— **Joy:** I'll have her over this weekend. We can all **get together** for dinner or something. Just, please! Be nice to her!

CHAPTER

5

PHRASAL VERBS

bend over

(몸을) 굽히다

To bend one's upper body forward and down while standing or kneeling

Bend over and touch your toes.
몸을 굽혀서 발끝에 손을 대세요.

tense up

(근육이) 긴장하다

To tighten the muscles

When I'm stressed out, I **tense up** my back and shoulders.
난 스트레스를 받으면, 등과 어깨가 뭉쳐.

take up

(배우기) 시작하다

To incorporate an activity into one's life; To begin doing something

first day

I've **taken up** yoga to help with my joint pain.
관절 통증에 도움이 될까 싶어 요가를 시작했어.

cool down

쿨다운 하다, (본 운동 후) 정리 운동하다

To allow your body to relax after exercise

A great way to **cool down** is to stretch.
운동을 마친 후 몸을 푸는 최고의 방법은 스트레칭을 하는 것이다.

SHORT DIALOGUE 1

Candace My back has really been hurting when I **bend over**.

Morgan Why don't you come to a yoga class with me? It will help if your muscles are all **tensed up**.

Candace I already go to kick-boxing classes, so I don't think I have time to also **take up** yoga.

Morgan But yoga will help! Plus, it's a great way to **cool down** after doing a cardio work out.

    Candace 몸을 굽히면 등이 정말 아파.
    Morgan 나랑 요가 강습 가는 게 어때? 근육이 뭉쳐 있으면 요가가 도움이 돼.
    Candace 이미 킥복싱 강습에 다니고 있어서, 요가를 시작할 시간이 없을 것 같아.
    Morgan 하지만 요가가 도움이 될 거야! 또, 유산소 운동 후에 정리 운동으로 몸을 푸는 데 요가가 아주 좋아.

work out
운동하다

To exercise

Do you want to **work out** with me after school?
방과 후에 나랑 같이 운동할래?

kick off
(경기를) 시작하다

To commence;
To start play in a game

I usually **kick off** my workout with some stretching.
저는 보통 스트레칭으로 운동을 시작한다.

get into
~에 빠지다, ~을 즐기다

To take interest in something, typically a hobby or pass-time

I first **got into** Taekwondo when I was 7.
난 7살 때 처음으로 태권도에 빠졌다.

pull through
~을 (성공적으로) 해내다

To succeed;
To persevere

I didn't think our team would win, but in the end we **pulled through**.
난 우리 팀이 이길 거라고 생각 안 했는데, 결국 해냈다.

SHORT DIALOGUE 2

Sonia How was the game last night? I went to the gym to **work out** after work and missed it.

Adam It was amazing from the moment they **kicked off** the game till the end. I was really **getting into** it!

Sonia Was our team able to **pull through**? Did we win?

Adam Yes, we did! It was tied until Williams scored the final goal in the last thirty seconds!

> **Sonia** 어젯밤 경기 어땠어? 일 마치고 헬스클럽에 가서 운동하느라 못 봤어.
> **Adam** 경기 시작할 때부터 마지막까지 정말 대단했어. 나 완전히 푹 빠져서 봤다니깐!
> **Sonia** 우리 팀이 해낸 거야? 이겼어?
> **Adam** 응. 우리가 이겼어! Williams가 마지막 30초 남겨 두고 결승 골을 넣을 때까지는 동점이었거든!

warm up

준비 운동하다

To prepare the body
or specific body parts
for strenuous activity

Jay hurt himself because he forgot
to **warm up** before running.

Jay는 달리기 전에 준비 운동을 깜박해서 다쳤다.

burn off

(칼로리를) 소모하다, 태우다

To get rid of through
exercise, typically
referring to fat or
calories

I **burned off** 200 calories on the
treadmill yesterday.

나는 어제 러닝머신으로 200칼로리를 소모했다.

work off

(운동을 통해서) 해소하다, 풀다

To reduce or get rid of
something through
exercise

Jason went to the boxing gym to try
and **work off** some stress.

Jason은 운동으로 스트레스를 해소해 보려고
복싱장에 갔다.

stretch out

스트레칭을 하다

To stress body parts
in a way that increases
flexibility or reduces
fatigue

I'll show you how to **stretch out**
your legs. So just follow along.

다리 스트레칭하는 거 보여 줄테니, 따라서 해 봐.

SHORT DIALOGUE 3

Evan   Hey, Gracie! Do you want to go for a run with me this afternoon? It's a great way
to **burn off** calories.

Gracie   I am tired. But I did have a big lunch, and it would be nice to **work** it **off**.

Evan   Great! Let's meet in the park near the fountain so we can **warm up** beforehand.

Gracie   Great idea! We should definitely **stretch out** before and after our run.

Evan   야, Gracie! 오늘 오후에 나랑 조깅하러 나갈래? 칼로리 태우는 데는 조깅이 정말 좋아.
Gracie   나 피곤한데. 그런데 점심을 많이 먹어서, 운동하면서 좀 빼는 게 나을 것 같기 하다.
Evan   좋아. 먼저 준비 운동부터 하게 분수대 근처 공원에서 만나자.
Gracie   좋아! 달리기 전후에 스트레칭은 꼭 해야 해.

MP3 **037**

take off
(일을 휴가 내고) 쉬다

To choose to have a period away from work

I'm going to **take off** work today because I'm sick.
몸이 안 좋아서 오늘은 일 쉬려고 해.

check in on
(전화, 방문, 글 등으로) 잘 있는지 확인하다

To visit, call, or write to them to find out how they're doing

I'm happy to **check in on** your mother while you're gone.
너 없는 동안 내가 네 어머니 잘 살필게.

rest up
푹 쉬다

To rest completely; To sleep until energy is restored

I need to **rest up** for a few days before going back to work.
직장에 다시 나가기 전에 나 며칠 푹 쉬어야 해.

bounce back
(아프고 나서) 회복하다

To return to health after being ill

My grandfather **bounced back** fully after his stroke.
우리 할아버지가 뇌졸중에서 완전히 회복되었다.

SHORT DIALOGUE 1

Ken   I can't come to work. I think I have a cold.

Supervisor That's perfectly fine. **Take** today **off** and **rest up**.

Ken   Thank you for understanding. I hope I'll **bounce back** tomorrow.

Supervisor Don't worry about that. There's no rush. And, I'll **check in on** you later, okay? Do you want me to bring you anything?

> Ken   출근 못 하겠어요. 감기 걸린 것 같습니다.
> Supervisor 정말 괜찮으니까, 오늘 나오지 말고 푹 쉬게나.
> Ken   이해해 주셔서 감사합니다. 내일은 나아질 거라 기대해 봐야죠.
> Supervisor 그건 걱정하지 말게. 급할 거 없으니까. 그리고 내가 좀 있다 잠깐 들르겠네, 알았나? 뭐 좀 가져다줄까?

cut down on
(~의 섭취를) 줄이다

To eat or drink less of a particular thing, usually in order to improve your health

You should **cut down on** sugar if you want to lose weight.
살을 빼고 싶으면 설탕 섭취를 줄여야 해.

fight off
(병을) 퇴치하다, 물리치다, 극복하다

To try hard to get rid of something especially an illness

Orange juice is good when you're **fighting off** an infection.
감염을 극복하는 데 오렌지 주스가 좋아.

break out
(피부에) 갑자기 뭐가 나다

To become inflamed or affected by spots on one's skin

A rash **broke out** all over my body.
난 온몸에 발진이 났다.

clear up
(증상 등이) 멈추다, 사라지다

To go away;
To cease or disappear;
To become more clear

I'm glad that my cold **cleared up** after some rest.
좀 쉬었더니 감기가 나아서 다행이다.

SHORT DIALOGUE 2

Julie   I need to **cut down on** chocolate. I think I'm allergic to it.

Evan   That's a shame. I can't imagine living without chocolate.

Julie   It's not good for my skin. It causes me to **break out** and I'm tired of **fighting off** this acne.

Evan   I see. I'm sure your skin will **clear up** once you stop eating chocolate.

Julie   나 초콜릿 섭취를 줄여야 해. 초콜릿 알레르기가 있나 봐.
Evan   너무 안타까운걸. 난 초콜릿 없이 사는 건 상상할 수도 없는데.
Julie   초콜릿이 내 피부에 안 좋더라고. 피부가 뒤집어지고, 여드름과 씨름하는 것도 지겨워.
Evan   그렇구나. 일단 초콜릿 먹는 걸 끊으면 확실히 피부가 깨끗해질 거야.

fend off

막다, 물리치다

To resist

I'm having trouble **fending off** all these negative feelings.

난 이 모든 부정적인 생각들을 물리치는 것이 힘들다.

build up

키우다, 강화하다

To strengthen;
To increase

Eat healthy food to **build up** resistance to illness.

병에 대한 저항력을 키우도록 몸에 좋은 음식을 먹어.

come down with

(병에) 걸리다

To become afflicted or infected with something

It seems I've **come down with** the flu.

나 아무래도 독감에 걸린 것 같아.

get better

나아지다

To heal

I know you're not feeling well, so I hope that you **get better** soon.

너 몸이 안 좋은 거 알아. 빨리 나아지면 좋겠다.

SHORT DIALOGUE 3

Carl   Should I really get the flu vaccine? Will it actually help me **fend off** an infection?

Angie   Of course, Carl! Why wouldn't you?! It's proven to help you **build up** resistance.

Carl   But, as far as I know, there are quite a few people that have **come down with** the flu even after they get vaccinated.

Angie   Maybe, but even if you get the flu, the vaccine helps you **get better** quicker.

    Carl   독감 백신을 맞아야 하나? 그게 감염을 막는 데 실제로 도움이 될까?
    Angie   물론이지, Carl! 도대체 왜 백신을 안 맞아?! 저항력을 강화하는 데 도움이 된다고 증명이 됐는데.
    Carl   하지만 내가 알기로는 백신 맞아도 독감에 걸린 사람들이 꽤 있던데.
    Angie   그렇기도 하겠지. 그런데 독감에 걸린다고 해도, 백신을 맞으면 더 빨리 회복되게 도와준다니까.

swell up

붓다, 부어오르다

To become larger and rounder than usual as a result of illness

Obviously you broke your toe. It's **swelling up**.

분명히 발가락이 부러진 거야. 부어오르잖아.

hold on

손으로 고정시키다, 계속 잡고 있다

To grasp or support something with one's hands

Hold this ice pack **on** your head.

아이스팩을 머리 위에 올리고 있어.

go down

(수치가) 줄어들다, 가라앉다

To reduce in number or size

Betsy was glad that her fever had **gone down**.

Besty는 열이 가라앉아서 기뻤다.

sleep through

깨지 않고 자다, 잠자느라 ~을 놓치다

To sleep without being awakened by; To miss something because of sleep

I had such a great night's sleep that I ended up **sleeping through** my morning workout.

잠을 아주 잘 자서, 난 아침 운동도 잊고 잤어요.

SHORT DIALOGUE 1

Jacob   Ouch! I fell over and hurt my knee at soccer practice. It **swelled up**, and now I can't walk.

Samantha   I'll get you some ice. **Hold** it **on** your knee and the swelling will **go down**.

Jacob   What I need is rest. Can you help me to my bed? It's hard to walk.

Samantha   Sure. And hopefully, the pain won't get worse, so you can at least **sleep through** the night.

Jacob   아야! 축구 연습하다가 넘어져서 무릎을 다쳤어. 부어서 지금 걸을 수가 없어.
Samantha   얼음 좀 가져다줄게. 무릎 위에 올리고 있으면, 부기가 가라앉을 거야.
Jacob   내가 필요한 건 휴식이야. 침대까지 나 좀 거들어 줄래? 걷기가 힘들어.
Samantha   그럼. 통증이 더 심해지진 않으면 좋겠다. 적어도 밤에 깨지 않고 푹 잘 수 있게 말이지.

throw up

토하다

To vomit

After Karl ate those oysters, he **threw up**.

Karl은 굴을 먹고 나서 토했다.

pick up

감염되다, 병에 걸리다

To become infected;
To get an illness

I **picked up** a virus from work.

난 직장에서 바이러스에 감염되었다.

sit down

앉다

To move from a standing to a sitting position

You don't look good. You better **sit down**.

너 안 좋아 보여. 앉아 있는 게 좋겠어.

pass out

쓰러지다, 기절하다

To lose consciousness

I almost **passed out** after a long day at work.

나는 직장에서 힘든 하루를 보내고서 거의 쓰러질 뻔했다.

SHORT DIALOGUE 2

Camilla Dad, I don't know what's wrong with me. I just **threw up**.

Dad Hmm. Maybe you **picked up** something from one of the kids at school. How do you feel now?

Camilla Really bad! I feel like I'm going to **pass out**.

Dad Okay, **sit down** for now. I'll take you to the doctor as soon as I can.

Camilla 아빠, 왜 그런지 모르겠는데. 저 방금 토했어요.
Dad 음. 학교 친구한테서 뭔가 옮은 거 같은데. 지금은 어때?
Camilla 정말 안 좋아요! 저 쓰러질 거 같아요.
Dad 그래, 일단 앉아 있어. 최대한 빨리 의사 선생님 보러 가자.

pass on

감염시키다

To infect
someone with
your illness

I don't want you to **pass on** your
infection to your coworkers. Stay
home.

다른 동료들에게 옮기면 안 되니, 집에 있어.

go around

(특정 지역에서) 퍼지다, 유행이다

To spread, typically throughout a
specific location

Some kind of virus has been **going
around** my school.

내가 다니는 학교에서 바이러스가 돌고 있다.

keep up

깨어 있게 하다,
잠들지 못하게 하다

To prevent
someone from
sleeping

The noise from upstairs neighbor
kept me **up** all night.

윗집에서 나는 소음 때문에 나는 밤새 잠을 못 잤다.

heal up

낫다, 아물다

To overcome an
ailment or injury

When Jamie was all **healed up**,
he traveled to France.

Jamie는 완전히 회복된 후에, 프랑스로 여행을
떠났다.

SHORT DIALOGUE 3

Rebecca   Make sure you wash your hands. There's a virus **going around**.

Louis   Come to think of it, my roommate had a stomachache that **kept** him **up** all
night.

Rebecca   Are you serious? I hope you don't **pass** that **on** me.

Louis   Don't be so dramatic. You'll **heal up** quickly if you do get sick.

Rebecca   손 꼭 씻어. 바이러스가 돌고 있으니까.
Louis   그러고 보니, 내 룸메이트가 복통으로 밤새 잠을 못 자던데.
Rebecca   정말? 네가 나한테 전염시키지 않아야 할 텐데.
Louis   오버 좀 하지 마. 넌 병에 걸려도 바로 회복될걸.

DIG IN

Food is ready.
Go ahead.
Dig in!

DRINK

UP

quickly!

LONG DIALOGUE

Alice: 안녕, Daniel. 잘 지내? 내일 중요한 경기 기대되니? 나 최근에 하키에 푹 빠졌거든.

— Daniel: 약간 긴장돼. 이 경기가 시즌 첫 경기인데. 팀의 반이 아픈 것 같아. 뭔가 돌고 있나 봐.

Alice: 정말? 같이 운동하니까 그런 것 같은데. 같은 병에 걸렸을 수도 있겠네. 그럼 경기가 취소된다는 말이야?

— Daniel: 선수들이 제대로 해내려고 하고는 있어. 하지만 팀의 반이 토하고 하는 상황이라면 어떻게 할 수 있을지 잘 모르겠어. 친한 친구 한 명이 팀에 있는데, 상황이 많이 안 좋대.

Alice: 오늘 밤까지 회복되지 않으면, 다시 일정을 잡아야겠는걸.

— Daniel: 그렇게 하는 게 현명한 거지. 전염병이랑 씨름하는 상황에서 어떻게 최고 실력을 발휘할 거라고 기대하겠어?

Alice: 오옷! 방금 문자 받았는데, 게임이 취소됐어!

— Daniel: 뭐라고 써 있는데?

Alice: Tracy한테서 온 건데, 선수 중 한 명이 준비 운동하다가 기절했대.

— Daniel: 상황이 많이 안 좋네. 음, 적어도 선수들이 다 집에 가서 쉴 수 있으니 다행이지. 그게 선수들이 회복할 수 있는 유일한 방법이야.

Alice: (경기를 못 봐서) 실망스럽기는 하지만, 이게 최선인 거지. 선수들이 더 아플 수 있는 위험을 감수하는 것보단, 빨리 회복하는 게 나으니까.

Alice: Hey, Daniel! How are you? Are you excited for the big game tomorrow? I've really been **getting into** hockey recently.

— Daniel: I'm a little nervous. This game is supposed to **kick off** the season, but half of the team seems to be getting sick. There's something **going around**.

Alice: Oh really? I guess they do all **work out** together. It makes sense that they'd all **come down with** the same thing. Does that mean the game is canceled?

— Daniel: They're going to try and **pull through**. But I don't know how they'll do it if half of the team is **throwing up**. One of my good friends is on the team, and he says that it's pretty bad.

Alice: Well, unless they **bounce back** before tonight, I'm sure they'll have to reschedule.

— Daniel: That's the smart thing to do. How can they be expected to do their best while **fighting off** an infection?

Alice: Oh wow! I just got a text. The game is canceled!

— Daniel: What does it say?

Alice: It's from Tracy. She said that one of the players **passed out** while they were **warming up**.

— Daniel: That's pretty bad. Well, I'm relieved at least they all get to go home and rest. That's the only way they'll **get better**.

Alice: It's disappointing, but it's for the best. Better for them to **heal up** than risk hurting themselves more.

blow down

(바람이 불어) 넘어뜨리다

To knock over
with gusts of
wind

The storm **blew down** the fence.
폭풍우가 울타리를 넘어뜨렸다.

pour down

(비가) 마구 쏟아지다, 퍼붓다

To rain intensely

It's going to **pour down** all night
because of the storm.
폭풍 때문에 밤새 비가 퍼부을 거야.

clear up

(날씨가) 개다, 맑아지다

To let more sunlight
through

The skies **cleared up** after the heavy
snowstorm.
강한 눈보라가 몰아친 후에 하늘이 맑아졌다.

blow over

누그러지다, 수그러들다

To come to an end;
To finish

We won't be able to drive until this
storm **blows over**.
우리는 이 폭풍우가 잦아들 때까지 운전할 수 없을
거야.

SHORT DIALOGUE 1

Tristan It seems like there's a bad storm coming. I hope it doesn't **blow down** any trees
on the road.

Vicky I heard it's really going to **pour down**. I'd be more worried about flooding.

Tristan We probably should stay in tonight. We shouldn't drive until the weather **clears
up**.

Vicky The storm won't **blow over** until midnight. Looks like we're spending our
Saturday indoors.

Tristan 강한 폭풍이 올 것 같아. 도로에 있는 나무가 쓰러지지 않으면 좋겠는데.
Vicky 비가 정말 세차게 내릴 거라고 들었어. 난 홍수가 더 걱정이 돼.
Tristan 오늘 밤은 그냥 집에 있는 게 좋을 것 같아. 날씨가 개기 전까진 운전하면 안 돼.
Vicky 폭풍이 자정까지 사그라들지는 않겠는걸. 토요일을 그냥 집 안에서 보내야 할 것 같네.

roll in

밀려들다, 몰려들다

To begin to cover
an area of the sky
or land

The dark clouds are **rolling in**, so
stay inside.

먹구름이 몰려들고 있으니, 집에 있어.

let up

멈추다, 약해지다

To stop or become
less intense

When's this rain going to **let up**?

이 비가 언제 그칠까?

freeze over

얼음으로 뒤덮이다, 다 얼어붙다

To become
covered in ice

The pool **froze over**, so we can't
swim!

수영장이 다 얼어서 우리 수영 못 해!

cool down

서늘해지다, 시원해지다

To grow colder;
To become less warm

This hot summer is almost over. It's
finally starting to **cool down**.

이 더운 여름도 거의 끝나가네. 이제야 시원해지기
시작하니 말이야.

SHORT DIALOGUE 2

Ronald   Cold weather is supposed to **roll in** over the next week.

Virginia   I can't wait. This hot weather has got to **let up** soon. I'm tired of it.

Ronald   I, for one, like the hot weather. I don't want everything to **freeze over**.

Virginia   I don't like it when everything is frozen, either! I just want it to **cool down**.

    Ronald   추운 날씨가 다음 주면 몰려올 거래.
    Virginia   빨리 추워지면 좋겠다. 이 뜨거운 날씨가 얼른 멈춰야지. 지겨워 죽겠어.
    Ronald   다른 사람은 모르겠지만, 난 더운 날씨가 좋아. 다 얼어붙고 하는 건 싫어.
    Virginia   나도 세상이 온통 얼어붙는 건 싫어. 그냥 좀 시원해지면 좋겠어.

hold up

지체되다, 지연시키다

To delay or block
the movement or
progress of someone
or something

We have to **hold up** our hike until
the storm passes.

폭풍우가 지나갈 때까지 우리 하이킹을 미뤄야 해.

open up

열다, 열리다

To unblock;
To create space

Soon the sky will **open up** and the
sun will shine!

곧 하늘이 열리고, 태양이 밝게 빛날 거야!

come out

나오다, 드러나다

To appear; To be
revealed or released

Later in the afternoon, it stopped
raining and the sun **came out**.

오후 늦게, 비가 그치고 해가 나왔다.

brighten up

밝아지다

To grow brighter

As the dark clouds cleared up, the
sun came out and the sky started to
brighten up.

먹구름이 걷히면서, 해가 나고 하늘이 밝아지기
시작했어요.

SHORT DIALOGUE 3

Roger   Look outside! I think our picnic is going to get **held up**. It's really cloudy. I think
it's going to rain.

Betty   No, it won't. Soon the sky will **open up** and the sun will shine!

Roger   I'm not sure if I believe you. The sun hasn't **come out** for days.

Betty   No, seriously, I just checked the weather forecast. It's going to **brighten up** soon.
Our picnic won't be ruined!

Roger   바깥을 봐! 소풍이 연기될 것 같아. 정말 흐리네. 곧 비가 오겠는데.
Betty   아냐. 곧 하늘이 열리고(구름이 걷히고), 태양이 빛날 거야!
Roger   네 말을 믿어야 할지 잘 모르겠다. 며칠 째 해가 안 나왔으니.
Betty   아냐, 정말이야. 방금 일기 예보를 확인했다고. 곧 날씨가 개고 환해질 거야. 소풍 가는 거 문제없다고!

MP3 **041**

fit in

적응하다, 딱 맞다

To belong to a group;
To have a place

I have trouble **fitting in** my new school.

난 새로운 학교에 적응하기 힘들어.

settle in

적응하다, 편안해지다

To grow comfortable;
To find peace in
a new place or
position

Thanks to my coworkers, it was easy to **settle in** to my new job.

동료들 덕분에, 난 새로운 일에 적응하기 쉬웠다.

move to

이사하다, 이동하다

To change homes;
To relocate

My family and I are **moving to** Portugal next spring.

가족들과 나는 내년 봄에 포르투갈로 이사를 간다.

branch off

갈라지다, 다른 길로 가다, 새롭게 시작하다

To break away;
To change direction
or focus

I'm looking to **branch off** in a completely new area.

난 완전히 새로운 분야에서 뭔가를 시작하려고 한다.

SHORT DIALOGUE 1

Diana   I'm a little bit worried we don't **fit in** with the people in this neighborhood.

Arnold   We just moved, Diana. It'll take us some time to **settle in**.

Diana   You don't think it was a mistake to **move to** this area?

Arnold   Not at all! We just have to **branch off** and make new friends. Then we'll feel at home.

Diana   난 우리가 이웃 사람들과 잘 어울리지 못할까 봐 좀 걱정이 돼.
Arnold   우리 방금 이사했어, Diana. 정착하고 적응하는 데 좀 시간이 걸리겠지.
Diana   이곳으로 이사 온 게 실수라고 생각하지 않아?
Arnold   전혀 그런 생각 안 하는데! 그저 새롭게 시작하고, 새로운 친구들을 만들면 되는 거야. 그러면 편안해질 거고.

lock up
(문 등을) 잠그다

To make a building safe
by locking
the doors

It's always wise to make sure you
lock up at night.
밤에는 항상 문을 꼭 잠그는 게 현명하다.

move out
이사 가다

To leave a place where
you have been living
or staying

The Japanese restaurant **moved
out** of the mall.
그 일식당이 쇼핑몰에서 이사를 나갔다.

put up
(벽에) 붙이다, 걸다

To put in place;
To hang

We need to **put up** more posters on
the wall.
우리는 벽에 포스터를 더 많이 붙여야 해.

move in
이사 오다

To go to a new
house and begin
to live there

My girlfriend is **moving in** with me
next month.
다음 달에 여자 친구가 내가 사는 집에 이사 와.

SHORT DIALOGUE 2

Ally   This neighborhood is a little dangerous. No wonder the previous couple wanted
to **move out**.

Carlos   Yeah. But at least we got a good price. And, we'll just have to remember to **lock
up** before we go to bed.

Ally   It still needs a lot of work. What do you think about **putting up** some curtains in
here?

Carlos   I'm sure we will make this apartment look lovely. You won't regret **moving in**
together. I promise.

Ally   이 동네는 조금 위험해. 전에 살던 커플이 이사 나가고 싶어 했던 것도 당연해.
Carlos   그래, 그렇지만 우리가 적어도 싼 가격에 구했잖아. 잠자기 전에 문 잠그는 것만 잊지 않으면 돼.
Ally   아직도 할 일이 많아. 여기 안에 커튼 치는 거 어떻게 생각해?
Carlos   우리가 이 아파트를 멋지게 보이게 할 거야. 같이 이사 온 거 후회 안 할 거야. 내가 약속할게.

take up

차지하다, 빼앗아 가다

To cover;
To consume

This sofa **takes up** too much space.
이 소파가 너무 많은 공간을 차지해.

pick up

치우다, 정리하다

To put something
away neatly;
To tidy up

We need to **pick up** the house before our guests come.
손님들이 오기 전에 우리 집을 정리해야 해.

tuck away

숨기다, (안 보이는 곳에)
보관하다

To store something
(in a hidden place)

The letter is **tucked away** in my album.
그 편지는 내 앨범에 보관되어 있다.

blend in

어울리다

To fit in with the
surroundings;
To belong

This new building **blends in** with the rest of the houses.
이 새 건물은 나머지 집들과 잘 어울린다.

SHORT DIALOGUE 3

Melanie Finally! You **picked up** the living room! But you still need to move this chair. It **takes up** too much space out here.

Connor Are you serious? It's **tucked away** in the corner! It hardly **takes up** any space.

Melanie It's a huge chair! And it doesn't **blend in** with the rest of the furniture.

Connor Fine, I'll move it, but you owe me.

Melanie 드디어, 거실 정리 다 했네! 그런데 너 이 의자 좀 옮겨. 여기 공간을 너무 많이 차지하잖아.
Connor 진심이야? 구석에 박혀서 잘 보이지도 않잖아! 공간도 거의 차지하지도 않고
Melanie 그거 엄청나게 큰 의자야! 나머지 가구들이랑 어울리지도 않아.
Connor 알았어. 옮길게. 근데 너 나한테 신세 진 거다.

TOPIC 33 PETS 반려동물

let out
나가게 해 주다

To allow outside

Don't **let** the dogs **out**. Keep the gate closed.
개들을 밖에 나가게 하지 마. 문 닫아 놓고 있어.

run around
이곳저곳 뛰어다니다

To run in an area while you are playing

There are some dogs **running around** outside. Be careful!
바깥에 개들이 뛰어다녀요. 조심하세요!

run away
도망가다

To escape

I left my door open and my dog **ran away**!
내가 문을 열어 놓았더니 개가 도망가 버렸어!

watch over
보호하다, 지켜보다

To protect;
To guard

I asked my mother to **watch over** my dog while I'm on a business trip.
나는 출장 가 있는 동안 엄마에게 개를 봐 달라고 부탁했다.

SHORT DIALOGUE 1

Maxwell Hey, Sara. Can you come over to feed and **let out** my dog on Saturday? I'll be out of town.

Sara I think I can do that. I can just let her **run around** in your backyard, right?

Maxwell Yes! Just make sure the gate is closed in case she tries to **run away**.

Sara No worries. I'll **watch over** her closely.

Maxwell 저기, Sara. 토요일에 와서 우리 개 먹이도 주고 밖에 나가게 해 줄 수 있어? 나 어디 가거든.
Sara 할 수 있을 거 같아. 그냥 너희 집 뒷마당에서 뛰어다니게 내버려 두면 되는 거야?
Maxwell 그렇지! 혹시나 도망가려고 할지도 모르니까, 대문만 꼭 닫아 놔.
Sara 걱정하지 마. 내가 잘 지켜볼 테니까.

132

freak out
기겁하다, 깜짝 놀라다

To suddenly feel extremely surprised, upset

My dog **freaks out** whenever I try to give her a bath.
내 개는 목욕시키려고 할 때마다 기겁을 해요.

fly away
멀리 날아가다

To escape by flight

When I was about to pull the trigger at the bird, it **flew away**.
내가 새한테 총을 겨누고 막 방아쇠를 당기려 할 때, 그 새는 날아가 버렸다.

put down
안락사시키다

To kill an animal without causing it pain typically because it is sick or old

My dad just had to **put down** the dog.
우리 아버지는 그 개를 안락사시켜야 했다.

cuddle up
부둥켜안다

To snuggle;
To show a lot of physical affection

I always **cuddle up** with my dog whenever I come back home.
난 항상 집에 돌아오면 강아지를 부둥켜안습니다.

SHORT DIALOGUE 2

Isaac   Your bird is so calm! My parrot would always **freak out** when I had friends over.

Frannie   I think she likes you! She tries to **fly away** whenever Karen comes over. By the way, what happened to your bird?

Isaac   She got an infection, and sadly, we had to **put** her **down**.

Frannie   I'm sorry. If you ever want to **cuddle up** with my bird, come over anytime.

Isaac   네 새는 정말 조용하구나! 내 앵무새는 내가 친구들 데리고 올 때마다 항상 기겁을 했는데.
Frannie   우리 새가 널 좋아하나 봐! Karen이 올 때는 항상 날아가려고 하는데. 근데 네 새는 어떻게 된 거야?
Isaac   감염이 됐거든. 그래서 애석하게도 안락사시켜야 했어.
Frannie   안됐네. 혹시 내 새 안아 보고 싶으면, 언제든 놀러 와.

LONG DIALOGUE

Shelia: 난 도시를 좀 벗어나 이사하고 싶어. 음, 남쪽 어딘가에 겨울마다 얼어붙지 않는 그런 곳으로.

— Osage: 뭐 생각해 놓은 곳 있어? 가령 태양이 내리쬐는 화창한 곳? 시카고에서는 햇빛 보는 게 힘들잖아. 구름이 걷히면 정말 예쁜데, 거의 보기 힘들지.

Shelia: 우리가 도시에 살 필요는 없잖아! 교외에 집을 구할 수도 있고. 그렇게 하면, 우리 개도 뛰어놀 공간이 생길 테고.

— Osage: 하루에 세 번이나 산책시키지 않고, 그냥 마당으로 내보내는 게 더 쉽잖아. 가끔은 나도 근처 산책시킬 시간이 없을 때도 있고.

Shelia: 음. 루이빌로 이사 가는 건 어때? 거기 아름답거든.

— Osage: 괜찮긴 한데, 우리한테 거기가 잘 맞을진 모르겠어. 마이애미는 어떨까?

Shelia: 플로리다는 시원한 날이 전혀 없잖아! 난 더 따뜻한 곳을 가고 싶지, 너무 더운 곳은 별로야.

— Osage: 내슈빌은?! 우리 거기 정말 좋아하잖아. 젊은 사람들도 많으니까 우리가 적응하고 정착해서 친구 사귀기도 어렵지 않을 거야.

Shelia: 우리가 모은 돈으로 도시에서 떨어진 한적한 곳에 있는 집을 확실히 살 수 있을 거고.

— Osage: 정말 좋은 생각인데. 내일 좀 더 조사해 보자.

Shelia: I want to **move out** of the city. Maybe somewhere south where it doesn't **freeze over** every winter.

— **Osage:** What did you have in mind? Maybe somewhere sunny? We hardly get any sunlight in Chicago. It is pretty when the clouds **open up**, but that's very rare.

Shelia: We don't even have to live in a city! We could get a house in the suburbs. That way, our dog would have some space to **run around**.

— **Osage:** It would be easier to just **let** her **out** in a yard than take her on three walks a day. Sometimes I don't have time to walk my dog around.

Shelia: Hmm. How about we move to Louisville? It's beautiful down there.

— **Osage:** It is okay, but I'm not sure we'd **fit in**. What about Miami?

Shelia: It never **cools down** enough in Florida! I want to move somewhere warmer but not too hot.

— **Osage:** Nashville! We love it there, and there are a lot of young people, so it wouldn't be too hard for us to **settle in** and make friends.

Shelia: We could definitely buy a house **tucked away** from the city with our savings.

— **Osage:** That sounds great. Let's do some more research tomorrow.

CHAPTER

6

PHRASAL VERBS

save up
저축하다

To build a reserve of money, typically with intent to buy something

I got a part-time job to **save up** money.
난 돈을 모으기 위해서 알바를 구했다.

put aside
돈을 따로 챙겨 두다, 저축하다

To set money in a secure account or location

I have to **put aside** some money for retirement.
은퇴 후 생활을 위해서 난 돈을 저축해야 한다.

get by
그럭저럭 살다

To have enough of something, usually money, to survive

When I was a kid, we had barely enough to **get by**.
내가 어렸을때, 우리는 간신히 먹고 살았다.

live off
~로 살아가다, ~에 의존해서 살다

To use something as the main source of what one needs to survive

Do you have enough money to **live off** of?
너 충분히 먹고 살 돈은 있니?

SHORT DIALOGUE 1

Becca   We need to **save up** a lot of money to buy a house.

Jack   What if we start **putting aside** twenty percent of our paychecks?

Becca   That may be too much. We still need some money to **get by** until we move.

Jack   Right. Let's calculate how much we need to **live off** of. The rest we'll save up.

> Becca   집을 사려면 저축을 많이 해야 해.
> Jack   우리 월급의 20%를 따로 떼서 저축하는 건 어떨까?
> Becca   그건 너무 많은 것 같아. 이사할 때까지 먹고 살 돈도 필요하잖아.
> Jack   맞네. 살기 위해 꼭 필요한 돈이 어느 정도 되는지 계산해 보자. 나머지는 저축하고.

rake in

(돈을) 긁어모으다, 쓸어 담다

To earn a lot of money without trying very hard

Once I get this business off the ground, I will be **raking in** a lot of money. 일단 이 사업을 시작하기만 하면, 난 돈을 쓸어 담을 거야.

* get ~ off the ground ~을 순조롭게 시작하다

roll in

굴러 들어오다, 도착하다

To come into something; To arrive

Money will be **rolling in** if you simply do what you love to do. 네가 그냥 하고 싶은 일을 하면, 결국 돈은 굴러 들어올 거야.

put back

제자리에 갖다 놓다

To return something to the place where it belongs

I can't afford to buy that for you, so please **put** it **back** on the shelf. 나 너한테 그걸 사 줄 형편이 안 되니까, 다시 진열대에 갖다 놔.

scrape by

근근이 살아가다, 입에 풀칠하다

To make barely enough money to survive

I'm making just enough to **scrape by**. 난 간신히 먹고 살 정도만 벌어.

SHORT DIALOGUE 2

Abigail I got a promotion at work! I'll be **raking in** a lot more money.

Harry I told you! If you put in the hard work, the money starts to **roll in**.

Abigail I spent so long just trying to **scrape by**, but now that's over!

Harry And soon you'll be able to **put** that money **back** into our account that you borrowed last month.

> Abigail 나 직장에서 승진했어! 훨씬 더 많은 돈을 아주 갈퀴로 긁어모을 거야.
> Harry 내가 말했지! 열심히 노력하면, 돈이 굴러 들어오기 시작한다고.
> Abigail 정말 오랫동안 입에 풀칠하면서 근근이 살았는데, 이제 그 시절도 끝이다!
> Harry 곧 우리 계좌에 지난달에 빌렸던 돈을 다시 넣어 놓을 수 있을 거야.

pay off

다 갚다, 갚아 버리다

To pay entirely

I finally **paid off** my student loans!

드디어 내가 학자금 대출을 다 갚았어!

come into

물려받다

To get something as a possession

I **came into** a lot of wealth after my grandmother died.

할머니가 돌아가신 후 나는 많은 재산을 물려받았다.

chip in

(돈을) 보태다

To pay in part for something

They all **chipped in** to buy a birthday cake for Jane.

그들 모두 Jane의 생일 케이크를 사는 데 조금씩 보탰다.

pay back

돈을 갚다

To return the money that is owed

I'll lend you some money with a low interest. But you have to **pay back**.

내가 저금리로 돈을 빌려줄게. 하지만 너 꼭 갚아야 한다.

SHORT DIALOGUE 3

Matt I don't know what I'm going to do. I lost my job, and now I have no way to **pay off** my debt.

Annabel Hmm. I've just recently **come into** a large sum of money. Maybe I could help.

Matt You'd be willing to **chip in** some cash? That would be great! Thank you. I'll repay you when I get a job.

Annabel Don't worry about **paying** me **back**. What are friends for?

Matt 나도 내가 뭘 어떻게 해야 할지 잘 모르겠어. 직장도 잃고, 이제 빚을 갚을 길이 없어.

Annabel 음, 내가 최근에 큰돈을 물려받았어. 내가 도와줄 수도 있어.

Matt 나를 도와주기 위해서 기꺼이 돈을 보태겠다고? 그래 준다면야 좋지! 고마워. 직장 잡으면 내가 꼭 갚을게.

Annabel 갚는 건 걱정하지 마. 친구 좋다는 게 뭐겠어?

MP3 **045**

cough up

(마지못해) 내놓다

To give unwillingly

Come on, **cough up**. It's your turn to pay.

야, 돈 내놔. 네가 낼 차례야.

run out

다 떨어지다

To be depleted;
To have no more of

I **ran out** of money to pay interest. So I eventually had to sell my house.

이자 낼 돈이 다 떨어져 버려서, 결국 나는 집을 팔아야 했다.

take out

꺼내다, 인출하다

To withdraw

Emily stopped by the bank to **take out** a hundred dollars.

Emily는 100달러를 인출하려고 은행에 들렀다.

pay up

빚을 다 갚다

To pay money that you owe, especially when you do not want to or you are late

Pay up or lose your home. It's your call.

돈을 갚든지, 아니면 집을 잃든지. 그건 너의 선택이야.

SHORT DIALOGUE 1

Landlord You haven't paid rent in three months! **Cough up** the money, or I'll kick you out!

Keegan Please! Give me more time! I just **ran out** of money from my last paycheck.

Landlord I don't care! **Take out** a loan or something. Whatever. Just **pay up**!

Keegan I can pay you in two weeks when I get paid. I just need more time!

> Landlord 지금 그쪽이 3개월이나 월세를 안 냈어요! 어떻게든 돈을 마련해 봐요. 안 그럼 내보낼 거니까!
> Keegan 제발, 조금만 더 시간을 주세요! 지난달 월급이 다 떨어졌어요.
> Landlord 그게 나랑 무슨 상관이에요! 대출을 받든 뭘 하든, 어떻게든지 빨리 갚아요!
> Keegan 2주 후에 월급 타면 드릴 수 있어요. 시간이 더 필요해요!

run up
돈을 많이 쓰다, 빚지다

To use so much of
something, or borrow
so much money; To
increase the amount of
something

I stayed at this fancy hotel for three
nights and **ran up** more than 2,000
dollars.

나는 이 고급 호텔에서 3일 밤을 묵었고, 2,000달러
이상이 들었다.

cut back
축소하다, 삭감하다

To limit; To show
restraint

I have to **cut back** on spending to
buy a car.

나 차 사려면 지출을 줄여야 해.

cut down
확 줄이다

To reduce greatly

I used to work more than 40 hours
but I recently **cut down** to 20.

나는 예전에 40시간 이상 일을 했었는데, 최근에
20시간으로 줄였어.

bring in
돈을 벌다, 가지고 오다

To make money;
To gather; To invite

If you want this restaurant to
run, you need to **bring in** more
employees.

이 식당을 계속 운영하고 싶으면, 더 많은 사람을
고용해야 해.

SHORT DIALOGUE 2

Manager I looked at the numbers, and we've **run up** a 2,000-dollar debt with the
suppliers.

Owner You're right. We need to **cut back** on spending, or this restaurant will fail.

Manager The easiest choice would be to **cut down** our costs by buying cheaper
ingredients.

Owner This month has been hard. Hopefully, this summer, we'll be able to **bring in**
more cash.

Manager 제가 숫자들을 살펴보니, 납품업체에게 2,000달러의 빚을 지고 있어요.
Owner 맞아. 우리가 지출을 줄이지 않으면, 이 식당 망할 거야.
Manager 가장 쉬운 선택은 좀 더 저렴한 식재료를 사서 비용을 줄이는 거예요.
Owner 이번 달은 힘들었어. 이번 여름에는 돈을 좀 더 많이 벌 수 있게 되면 좋겠어.

settle up

지불하다, 처리하다

To pay a bill;
To pay someone
what you owe them

I owe you $100. I'll **settle up** now and take care of it.

내가 너한테 100달러 빚졌지. 지금 갚아서 처리할게.

amount to

(합계가) ~이 되다

To come to a total

The car payment **amounted to** $200 a month.

차 할부금이 한 달에 200달러였어.

add up

합산하다, 늘어나다

To calculate the sum of; To grow to the point overwhelming

Planning a trip can **add up** to be quite expensive.

여행 계획을 짜서 다 합계해 보면 꽤 많은 돈이 들어간다.

fork out

(마지못해) 돈을 쓰다

To spend a lot of money, typically with reluctance

I really didn't want to **fork out** for that expensive dinner.

난 정말 그 비싼 저녁 식사에 돈을 쓰고 싶지 않았다.

SHORT DIALOGUE 3

Server　We're closing soon, sir. I'm afraid you have to **settle up** your tab.

Tim　Alright, that's fine. What does the total **amount to**?

Server　The total **adds up** to eighty dollars and sixty cents.

Tim　Craig, I'll let you **fork out** the money for this one. And don't forget to leave her a good tip!

Server　손님, 저희가 곧 문을 닫습니다. 죄송합니다만, 먼저 계산 좀 부탁드리겠습니다.
Tim　네, 괜찮습니다. 전부 해서 얼마인가요?
Server　총 80달러 60센트입니다.
Tim　Craig, 이건 네가 돈 좀 내라. 팁 두둑이 남기는 것도 잊지 말고!

fly by

(시간이) 매우 빨리 가다, 후딱 가다

To pass quickly

The movie was amazing. Those two hours **flew by**.

영화가 정말 대단했다. 2시간이 후딱 갔다.

clock in

출근 시간을 기록하다, 출근하다

To note the starting time of a shift

I forgot to **clock in** at my job yesterday.

난 어제 직장에서 출근 시간 기록하는 것을 깜빡했다.

pass by

(시간이) 지나다, 지나가다

To move forward and get further away from the present moment

The hours **pass by** slowly when I'm at school.

학교에 있을 때는 시간이 정말 느리게 간다.

go by

시간이 가다

To move past

Time **goes by** faster as you get older.

나이가 들수록 시간이 더 빨리 간다.

SHORT DIALOGUE 1

Abby   This shift is **flying by** really quickly.

Dave   It's because we're so busy. I feel like I **clocked in** an hour ago.

Abby   In reality, the whole day has **passed by**. I wish it was always like this.

Dave   It would be nice if every shift could **go by** this quickly.

> Abby   이번 교대 근무 시간은 정말 빨리 가네.
> Dave   아주 바쁘니까 그래. 난 한 시간 전에 출근 기록 찍은 것 같은데.
> Abby   실제로는 하루가 다 가 버렸어. 정말 항상 이러면 좋겠다.
> Dave   교대 근무할 때마다 이렇게 시간이 빨리 가면 좋겠다.

hurry up

서두르다

To increase one's
speed or pace

Hurry up and get in the car. We
need to go now.
서둘러서 빨리 차에 타. 지금 가야 해!

drag on

질질 끌다

To go by slowly

This song is so boring. It's just
dragging on!
이 노래 너무 지루해. 계속 늘어지잖아!

put back

지체시키다, 지연시키다

To delay;
To reverse progress

The accident **put back** the opening
of our business.
그 사고 때문에 우리 사업장 오픈을 미뤄야 했다.

rush off

급하게 떠나다, 재촉하다

To depart in a hurry;
To force someone
to do something
too quickly

I had to **rush off** after the meeting
to catch a flight.
비행기 시간 때문에 난 미팅 끝나고 황급히
가야 했다.

SHORT DIALOGUE 2

Hazel   **Hurry up**, Kay! I don't want to miss the plane. Come on! You're walking too
slowly.

Kay   It's not my fault! The line to check in was **dragging on** and getting through the
security took up more time than we thought.

Hazel   Yeah. Security did **put** us **back** a little bit. That's why you need to walk faster!

Kay   Don't **rush off**. I'm walking as fast as I can.

     Hazel   서둘러, Kay! 나 비행기 놓치기 싫다고. 어서! 너 너무 천천히 걷는다.

     Kay   내 잘못이 아니잖아! 체크인 줄이 길게 늘어져 있어서 보안 검색대 통과하는 데 생각보다 오래
            시간을 잡아먹었어.

     Hazel   그래. 검색대 때문에 조금 지체되기는 했지. 그러니까 더 빨리 걸어야지!

     Kay   재촉하지 마! 나도 지금 최대한 빨리 걷고 있다고.

stick (it) out
끝까지 남아 있다, 버티다

To remain till
the end;
To persevere

You have to **stick** it **out** until you're
done with this project.

너, 이 프로젝트 마무리지을 때까지 끝까지 남아서
버텨야 해.

clock out
퇴근 시간을 기록하다

To register one's
departure from work,
especially by means
of a time clock

I **clock out** at 5 PM every day.

난 매일 오후 5시에 퇴근한다.

fit in
시간을 내다, 짬을 내다

To give a place or
time to

It's tight, but I think I can **fit** you **in**
tomorrow morning.

시간이 빠듯하지만, 제가 내일 아침에 시간을 낼 수
있을 거 같아요.

sneak up on
몰래·조용히 다가가다, (모르는 사이에 벌써)
~이 되다

To approach
carefully and
quietly

This event has really **snuck up on**
us. It's Friday already.

그 행사가 눈 깜짝할 사이에 다가왔어. 벌써
금요일이잖아.

SHORT DIALOGUE 3

Masseuse   Oh my! The time has really **snuck up on** me today. It's already 6:00!

Receptionist   You still have one more appointment. Do you think you can **stick** it **out** a little
longer to massage Mrs. Miller before you leave for the day?

Masseuse   I really wanted to **clock out** on time today. I have a dinner reservation.

Receptionist   I'm sure she would really appreciate it if you could **fit** her **in**.

Masseuse   오, 이런! 오늘 시간이 정말 빨리 지나갔네. 벌써 6시라니!

Receptionist   아직 예약이 하나 더 있어요. 오늘 퇴근 전에 좀 더 시간 내서 Miller 여사님 마사지를
할 수 있겠어요?

Masseuse   오늘은 정말 정시에 퇴근하고 싶어요. 저녁 식사 예약을 해놨어요.

Receptionist   시간을 내서 Miller 여사님 마사지를 해 주시면 그분이 진짜로 고마워할 거예요.

POUR DOWN

LET UP

When's this rain going to **let up?**

LONG DIALOGUE

Tammy: 얼마나 더 남았어? 차로 가니까 정말 끝이 없는 것 같아. 시간이 정말 천천히 간다.

— Owen: 피닉스까지 3시간 넘게 남았어.

Tammy: 왜 우리가 비행기를 타지 않았을까? 이렇게 이틀이나 걸리지 않았을 텐데.

— Owen: 집 사려고 아끼는 중이잖아! 비행기 타고 갈 여유 없다고. 우리 대출받고, 그거 다 갚으려면 한 푼이라도 더 아껴야 해. 3시간만 더 가면 돼. 그때까지만 견디면 된다고.

Tammy: 넌 돈에 대해서 걱정이 너무 많아! 지난 6개월 동안 우리 거의 손가락 빨고 살았어. 나도 씀씀이 줄이고 절약해야 한다는 건 이해하는데, 이렇게 살 수는 없어!

— Owen: 우리 이제 곧 집 사잖아! 그럼 지금보다는 조금 더 인생을 즐길 수 있을 거야. 별거 아닌 것 같지만, 외식이랑 비행기 표 같은 것도 합치면 꽤 된다고. 그러면, 막상 집 살 때가 돼서 돈 써야 할 때는 돈이 다 떨어져 있을 수 있고.

Tammy: 무슨 말인지는 알아. 그게 돈을 저축해야 하는 타당한 이유고. 난 그저 너처럼 걱정하진 않아. 게다가, 피닉스가 LA보단 살기에 물가가 더 싸잖아. 그리고 피닉스에서 우리가 일을 새로 시작하면 돈이 들어올 거라고.

— Owen: 너만 이미 일자리 제안을 받았지. 난 아직 못 찾았잖아.

Tammy: 너도 곧 찾을 거야. 내가 장담해. 그러고 나면 우리가 현금을 쓸어 담을 거야! 돈 때문에 네가 너무 스트레스 받는 것 같아. 모든 게 괜찮아질 거라고.

Tammy: How much longer do we have? I feel like this car ride has **dragged on** forever. The hours are **passing by** very slowly.

Owen: We have three more hours until we get to Phoenix.

Tammy: Why didn't we just fly there? It wouldn't have taken up two days of our time.

Owen: We're **saving up** to buy a house! We can't afford to fly. We need every penny we can get if we're going to **take out** a loan and **pay** it **off**. We only have three more hours. You can **stick** it **out** until then.

Tammy: You're so worried about money! We've been **scraping by** on almost nothing for the past six months! I understand that we need to **cut down** on spending, but I can't live like this!

Owen: We're about to buy a new house! Then we can enjoy life a little more. I know it seems like nothing, but things like eating out and plane tickets **add up**. Then when the time comes that we have to **cough up** the money for a house, we've **run out**.

Tammy: I understand your point. This is a good reason to **put** money **aside**. I'm just not as worried as you are. Besides, Phoenix is a cheaper place to live in than Los Angeles. And the money will start **rolling in** when we start our new jobs in Phoenix.

Owen: You're the only one that already got a job offer! I haven't found one yet.

Tammy: Well, you will find one soon. I'm sure of it. And then we'll be **raking in** cash! I think you're way too stressed about money. Everything is going to be alright.

turn up

소리를 키우다, 올리다

To increase, typically referring to volume

I love this song! **Turn** it **up**!
이 노래 나 너무 좋은데! 소리 좀 키워 봐!

fade in

(소리가) 점점 커지다

To gradually become louder

His voice **fades in**. It's low and soothing.
그의 목소리가 조금씩 커진다. 낮고 부드럽다.

come out

나오다, 발매하다

To be released

When is his new song **coming out**?
그의 신곡이 언제 나오지?

turn down

소리를 줄이다, 낮추다

To reduce the intensity or volume of something

Turn down the music when people are trying to sleep.
사람들이 자려고 할 때는 음악 소리 좀 줄여.

SHORT DIALOGUE 1

Kenny   I'm going to play my new album for you. **Turn up** the volume.

Judith   Ooh. I like the introduction. The way the music **fades in** is cool.

Kenny   Thanks! You're the first person to hear this. The album **comes out** in three days.

Judith   The first song is very cool so far, but can you **turn it down** now? I need to get back to studying.

Kenny   내가 새로 나온 내 앨범 틀어 볼게. 소리 좀 키워 봐.
Judith   오, 시작 부분이 좋은데. 음악 소리가 점점 커지는 게 좋다.
Kenny   고마워! 네가 이거 처음으로 듣는 거야. 앨범이 3일 후에 나오거든.
Judith   첫 번째 노래는 지금까지 정말 좋다. 그런데 이제 소리 좀 줄여 줄래? 나 이제 공부해야 해.

put on

제작하다, 공연하다

To produce;
To put together
a performance
or show

Given their lack of experience, they **put on** a great show.

경험 부족을 고려해 보면, 그들이 정말 대단한 공연을 했다.

belt out

큰 소리로 노래하다

To sing loudly

Everyone was surprised when he **belted out** a song.

그가 큰 소리로 노래를 했을 때 모두 깜짝 놀랐다.

rock out

열정적으로 연주하다

To play instruments passionately

Sarah and John **rocked out** together at the concert.

Sarah와 John은 콘서트에서 정말 열정적으로 연주했다.

put out

출시하다, 생산하다

To create and release media or art

You can subscribe if you like. I **put out** new videos every Friday.

마음에 드시면 구독해 주세요. 저는 매주 금요일마다 동영상을 올려요.

SHORT DIALOGUE 2

Callie   Hey, Gerald. Coldplay is **putting on** a show in New York City. We should go see it.

Gerald   Let's do it. Their shows are awesome. I love the way Chris Martin **belts out**.

Callie   They really do **rock out**. I hope that they find success in New York City.

Gerald   They just **put out** a new album. I'm sure it will be very popular.

    Callie   야, Gerald. Coldplay가 뉴욕에서 공연한대. 가서 봐야지.
    Gerald   그러자. 그 밴드 공연은 최고지. 나는 Chris Martin이 열창하는 모습이 너무 좋더라.
    Callie   정말 연주 끝내주게 잘하잖아. 뉴욕 공연에서도 성공하면 좋겠다.
    Gerald   최근에 새 앨범 냈거든. 확실히 아주 인기가 있을 거야.

throw up

(빠르게) 보여 주다, 전시하다

To display in a hurry, not with much care

Throw up that music video on the projector screen.

프로젝터 스크린에 빨리 그 뮤직 비디오를 띄워 봐.

throw together

(빠르게) 준비하다

To create, typically quickly or without attention to detail

I'm just going to **throw together** a quick sketch.

내가 빠르게 스케치를 해 볼게.

come together

완성되다, 정리되다

To be completed or nearing completion

My new song is really **coming together**.

내 신곡이 거의 완성돼 가고 있어.

pack out

사람들을 채우다

To cause a place to be filled with people

We are going to **pack out** the theater the first night.

우리는 첫날 저녁에 극장을 다 채울 거야.

SHORT DIALOGUE 3

Eddie   Sally! What are you doing on Thursday? Can you help me **throw up** posters for my art show?

Sally   Of course. But you're always so busy. How did you find the time to **throw together** a show?

Eddie   I've spent every weekend working on it. I'm glad it's all **coming together**.

Sally   I'll have to come and see it. And these posters look really cool. You'll **pack out** the gallery for sure!

Eddie   Sally! 목요일에 뭐해? 내 미술 전시회 포스터 전시하는 것 좀 도와줄래?
Sally   그럼. 근데 너 항상 바쁘잖아. 어떻게 전시회 준비할 시간이 있었어?
Eddie   전시회 준비를 하느라 주말마다 작업했어. 이제 다 완성돼 가고 있어서 기뻐.
Sally   꼭 가서 볼게. 이 포스터들 정말 너무 멋지다. 확실히 미술관을 관람객들로 가득 채울 거야!

MP3 **049**

sign up for

등록하다, 가입하다

To register for
a service

I decided to **sign up for** this class.
난 이 강좌를 등록하기로 했다.

fall behind

뒤처지다

To perform worse
than one's peers

My son is **falling behind** in English.
우리 아들은 영어가 (다른 애들에 비해) 뒤처지고
있어.

buckle down

열심히 하다

To start
working hard

You should **buckle down** if you
really want to get accepted.
네가 정말 합격하고 싶으면 열심히 해야 해.

keep (it) up

계속 나아가다, 힘내다

To continue a level of
effort or progress

Your grades are nice! **Keep** it **up**.
성적이 좋구나! 계속 열심히 하렴.

SHORT DIALOGUE 1

Phil   Mom! I **signed up for** the chess team. I'm going to have to stay at school till four
o'clock on Thursdays.

Mom   Phil! Why didn't you ask me? You're **falling behind** in math! How can you make
time for the chess team?

Phil   I love chess, Mom! I promise I'll **buckle down** and get my grades up in math.

Mom   Fine. If you get good grades and **keep** it **up**, you can stay on the chess team.

Phil   엄마! 나 체스팀에 가입했어요. 목요일마다 4시까지 학교에 있어야 해요.
Mom   Phil! 왜 엄마한테 안 물어봤어? 너 수학 뒤처져 있잖아! 어떻게 체스팀 할 시간이 있어?
Phil   나 체스 엄청 좋아해요, 엄마! 열심히 해서 수학 성적 올릴게요.
Mom   알았어. 네가 좋은 성적 받고 잘 유지하면, 체스팀에 있어도 좋아.

get in

합격하다

To be admitted into
a program or school

Did you **get in** that school you were
talking about?

너 네가 말했던 그 학교에 합격한 거야?

major in

전공하다

To get a degree in;
To focus on one
subject in college

I **majored in** economics back in
college.

난 대학에서 경제학을 전공했다.

keep up with

(뒤처지지 않고) ~을 따라가다

To go or make progress at the
same rate as (others); To be able to
complete something

Jesse was having trouble **keeping
up with** his school work.

Jesse는 학교 과제를 따라가느라 힘들었다.

get through

(힘들지만) 잘 해내다

To persevere; To live
through a difficult
experience

Once we **get through** this semester,
we are going to throw a huge party.

일단 이번 학기만 잘 넘기면, 우리가 큰 파티를 열
거야.

SHORT DIALOGUE 2

Cheryl   I've got some good news! I applied for my dream college, and I **got in**.

Benjamin   That's amazing! Congratulations! What are you going to **major in**?

Cheryl   I'll be studying microbiology. I'm nervous. I will have a lot of work to **keep up
with**.

Benjamin   I'm sure you'll **get through** it just fine. You're super smart.

Cheryl   나 좋은 소식 있어! 내가 평소에 가고 싶어 하던 대학에 지원했는데, 합격했어.
Benjamin   잘됐다! 축하해! 전공은 뭐 할 거야?
Cheryl   나 미생물학을 공부하려고. 긴장된다. 따라가려면 정말 공부 많이 해야 할 거야.
Benjamin   넌 분명 잘 해낼 거야. 너 완전 똑똑하잖아.

pore over

꼼꼼히 살피다

To study intensely

You will need to **pore over** your notes if you want to pass this test.

이 시험 통과하고 싶으면 노트를 꼼꼼히 봐야 할 거야.

skim over

대충 훑어보다

To read quickly;
To study without attention to detail

Let me **skim over** the instructions before we get started.

시작하기 전에 설명을 대충 훑어 볼게요.

brush up

(예전에 했던 것을) 다시 살펴보다, 기억을 새로이 하다

To study something already known

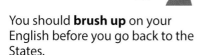

You should **brush up** on your English before you go back to the States.

너 미국으로 돌아가기 전에 영어 공부를 다시 해 봐.

sail through

쉽게 해내다, 별 탈 없이 해내다

To complete something easilly

You can **sail through** anything if you put in the work.

넌 노력하면 그 어떤 것도 해낼 수 있어.

SHORT DIALOGUE 3

Britany: Are you ready for the math test? I **pored over** my notes until midnight last night.

Josey: I'm not sure. I just **skimmed over** my notes. Honestly, I didn't study a lot.

Britany: You're a good student. Maybe you just need to **brush up** on them before the test.

Josey: We'll see. I've **sailed through** this class so far. I'm not worried.

> Britany 수학 시험 준비는 다 했어? 난 어젯밤에 자정까지 꼼꼼히 노트 살펴봤다.
> Josey 솔직히 잘 모르겠어. 그냥 노트만 대충 훑어봤어. 솔직히, 많이 공부하진 않았어.
> Britany 너 모범생이잖아. 시험 보기 전에 그냥 한번 보기만 하면 되지 않을까?
> Josey 곧 알게 되겠지. 지금까지 내가 이 수업 쉽게 잘해 왔으니까. 걱정하지 않아.

talk over

~에 대해 자세히 이야기 나누다

To discuss the details of something

Can we **talk over** your plan one more time?

다시 한 번 너의 계획에 대해서 자세히 이야기 나눌 수 있을까?

touch up

약간 수정하다, 보정하다

To improve something with small changes

I need to **touch up** a few mistakes on my essay.

내 에세이에서 실수 몇 개를 수정해야 해.

go over

검토하다

To check something carefully

Can you **go over** this report before I hand in?

내가 보고서 제출하기 전에 네가 한번 검토해 줄래?

deal with

~을 다루다

To concern; To involve details of something or someone

This book **deals with** the darkside of being famous.

이 책은 유명해진다는 것의 어두운 면을 다룬다.

SHORT DIALOGUE 1

Malcolm   Hello, Professor. I need some help with my paper. Do you have time to **talk it over** with me?

Professor   Sure, Malcolm. What part did you want to **go over**?

Malcolm   Mainly this section here that **deals with** my theory. Do you think I need to add more?

Professor   Let me see… No, I think this is good. But you do have a few minor mistakes you need to **touch up** before you submit it.

Malcolm   안녕하세요, 교수님. 제 논문과 관련해서 도움이 좀 필요해서요. 얘기 좀 나눌 수 있을까요?
Professor   그래, Malcolm. 어느 부분을 검토하고 싶은 거지?
Malcolm   주로 제 이론을 다루는 여기 이 부분이요. 여기서 더 추가를 하는 게 좋을까요?
Professor   어디 보자… 아니, 내 생각은 지금 이대로가 좋아. 하지만 제출하기 전에 수정해야 할 사소한 오류들이 좀 있네.

get into

~에 처하게 되다

To become involved in

I don't want to **get into** an argument with you.

나 너랑 논쟁하고 싶지 않아.

bring up

언급하다, 말을 꺼내다

To mention a subject

Why did you have to **bring up** my ex-husband?

너 왜 내 전 남편 이야기를 꺼내야만 했던 거야?

point out

지적하다

To draw attention to a specific detail

Please **point out** my mistakes if I do something wrong.

제가 잘못하면 제 실수를 지적해 주세요.

go into

자세히 설명하다

To explain something in detail

Nate didn't want to **go into** details about his divorce.

Nate는 그의 이혼에 대해서 자세하게 설명하고 싶지 않았다.

SHORT DIALOGUE 2

Cindy　Hey, Bert. Are you alright? It seems like you've been sad all day.

Bert　Why do you **bring** it **up**? Am I acting differently?

Cindy　I didn't mean to **point** it **out**, but you've been very quiet today.

Bert　Actually, I **got into** a fight with my mother. I don't want to **go into** the details.

Cindy　야, Bert. 괜찮아? 너 하루 종일 슬퍼 보여.
Bert　왜 그런 말을 해? 내가 좀 다르게 행동하니?
Cindy　지적하려는 건 아니었는데, 네가 오늘 너무 조용해서.
Bert　실은 엄마하고 다퉜어. 자세히 말하고 싶지 않아.

run by

~에게 의견[조언]을 구하다

To bring to someone's attention, typically in search of approval or advice

Before I close the deal, I want to **run** this **by** my wife last time.

이 계약을 마무리하기 전에, 마지막으로 아내에게 의견을 구해 볼게요.

get back

(답을 가지고) 나중에 다시 연락하다, 다시 알려 주다

To return later with an answer or a clarification

I'll **get back** to you later about the price of the car repairs.

차 수리비는 나중에 다시 알려 드릴게요.

go ahead

진행하다, 어서 하다

To proceed

If you have any questions, **go ahead** and ask. I'm happy to help.

궁금한 점이 있으면, 언제든지 알려 줘. 내가 기꺼이 도와줄게.

think about

(곰곰이) 생각하다

To ponder;
To consider

I need some time to **think about** this. Can I get back to you later?

이것에 대해 생각할 시간이 좀 필요해요. 나중에 알려 드려도 될까요?

SHORT DIALOGUE 3

Peter Jonathan! How are you? I wanted to **run** something **by** you.

Jonathan I don't have a lot of time, but you can **go ahead** and ask.

Peter Do you want to be my roommate this fall? You can **get back** to me later if you want.

Jonathan Hmm. I have to **think about** it. How about I give you a call tomorrow?

Peter   Jonathan! 잘 지내? 너한테 의견 구하고 싶은 게 있어서.
Jonathan 나 시간이 많이 없기는 한데, 어서 물어봐!
Peter   너 이번 가을에 내 룸메이트 되고 싶어? 그러고 싶으면 나한테 알려 줘.
Jonathan 음. 생각해 봐야겠다. 내일 내가 전화하는 건 어때?

MP3 **051**

make out

이해하다, 알아보다

To understand something

I can't **make out** what he was talking about.
난 걔가 무슨 말을 하는지 모르겠어.

help out

도와주다, 거들다

To do work for someone or provide the person with something that is needed

Thanks a lot for **helping** me **out** with my essay.
나 에세이 쓰는 거 도와줘서 정말 고마워.

grapple with

~을 해결하려고 애쓰다, 고심하다

To struggle with something; To deal with a difficult question

I'm **grappling with** the financial situation.
난 재정 상황을 이해하고 해결하려고 고심하고 있어.

sink in

실감 나다, 깨닫다

To realize over time; To come to terms with

It just **sunk in** that I'm getting older.
내가 나이가 들고 있다는 게 딱 실감이 났다.

SHORT DIALOGUE 1

Stu   Are you alright, Lucy? I couldn't **make out** what happened at the party.

Lucy   I was in the kitchen, **helping out** with the food, when I saw that Jason was there.

Stu   I know that it's hard to **grapple with** seeing him, but you need to move on.

Lucy   I know, I know. I guess it just hasn't **sunk in** that we'll never live together again.

Stu   Lucy, 괜찮아? 파티장에서 무슨 일이 생겼는지 알 수가 없어서.

Lucy   음식 하는 거 도와주면서 부엌에 있었는데, 그때 Jason이 거기 있는 걸 봤어.

Stu   Jason을 보는 게 쉽지 않은 건 아는데, 이제 잊고 너도 네 갈 길 가야지.

Lucy   나도 알아, 알지. 그냥 우리가 다시는 함께 살 수 없다는 게 실감이 나지 않아서 그런 것 같아.

find out

알아내다, 알게 되다

To discover

When did you **find out** that you were adopted?

네가 입양되었다는 것을 언제 알게 된 거야?

mix up

혼동하다, 착각하다

To confuse;
To switch two or
more people or
subjects

They're identical twins. It's very easy to **mix** them **up**.

걔네들 일란성 쌍둥이야. 혼동하기가 매우 쉬워.

piece together

(종합하여) 이해하다, 파악하다

To make a discovery
through analyzing
details; To come to
a realization

I finally **pieced together** why we're always out of ice cream. You've been eating it when I'm asleep. Right?

내가 드디어 왜 아이스크림이 항상 없어지는지 파악했어. 내가 잘 때 네가 먹은 거지, 그렇지?

clear up

(오해, 문제 등을) 말끔히 해결하다

To get rid of confusion;
To clarify

Let me **clear up** your confusion about this.

내가 이것에 관해 네가 혼동하는 점을 말끔히 해결해 줄게.

SHORT DIALOGUE 2

Phyllis   Did you **find out** what happened to the T-shirt you ordered, Heidi?

Heidi   Yeah. I called the store, and they told me that they had **mixed up** my order.

Phyllis   What does that mean? Were you able to **piece together** what happened?

Heidi   It was just a misunderstanding. They sent it to the wrong address. I **cleared** it **up**.

Phyllis   네가 주문한 티셔츠 어떻게 되었는지 알아냈어, Heidi?
Heidi   응. 가게에 전화했는데, 내 주문을 다른 것과 혼동했대.
Phyllis   그게 무슨 말이야? 어떻게 된 일인지 파악할 수 있었다는 거야?
Heidi   약간 오해가 있었던 것뿐이야. 잘못된 주소로 배송했더라고. 내가 다 해결했어.

put together

취합하다, 이해하다

To create something by gathering parts together;
To understand

I can't **put together** why Amy doesn't like me at all.

왜 Amy가 날 좋아하지 않는지 이해가 안 돼.

dawn on

처음으로 깨닫다, 명확해지다

To realize for the first time

It just **dawned on** me that I've been following money over passion all my life.

난 내가 평생 열정이 아닌 돈을 좇았다는 것을 처음으로 깨닫게 되었다.

relate to

공감하다, 이해하다

To feel that you can understand a person, a situation

We all can **relate to** your story.

우리 모두 너의 이야기에 공감할 수 있어.

come to

~하게 되다

To begin to have a feeling or opinion

I **came to** believe that I need more healthy relationships.

내게는 더 건강한 관계가 필요하다는 것을 믿게 되었다.

SHORT DIALOGUE 3

Pierce   So why did you break up with Chandler? I was never able to **put together** the story.

Leslie   It's not complicated. One day it just **dawned on** me that I didn't want to be with him.

Pierce   I can **relate to** that. But I can also understand how hard it must be for him.

Leslie   Yeah, I'm sure one day, he'll **come to** realize that I wasn't right for him, either.

Pierce   너 Chandler랑 왜 깨진 거야? 어떻게 된 건지 난 도저히 이해가 안 돼.
Leslie   복잡하지 않아. 어느 날 그냥 걔랑 함께하고 싶지 않다는 걸 깨닫게 된 거지.
Pierce   그건 나도 공감해. 그렇지만 Chandler가 얼마나 힘들지도 이해할 수 있어.
Leslie   그래. 언젠가 Chandler도 내가 자기 인연이 아니었다는 걸 깨닫게 될 거야.

LONG DIALOGUE

Ned: 사랑이나 비통함에 관한 곡을 써야 해. 그 수업에서 뒤처져 있어서 나 잘해야 하거든.

— **Regina:** 왜 그걸 나한테 말하는 건데?

Ned: 네가 음악 이론을 전공했으니까. 우리가 그것에 대해 이야기 좀 나눌 수 있을까 하는데. 난 전에 곡을 써 본 적이 없어서, 도움이 필요해.

— **Regina:** 음, 나도 작곡 기술에 대해서는 다시 한번 살펴봐야 해. 예전 노트 좀 대충 훑어 보고 나서 도와줄게. 사람들이 공감할 수 있는 음악을 만드는 게 중요하잖아.

Ned: 음. 그렇지. 공감할 수 있는 것과 없는 것을 파악하는 게 난 어렵더라.

— **Regina:** 곡을 쓸 때, 너무 많이 생각하지 마. 생각을 너무 많이 하면, 뒤죽박죽이 돼. 긴장 풀고, 자신의 이야기를 쓰다 보면, 노래가 자연스럽게 만들어져. 너 사랑에 빠진 적 있어? 상처받은 적은?

Ned: 실은 그런 경험이 있어. 있잖아, 방금 생각났는데, 절친이랑 멀어진 일에 대해 곡을 써야겠어.

— **Regina:** 좋은 생각이야. 마이크 가져 와서 네가 느끼는 감정이 뭐든 내뱉어 봐. 내가 기타 가지고 올게. 그리고 네가 원하면 같이 연주해 보는 거야.

Ned: 좋아! 내일 만나서 녹음하자. 내가 오늘 밤에 열심히 해서 써 볼게. 도와줘서 고마워!

Ned: I have to write a song that **deals with** love or heartbreak, and I need to do well because I'm **falling behind** in that class.

— Regina: Why are you **bringing** it **up** to me?

Ned: Because you **majored in** music theory. I thought we could **talk** it **over**. I've never written a song before, and I need help.

— Regina: Well, I do need to **brush up** on my songwriting skills. I can **skim over** some of my old notes and then **help** you **out**. It's important to make music that people can **relate to**.

Ned: Hmm. That makes sense. It's just hard for me to **piece together** what is relatable or not.

— Regina: When you write music, don't **think about** it too much. If you think too much, you'll just get **mixed up**. When you relax and just write something personal, then the song **comes together** naturally. Have you ever been in love? Have you ever had your heart broken?

Ned: Yes, actually. You know what? It just **dawned on** me. I should write a song about falling out with my best friend.

— Regina: Good idea. Just get a microphone and **belt out** whatever you're feeling into it. I can get my guitar, and we can **rock out** together if you want.

Ned: Perfect! Let's meet tomorrow and record. I'll **buckle down** and start writing tonight. Thanks for the help!

CHAPTER

7

PHRASAL VERBS

whittle away

조금씩 줄이다, 깎아내다

To deplete slowly;
To tear down piece
by piece

The impact of high interest will
eventually **whittle away** the
housing market value.
고금리 영향은 결국 주택 시장의 가치를 줄일 것이다.

come up with

~을 생각해 내다

To suggest or think of
an idea or plan

I just **came up with** an idea to
increase the number of my clients.
나 방금 고객 수를 늘릴 수 있는 아이디어를 생각해
냈어.

blow off

(책임 등을) 무시하다

To neglect
a responsibility or
person

Don't **blow off** your responsibility
while the rest of us are working
hard.
우리 나머지 사람들은 열심히 일하는데, 너 책임
피하려고 하지 마!

pick up

증가하다, 나아지다

To improve or
become better

Hopefully, business will **pick up** in
the summer.
바라건대, 여름에 사업이 좀 나아지면 좋겠다.

SHORT DIALOGUE 1

CEO Ever since that new shopping mall opened, our sales have started to **whittle away**.

Director I told Shay from advertising to do something about it, but she just **blew** me **off**.

CEO I expect you to **come up with** some solutions before the board meeting tomorrow.

Director Yes, ma'am. By next quarter sales will **pick** back **up**.

CEO 새 쇼핑몰이 오픈한 후로, 우리 매출이 조금씩 줄어들기 시작했어요.
Director 광고팀 Shay에게 그것과 관련해서 뭔가 좀 하라고 말을 했습니다만, 제 말을 듣지 않네요.
CEO 내일 이사회 회의 전에 해결책을 생각해 오셨으면 합니다.
Director 네, 알겠습니다. 다음 분기 때까지는 매출이 다시 나아질 겁니다.

set back

방해하다, 지연시키다

To delay an event, process, or person

Poor writing could **set back** your own career.

글솜씨가 부족하면 당신의 커리어에 문제가 될 수 있다.

forge on

계속하다, 지속하다

To continue, typically despite hardship

Even though we lost our main client, we still have to **forge on**.

비록 주 거래처를 잃었지만, 우리는 계속 앞으로 나아가야 합니다.

get past

넘어가다, (어려운 일을 잊고) 나아가다

To transcend or leave something behind

I cannot **get past** the fight I had with my girlfriend.

내 여자 친구하고 다툰 것을 잊고 그냥 넘어갈 수가 없어.

look back

돌아보다, 회상하다

To reflect; To consider the past

Sometimes I **look back** and remember all of the friends I used to have.

가끔 과거를 회상하면서 난 함께했던 옛 친구들을 모두 기억한다.

SHORT DIALOGUE 2

Ross   Losing one of our main clients will certainly **set back** our business for a while.

Barbara   It is bad news, that's for sure. But we have to **forge on** anyway.

Ross   I know. If we work hard, we'll be able to **get past** this.

Barbara   In a year, we'll **look back** and see how much progress we've made.

> Ross   우리 주 거래처를 하나 잃은 게 한동안은 사업 발전에 문제가 될 거야.
> Barbara   확실히 안 좋은 소식이네. 하지만 어쨌든 계속 나아가야지.
> Ross   맞아. 열심히 하면, 이 어려운 시간도 잘 넘어갈 수 있을 거야.
> Barbara   일 년 후에는, 돌아보면서 우리가 얼마나 발전했는지 알게 될 거야.

pick up

픽업하다, 차를 태우다

To go somewhere
and collect someone

I'll **pick** you **up** at 6:00 AM. You
should be ready by then.
내일 오전 6시에 픽업할게. 그때까지 준비하고
있어야 해.

stick with

~을 지속하다, 계속하다

To continue with
something or
someone

We tend to **stick with** enjoyable
activities.
우리는 즐거워하는 일은 더 오래 지속하는 경향이
있다.

pan out

전개되다, 진행되다

To develop or happen

Things really didn't **pan out** as
I wanted.
실제로는 일이 내가 원하는 대로 진행되지 않았다.

keep at

계속 밀고 나가다

To persist with
something

We've made some progress and
we're going to **keep at** it.
우리는 어느 정도의 진척을 이뤄냈고, 계속 밀고 나갈
거예요.

SHORT DIALOGUE 3

Sue　　It's always been my dream to be a painter, but I've never been able to **stick with**
　　　　it.

Jeffery　That's because you're always so busy running errands, **picking** your kids **up**, and
　　　　driving them around...

Sue　　You're right. I just need to find the time to paint and then **keep at** it.

Jeffery　I'm sure everything will **pan out** for you once you make painting a priority.

Sue　　난 항상 화가가 되는 게 꿈이었어. 그런데 그것을 결코 지속할 수가 없었어.
Jeffery　그건 네가 자잘한 바깥일에 아이들 픽업하고, 운전해 주느라 항상 바빠서 그렇지.
Sue　　맞아. 그림 그릴 시간을 확보하고 계속 그려야 하는데 말이야.
Jeffery　일단 네가 그림 그리는 것을 우선순위로 하면, 다 잘 진행될 거야.

MP3 **054**

pull off

해내다, 성공하다

To achieve something;
To do something
successfully

It was not an easy task, but I
managed to **pull** it **off**.
쉬운 일은 아니었지만, 난 결국 해냈다.

win over

설득하다, 마음을 돌리다

To persuade someone
to support you
or agree with you

My boyfriend really **won over** my
parents when he met them.
남자 친구가 우리 부모님을 만났을 때 그분들의
마음을 사로잡았다.

fall through

무산되다, 실패하다

To be ruined;
To fail

The deal to open a new business in
Korea **fell through**.
한국에서 새로운 사업체를 열기로 한 계약은
무산되었다.

give off

풍기다, 내다, 발산하다

To radiate

Elon always **gives off** an air of
confidence.
Elon은 항상 자신감 넘치는 기운을 뿜어낸다.

SHORT DIALOGUE 1

Katrina   I'm nervous about this interview. I want this job, but I don't know if I can **pull** it
off.

Stewart   You're a very smart person, Kat, and you always **give off** confident energy. I'm
sure you'll **win** them **over**.

Katrina   Thank you. Even if this **falls through**, I have another interview next week.

Stewart   Well, there you go, no pressure!

Katrina   나 이번 면접 긴장돼. 정말 원하는 일인데, 잘할 수 있을지 모르겠어.
Stewart   넌 정말 똑똑해, Kat. 넌 항상 자신감 넘치는 에너지를 내. 분명히 면접관들 마음을 사로잡을 거야.
Katrina   고마워. 이 면접 떨어져도 다음 주에 다른 면접이 잡혀 있어.
Stewart   음, 거 봐. 부담 없잖아!

get ahead

앞서가다, 더 잘 해내다

To be successful and
do better than other
people

Working hard and consistently is
the best way to **get ahead**.

열심히, 꾸준히 하는 것이 앞서 나갈 수 있는 최고의
방법이다.

rise above

극복하다, 넘어서다

To get better than;
To get over

How were you able to **rise above**
that criticism and pursue your
dreams?

어떻게 그런 비난들을 극복하고, 꿈을 향해서 달려갈
수 있었어요?

work out

잘 되다

To be okay in the end

Don't worry, everything is going to
work out.

걱정하지 마. 모든 게 다 잘 될 거야.

win back

다시 얻다, 되찾다

To earn something
that had been lost;
To regain

You have to work really hard to **win
back** my trust.

내 신뢰를 다시 얻으려면 너 정말 열심히 일해야 해.

SHORT DIALOGUE 2

Joyce — We need to get new clients if we want to **rise above** this setback.

Richard — No, we don't need new clients to **get ahead**. Instead, we need to **win back** the clients that we've lost.

Joyce — Richard! That's crazy. There's no way they will come back to us!

Richard — Just trust me. I know what to do. Everything will **work out**.

Joyce — 이 차질을 넘어서려면 새로운 고객을 구해야 해요.

Richard — 아뇨, 앞서 나가기 위해 새로운 고객이 필요하진 않습니다. 대신, 우리가 놓친 고객을 되찾아야 합니다.

Joyce — Richard! 그건 말도 안 돼요. 그 고객들이 우리에게 다시 돌아오는 것은 불가능합니다!

Richard — 절 믿어 주세요. 뭘 해야 할지 압니다. 모든 게 다 잘 될 거예요.

succeed in

성공적으로 해내다

To execute a specific
task successfully

You need to focus if you're going to
succeed in your new project.
새로운 프로젝트를 성공적으로 해내려면 집중해야 해.

lose out

(기회를) 놓치다, 손해를 보다

To miss or fail to seize an
opportunity

Don't **lose out** on this great
opportunity! Just one seat remains.
이 좋은 기회를 놓치지 마세요! 딱 한 자리만 남아
있어요.

get away

모면하다, (처벌을) 피하다

To escape; To face no
consequences

I won't let you **get away** with
mistakes.
난 너의 실수를 용인하지 않을 거야.

come off as

~로 보이다

To be perceived
in a way

I don't want to **come off as** a snob.
난 속물처럼 보이고 싶지 않아.

SHORT DIALOGUE 3

Chef   We've **succeeded in** cutting down our costs, but we need more customers.

Owner   I think we're **losing out** on many guests because we don't have a big menu.

Chef   I disagree. We **get away** with not having many options because the food we
        have is delicious.

Owner   I'm telling you; our menu **comes off as** too limited! We need to expand it.

    Chef   비용을 줄이는 건 성공했지만, 손님이 더 있어야 합니다.
    Owner   내 생각엔 우리 메뉴가 다양하지 않아서 손님들을 많이 놓치는 것 같네.
    Chef   제 생각은 다릅니다. 우리 음식들이 맛있어서, 메뉴가 많이 없는 것은 문제가 되지 않아요.
    Owner   내 말이 맞다니깐. 우리 메뉴가 너무 한정되어 있는 것처럼 보여. 메뉴를 더 늘려야 해.

talk into

설득해서 ~하게 하다

To convince

Jamie **talked** me **into** going to a bar tonight.

Jamie가 오늘 밤에 술집에 가자고 나를 꼬드겼어.

insist on

주장하다, 고집하다, 우기다

To say or show that one believes that something is necessary or very important

I **insist on** you reading this book.

너 이 책 꼭 읽어 봐!

plan ahead

미리 계획하다, 장래의 계획을 세우다

To make arrangements in advance

We need to **plan ahead** if we're going to go camping.

우리가 캠핑을 갈 거라면, 미리 계획을 세워야 해.

allow for

~을 감안하다

To think about or plan for something that might happen in the future

If you **allow for** inflation, he's actually making less money now than 15 years ago.

물가 상승을 감안하면, 그는 15년 전보다 오히려 지금 돈을 덜 버는 셈이다.

SHORT DIALOGUE 1

Bob   Phoebe's trying to **talk** me **into** going to the movies tonight. I'm so tired, though.

Leah   Then, just say, "No." She can't **insist on** making you go if you don't want to.

Bob   I just wish she would **plan ahead** more instead of asking me right before the movie starts.

Leah   She should have **allowed for** a bit of time so that you can get ready!

Bob   Phoebe가 오늘 밤에 영화 보자고 날 꼬드기고 있어. 그런데 나 너무 피곤해.
Leah   그럼 그냥 안 본다고 해. 네가 싫다는데, 걔도 나가자고 고집 부리면 안 되지.
Bob   영화 시작 직전에 나한테 물어보지 말고, 미리 좀 계획하면 좋을 텐데 말야.
Leah   네가 준비할 수 있게 시간을 두고 감안했어야지.

MP3 055

cave in

마지못해서 ~하다, 설득되다

To concede;
To be convinced

I finally **caved in** when I heard it was the last offer.

나는 그게 마지막 제안이라는 말을 듣고 마침내 응했다.

mull over

~에 대해 숙고하다, 고민하다

To ponder;
To think about

Hmm...

I have to **mull over** the offer I received before I decide.

결정하기 전에 제가 제안받은 것을 고민해 봐야 해요.

bring around

(의견을 받아들이도록) ~를 설득하다

To change someone's mind; To convince someone to think differently

Let me talk to Jayden.
I'm sure I can **bring** him **around**.

내가 Jayden하고 이야기 좀 해 볼게. 내가 설득할 수 있을 거야.

think over

~을 심사숙고하다, 곰곰이 생각하다

To consider all the details of something

When someone asks a favor, **think** it **over** to see if you have time to do it.

누가 너에게 부탁을 하면, 그것을 할 시간이 있는지 곰곰이 생각해 봐.

SHORT DIALOGUE 2

Christina Do you want to go to a baseball game with me this weekend?

Paul I'll have to **mull** it **over** a little. I have a lot of work to do.

Christina Oh, come on! I know I can get you to **cave in**. What do I have to do to **bring** you **around**?

Paul I didn't say I wasn't going! I said that I'd **think** it **over**. I'll text you later.

Christina 이번 주말에 나랑 야구 경기 보러 갈래?
Paul 생각 좀 해 봐야겠다. 할 일이 많아서.
Christina 에이, 왜 그래! 네가 내 말대로 할 거라는 거 알고 있어. 네 맘 돌리려면 내가 어떻게 해야 할까?
Paul 안 간다고는 안 했잖아! 생각 좀 해 본다고 했지. 나중에 문자 보낼게.

LONG DIALOGUE

Brittney: Ted, 얘기 좀 할 수 있어? 아까 너한테 소리 지른 건 내가 실수했어. 잠시 화가 났지만, 우리가 함께했던 즐거운 시간들을 돌아봤어. 그리고 다시 너랑 친구가 되기 위해 노력해야 한다는 걸 깨달았어.

— **Ted:** 너무 늦었어, Brittney. 네가 날 그렇게 대한 게 용서가 안 돼. 친절하게 말한다고 해서 내 맘이 돌아서지 않아.

Brittney: 널 설득하려는 게 아냐. 단지 우리 사이가 멀어진 게 안타깝다고 말하고 싶은 거지.

— **Ted:** 단지 상황이 안 좋아진 게 아니야. 넌 나를 막 대했어. 나한테 계속 소리 지르고. 내가 네 도움이 필요할 때마다 무시했어. 넌 네 행동 때문에 내가 어떤 심정이었는지는 한번도 생각한 적이 없어.

Brittney: 나도 알아. 진심으로 미안해. 내가 원하는 건, 이 의견 차이를 극복하는 거야. 그렇지만 계속 나에게 화를 내고 싶다면… 나도 이해해.

— **Ted:** 나 아직도 화는 나. 하지만… 네가 정말 이 일을 잊고 앞으로 잘하고 싶다면 고민해 볼게.

Brittney: Ted, can I talk to you? I know I made a mistake earlier when I yelled at you. I was angry for a while. But then I **looked back** at all the fun times we had, and I realized that I need to try and **win** you **back** as my friend.

— **Ted:** It's too late, Brittney. You can't **get away** with the way you treated me. You're not going to **win** me **over** with kind words.

Brittney: I'm not trying to **talk** you **into** anything. I just want to say that I'm sorry things **fell through** between us.

— **Ted:** Things didn't just **fall through**. You didn't treat me right. You constantly yelled at me. You **blew** me **off** when I needed your help. You never considered how your actions made me feel.

Brittney: I know. And I'm truly sorry. All I want is to **rise above** this disagreement. But if you **insist on** being angry at me… I understand.

— **Ted:** I am still mad. But… I guess if you really want to **get past** this, I can **think** it **over**.

set off

화나게 하다

To make angry;
To upset

When Jane started to talk to me like a child, it really **set** me **off**.

Jane이 날 어린애 취급하며 말을 걸었을 때, 난 정말 화가 났다.

fly into

버럭 화를 내다

To suddenly become very angry

I never saw Luke **fly into** a rage like that.

난 Luke가 그렇게 화내는 것을 한 번도 못 봤어.

flare up

갑자기 확 타오르다,
벌컥 화를 내다

To increase suddenly;
To show sudden anger
towards somebody

My depression starts to **flare up** whenever I hear this song.

나는 이 노래를 들을 때마다 우울감이 치솟는다.

cut off

~을 가로막다, 끼어들다

To prevent someone from having access to somewhere or someone

The other car **cut** me **off** on the highway.

다른 차가 고속도로에서 내 앞에 끼어들었다.

SHORT DIALOGUE 1

Peggy   I really shouldn't drive. Every time I do, someone **sets** me **off**.

Brett   I know what you mean. The other day, someone **cut** me **off**, and I **flew into** a rage.

Peggy   I really don't get these people. Something about reckless driving makes my anger **flare up**.

Brett   It's not our fault. Some people really shouldn't drive.

Peggy   나 정말 운전하면 안 돼. 내가 운전할 때마다, 누군가 때문에 내가 꼭 열이 받거든.
Brett   무슨 말인지 나도 알아. 일전에, 누군가 내 앞에 끼어들어서 나도 엄청 화가 났거든.
Peggy   이런 사람들이 도무지 이해가 안 돼. 주위를 살피지 않고 운전하는 걸 보면 정말 화가 막 끓어오른다니까.
Brett   그게 우리 잘못은 아니지. 어떤 사람들은 정말 운전하면 안 돼!

knock out

기절시키다

To strike unconcious

The drunk man **knocked out** Stephen at the bar.

그 술 취한 남자는 술집에서 Stephen을 기절시켰다.

break up

갈등을 끝내다, 싸움을 말리다

To end a conflict; To separate a fight

Sometimes it's dangerous to try and **break up** a dog fight.

때로는 개싸움을 말리는 게 위험하다.

drag into

~을 (어떤 일에) 끌어들이다

To involve someone against their wishes

I don't want to **drag** my friends **into** my problems.

나는 친구들을 내 문제에 끌어들이고 싶지 않아.

calm down

진정하다

To become less stressed or angry

Whenever I get too angry, I try to take a deep breath to **calm down**.

화가 너무 날 때마다, 나는 진정하려고 심호흡을 한다.

SHORT DIALOGUE 2

Nina Last night was crazy. Andre **knocked** someone **out**.

Marcus That's not cool. You saw a fight, and you didn't **break** it **up**?

Nina I didn't want to get **dragged into** it.

Marcus He's your friend! You could have at least tried to **calm** him **down**.

> **Nina** 어젯밤 장난 아니었어. Andre가 어떤 애를 기절시켰잖아.
> **Marcus** 그건 정말 별로다. 넌 싸우는 거 봤으면서, 말리지 않은 거야?
> **Nina** 거기에 별로 엮이고 싶지 않았어.
> **Marcus** 걔는 네 친구잖아! 적어도 Andre를 진정시킬 수는 있었잖아.

fall in with

~와 어울리다

To spend time with;
To become friends
with

Mark really **fell in with** a group of
bad people.

Mark는 정말로 질 나쁜 사람들과 어울려 다녔다.

mix up

연루시키다, 어울리다

To involve;
To be part of

I got **mixed up** with the bad people
back in college.

나는 대학 때 나쁜 사람들하고 어울렸었다.

break into

침입하다

To enter a house or
building illegally

If we want that money, we'll need to
break into the bank.

만약 우리가 그 돈을 원한다면, 은행에 침입해야
겠지.

hold up

털다, 강탈하다

To rob

In the old days, gangsters would
hold up banks.

예전에는 조직폭력배들이 은행을 털곤 했다.

SHORT DIALOGUE 1

Anthony   Man. Elijah has really **fallen in with** the wrong people.

Ruth   Why do you say that? What did he get **mixed up** in this time?

Anthony   He **broke into** some cars, and then some guy talked him into trying to **hold up**
a gas station.

Ruth   Wow. Did he get arrested?

    Anthony   아. Elijah가 질 나쁜 사람들이랑 어울리네.
    Ruth   왜 그러는데? 이번에는 걔가 어떤 문제에 연루된 거야?
    Anthony   차량을 털고, 어떤 녀석이 시켜서 주유소도 털려고 했어.
    Ruth   와우. Elijah는 체포된 거야?

bring in
체포하다

To arrest

Don't kill the spy. **Bring** him **in** alive.
그 스파이를 죽이지 말고, 산 채로 잡아 와.

carry out
복역하다, 징역을 살다

To serve a sentence;
To execute a
punishment

Jake **carried out** his sentence
in a prison.
Jake는 감옥에서 형을 살았다.

get off
풀려나다

To be released;
To avoid criminal
conviction

Because Ashley was so young, she
got off with just a warning.
Ashley는 너무 어려서, 경고만 받고 풀려났다.

walk away
(가벼운 처벌만 받고) 풀려나다

To get away with
a minor sentence

Jeremy was able to **walk away**
because he bribed the judge.
Jeremy는 판사를 돈으로 매수해서 풀려날 수 있었다.

SHORT DIALOGUE 2

Rona Did you see the news? The police **brought in** a suspect for that robbery.

Bruno It's about time. How long do you think the trial will be? I'm sure he will have to **carry out** a long sentence.

Rona Actually, it was a "she." And, I'm not sure. The reports say the woman might **get off**.

Bruno What? No! Nobody should get to just **walk away** without punishment for that.

Rona 그 뉴스 봤어? 경찰이 강도 사건 용의자를 체포했어.
Bruno 그럴 때가 됐지. 재판은 어느 정도 걸릴 것 같아? 확실히 그 용의자는 오랫동안 복역해야 할 거야.
Rona 그게 말야, 용의자가 여자였어. 그리고 잘 모르겠어. 뉴스에서는 그 여자가 풀려날지도 모른다고 하던데.
Bruno 뭐? 안 돼! 그 누구도 그런 범죄에 대해 처벌도 받지 않고 풀려나면 안 되지.

spy on

감시하다, 염탐하다

To watch someone
secretly in order to
find out what they
are doing

I think the equipment helped the
detective **spy on** the suspects.

그 장비가 형사가 용의자들을 감시하는 데 도움이 된
것 같다.

narrow down

(선택지를) 좁히다

To reduce the
number of options

We've **narrowed down** the suspects
to just two men.

우리는 용의자들을 두 남자로 좁혔다.

rule out

배제하다, 제외시키다

To no longer consider
someone or something
as a possibility after
careful study

Jake was out of the country, so we
have to **rule** him **out** as a suspect.

Jake는 국외에 있었어. 그래서 용의선상에서 배제해
야 해.

dig up

(세부사항 등을) 캐내다

To uncover details
from the past

Let me **dig up** something from his
past.

제가 그의 과거에 대해서 한번 캐 볼게요.

SHORT DIALOGUE 1

Police Chief　We've been **spying on** this building for almost a year, and we still don't know
who's selling drugs.

Detective　Yeah, you're right. But we've at least **narrowed down** the suspect to one of
the three men who live upstairs.

Police Chief　How can we **rule out** the people that live below them?

Detective　We can't **dig up** anything on them. They have no criminal record or motive.

Police Chief　우리가 거의 일 년이나 이 건물을 감시했는데, 여전히 누가 마약을 파는지 모르겠네.
Detective　네, 맞습니다. 하지만 적어도 용의자는 위층에 사는 세 남자 중 한 명으로 좁혔잖아요.
Police Chief　거기 아래층에 사는 사람들은 어떻게 배제할 수 있는 거지?
Detective　더 이상 그들에게 파낼 수 있는 게 없어요. 범죄 이력도 없고 동기도 없거든요.

rat out

고자질하다, 꼰지르다,
일러바치다

To tell the authorities
about a crime
someone committed

I thought Alex was my best friend,
but he **ratted** me **out** to the police.

난 Alex가 내 절친이라고 생각했는데, 걔가 날 경찰에
꼰질렀어.

root out

근절하다, 뿌리 뽑다

To uncover and
remove

We need to **root out** the corruption
in this city's government.

우리는 이 시 정부의 부정부패를 뿌리 뽑아야 한다.

look into

조사하다

To investigate

Police often have to **look into**
suspicious activity.

경찰은 종종 미심적인 행동을 조사해야 한다.

barge in on

~에 불쑥 들어오다, 불쑥 끼어들다

To suddenly and
rudely interrupt
or disturb

I just **barged in on** my husband
having an affair with another man.

난 남편이 딴 여자와 외도하는 현장에 불쑥 들어갔다.

SHORT DIALOGUE 2

Connie Have you seen the latest episode of *Law and Order*?

Jared I have! I had no idea that the delivery boy was the one who was **ratting**
everyone **out** to the police.

Connie Me neither! The gangsters were so close to **rooting** him **out** too! If only they
spent a little more time **looking into** his delivery route…

Jared And what about the fight scene where the officers **barged in on** the boss's
meeting at their hideout? Such a good episode!

Connie 〈Law and Order〉 최근 에피소드 봤어?
Jared 봤어! 나는 그 배달하는 소년이 경찰에 다 고자질할 거라는 건 전혀 몰랐어.
Connie 나도 몰랐어! 그 갱단도 거의 그를 찾아서 뿌리 뽑을 뻔했는데! 갱단들이 그의 배달 경로를 찾는 데
좀 더 시간을 썼으면 상황이 달라질 수 있었는데 말야.
Jared 은신처에서 경찰관들이 보스 회의에 끼어들었던 싸움 장면은 어땠어? 정말 괜찮은 에피소드였어!

stand back

뒤로 물러서다

To move a short distance away from something or someone

If you **stand back**, you will be able to see better.
뒤로 좀 물러서면 더 잘 볼 수 있을 거야.

track down

찾다, 추적하다

To find; To follow the trail left by someone or something

I'm trying to **track down** the missing child.
나는 실종된 아이를 찾으려고 하고 있다.

stake out

잠복 근무하다, 감시하다

To watch a place secretly and continuously

The detective **staked out** the building to catch the suspect.
형사는 용의자를 잡기 위해 그 건물을 감시했다.

give up

항복하다

To surrender; To hand something or someone over

I have nowhere to run. I have to **give** myself **up**.
난 더 이상 도망갈 곳이 없어. 항복해야 해.

SHORT DIALOGUE 3

Gabriella What are you watching?

Henry There is a hostage situation downtown. The police **tracked down** a robbery suspect to an apartment building, but he's holding some people hostage.

Gabriella Oh, no! That's terrible! Why are all the police **standing back** like that? Why don't they go in and arrest him?

Henry It's too dangerous for them to go in. They've **staked out** the building and are hoping he will **give** himself **up**.

Gabriella 뭐 보고 있어?

Henry 시내에서 인질극이 벌어지고 있대. 경찰이 강도 용의자를 아파트까지 추적했는데, 그 용의자가 사람들을 인질로 잡고 있어.

Gabriella 아이고! 정말 최악이네! 그런데 왜 경찰이 다 저렇게 뒤로 물러나 있는 거야? 왜 들어가서 체포를 안 하는 거지?

Henry 경찰이 들어가는 것은 너무 위험해. 경찰이 그 건물에서 잠복 중이고, 스스로 항복하길 바라는 거야.

MP3 060

abide by

(법률·규율 등을) 지키다

To conform to the standard or rules of something

When driving, you have to **abide by** the laws.

운전 중에는 법규를 지켜야 한다.

crack down

엄중 단속하다, 탄압하다

To treat more harshly than before

The Chinese government started to **crack down** on online tutoring companies.

중국 정부는 온라인 과외 업체 단속을 시작했다.

push back

저항하다, 반대하다

To resist

The time has come to **push back** against Asian hate crimes.

아시아인 혐오 범죄에 맞서야 할 때가 왔다.

step up

책임을 지다

To take responsibility

It's time for you to **step up** and make some money for your family.

이제 너도 책임을 갖고 가족을 위해서 돈을 벌어야 할 때야.

SHORT DIALOGUE 1

Dad   This is my house, and you have to **abide by** my rules! Now clean your room!

Bella   I don't get it! Why have you been **cracking down** on me so much lately?

Dad   You're getting older, and it's time you stop **pushing back** every time I ask you to do something. You need to **step up** and start helping out more around the house.

Bella   Fine! I'll do it!

    Dad   여긴 내 집이야. 너는 내가 정한 규칙대로 따라야 한다고! 그러니 네 방 청소해!

    Bella   이해를 못 하겠어요! 요즘 왜 이렇게 절 심하게 통제하는 건데요?

    Dad   너도 나이가 들고, 아빠가 하라는 것에 대해서 매번 반대하는 것도 이제 그만할 때가 되었어. 너도 책임을 지고, 집안일을 더 도와야지.

    Bella   알았어요! 그렇게 하겠다고요!

shut down

페기하다

To dismiss something aggressively

The government **shut down** the citizen's petition.
정부는 그 시민 청원을 페지했습니다

go against

반대하다, 말을 안 듣다

To oppose someone or something

My son is trying to **go against** me and attend a party tonight.
아들이 내 말을 안 듣고 오늘 밤 파티에 가려고 하네.

go through

통과하다, 이루어지다

To pass; To be approved

My request for a meeting with the mayor **went through**.
내가 요청한 시장과의 미팅이 받아들여졌다.

vote on

투표로 결정하다

To make a decision about something by voting

We'll **vote on** these issues.
우리는 이 문제들에 대해서 투표할 것이다.

SHORT DIALOGUE 2

Oliver   Soon, it will be time for the city to **vote on** our proposal to fix up the roads.

Charlotte   I'm just afraid the mayor will **shut down** this bill before it even passes.

Oliver   He doesn't like it, but the people do. And he won't **go against** the people.

Charlotte   You're right. I'm sure that the bill will **go through**. I worry too much sometimes.

Oliver   곧, 도로를 정비하자는 우리 제안에 시가 투표로 결정할 때가 됐군.
Charlotte   시장이 통과도 되기 전에 이 법안을 페기할까 봐 좀 걱정이 돼.
Oliver   시장은 안 좋아하지만, 사람들이 그 제안을 좋아하잖아. 시장도 사람들 의견에 반대하진 않을 거야.
Charlotte   맞아. 나도 법안이 통과될 거라고 확신해. 난 가끔 걱정이 너무 지나친 게 탈이야.

get through

(법안이) 통과되다

To be accepted or approved by an official group

The bill **got through** the House and the Senate.

법안이 하원과 상원을 통과했다.

take over

지배하다, 장악하다

To dominate or control

Social media has **taken over** all of our lives.

소셜 미디어가 우리의 모든 삶을 점령했다.

tighten up

강화하다

To grow more thorough or strict

We have to **tighten up** the rules about the dress code at school.

우리는 학교의 복장 규정을 더 강화해야 한다.

lock up

감옥에 집어넣다, 감금하다

To imprison

When someone commits murder, they need to be **locked up**.

누군가 살인을 저지르면, 감옥에 가야 한다.

SHORT DIALOGUE 3

Officer Wyatt It's a shame. This used to be a great neighborhood, but crime has **taken over**.

Officer Riley Ever since that new legislation on government housing **got through**, it's only gotten worse.

Officer Wyatt I just don't understand. We've been **locking up** more criminals, but the streets still aren't any safer.

Officer Riley If only we had more officers to help **tighten up** our watch over this area.

Officer Wyatt 안타깝다. 정말 좋은 동네였는데, 범죄 소굴이 되어 버리다니.
Officer Riley 정부 주택에 대한 새로운 법안이 통과된 이후로, 상황이 계속 악화되어 왔어.
Officer Wyatt 이해가 안 돼. 더 많은 범죄자를 감옥에 보냈는데도, 도시가 아직도 더 안전하지 않다니.
Officer Riley 우리가 이 지역에 대한 감시를 강화할 수 있게 더 많은 경찰이 충원되면 좋을 텐데.

LONG DIALOGUE

Striker: 제게 조사해 보라고 했던 문제 기억나세요, 대장님?

— **Mob Boss:** 쥐새끼 문제? 그래. 뭘 좀 찾아냈어?

Striker: 우리를 몰래 고자질하는 놈을 추적했습니다. 생각하시는 것보다 상황이 더 안 좋은데, 우리가 내부에서 감시를 당하고 있습니다.

— **Mob Boss:** 그럼 그렇지! 누구야?

Striker: 아직은 잘 모르겠습니다. 하지만 신입들 중 하나로 범위는 좁혔습니다. 사실 그중 아무도 배제할 수는 없어요. 어쩌면 밀고자가 한 명이 아닐 수도 있습니다.

— **Mob Boss:** 우리 조직에 들어와서, 정보를 캐내고, 나가겠다고 생각했다?

Striker: 상황이 더 심각합니다. 제보를 받았는데, 곧 경찰이 조직이 하는 일을 막아버린다고 합니다. 우리가 말하는 지금 이 순간에도 잠복하고 있다가, 우리가 이동하기를 기다려 체포하고 감옥에 처넣으려 한다고 해도 전 놀라지 않을 겁니다.

— **Mob Boss:** 아니야, 아니야! 걔들이 날 체포할 수 있다고 생각한다고?! 사람 잘못 보고 엮였구먼. 그 놈들 중 하나가 자기가 쥐새끼라고 인정할 때까지 내가 모두 엄중하게 처리할 거야.

Striker: 저도 뭔가를 해야 한다는 것에는 동의합니다, 대장. 그런데 화를 내는 것은 도움이 안 됩니다. 침착해야 합니다.

— **Mob Boss:** 침착, 침착하라고?! 내가 지금 당장 가서 직접 다 조져 버릴 거야.

Striker: 잠깐만요! 좋은 생각이 있습니다. 오늘 밤에 할 일이 있다고 하고, 각자에게 다른 주소를 주는 겁니다. 밀고자가 누구이건, 대장이 직접 내린 명령을 거부할 수 없을 거예요. 그놈들이 그 주소를 경찰에게 말할 거예요.

— **Mob Boss:** 경찰이 어느 장소에서 나타나건, 누가 쥐새끼 인지 알게 되겠군! 좋은 계획이야. 첫 번째 애를 여기로 들여보내.

Striker: You remember you asked me to **look into** that little problem you had, Boss?

— **Mob Boss:** The rat problem? Yeah. What did you find?

Striker: I've **tracked down** the person who wants to **rat** us **out**. And it's worse than you think. We're being **spied on** from the inside.

— **Mob Boss:** Well, of course we are! Who is it?

Striker: I'm not sure yet, sir, but I've **narrowed** it **down** to one of the new hires. In fact, I can't **rule** any of them **out**, so maybe more than one is a snitch.

— **Mob Boss:** They think they can **break into** my organization, **dig up** information about us, and then just **walk away**?

Striker: It's worse, I got a tip that pretty soon, the police will be shutting us down. I wouldn't be surprised if they're **staking out** this building as we speak; just waiting for us to leave so they can arrest us and **lock** us **up**.

— **Mob Boss:** No, no, no! One of them thinks they can **bring** me **in**?! Well, they've gotten **mixed up** with the wrong people. I'm going to **crack down** on all of them until one of them admits they're the rat.

Striker: I agree we need to do something about this, Boss. But **flying into** a rage won't help you. You need to **calm down**.

— **Mob Boss:** Calm? Calm?! I'm going to go down there and **knock** them all **out** myself!

Striker: Wait! I have an idea. Tell each one of them that they are in charge of the next job we're going to do tonight, but give each one a different address. They won't **go against** a direct order from you, but whoever the snitch is, they will tell the cops the address.

— **Mob Boss:** And whichever place the cops show up at, that will tell us who the rat is! It's a good plan. Send the first one in here.

CHAPTER

8

PHRASAL VERBS

get on

해 나가다, 꾸려 나가다

To deal with;
To handle

How have you been **getting on** with your studies?

공부는 어떻게 잘 되고 있니?

work through

(힘들게) 해결하다

To deal with or handle, typically with difficulty

I'm **working through** some financial issues right now. I need a new job.

지금은 내가 재정적인 문제를 해결하는 중이야. (그래서) 내게 새 일자리가 필요해.

be riddled with

~ 투성이다, ~로 가득 차다

To have in abundance;
To feature a lot of something

This road **is riddled with** hazards and dangerous obstacles.

이 도로는 위험 요소와 장애물 투성이야.

stick together

함께 뭉치다

To stay with a person or group of people

We're a family. We have to **stick together**.

우리는 가족이야. 함께 뭉쳐야 해.

SHORT DIALOGUE 1

Melina   How are you **getting on** with the move, Aaron? Is it going well?

Aaron   It's been difficult. We're **working through** a lot of problems. We didn't expect there to be so many issues with owning a house.

Melina   I'm sure buying a house **is riddled with** complications that I can't even imagine.

Aaron   At least I have Luna. As long as we **stick together**, I feel like we can get through it.

> **Melina**   이사는 어떻게 되고 있어, Aaron? 잘 되는 거야?
> **Aaron**   힘들었지. 지금도 많은 문제를 해결하는 중이야. 집을 소유하는 데 이렇게 많은 문제가 있을 거라고는 생각 못 했어.
> **Melina**   집을 사는 건 내가 상상조차 못하는 복잡한 일 투성일 거야.
> **Aaron**   적어도 난 Luna가 있잖아. 우리가 함께 뭉치면, 이 상황을 잘 해결할 수 있을 거란 느낌이 들어.

land in

결국 ~하게 되다

To find oneself in a particular situation, often unexpectedly

Jeff **landed in** a lot of debt after he lost his job.

Jeff는 실직 후, 큰 빚더미에 앉게 되었다.

get out of

~에서 벗어나다

To escape or leave a place or situation

Let me explain to you how we can **get out of** this struggle.

우리가 이 힘든 상황에서 벗어날 수 있는 방법을 설명해 드리겠습니다.

work together

함께 일하다, 힘을 합치다

To combine skills or effort with another

If we want to find our way back home, we have to **work together**.

우리가 집으로 돌아가는 길을 찾고 싶다면, 함께 노력해야 해.

crop up

(갑자기·불쑥) 등장하다, 나오다

To appear unexpectedly

A new job opportunity may **crop up** for you in the next months.

앞으로 몇 달 안에 너에게 새로운 일자리 기회가 생길지도 모른다.

SHORT DIALOGUE 2

Ava   It seems as if every month, we **land in** more and more debt.

Theo   And with the way the economy is going, it's going to be difficult to **get out of**.

Ava   I used to think that if we **worked together**, we could do anything. I don't know anymore.

Theo   Have faith. We promised we would face whatever problems **crop up** together.

Ava   정말 매달 점점 더 많은 빚더미에 앉게 되는 것 같아.
Theo   경제 굴러가는 상황을 보니까, 벗어나긴 어려울 거야.
Ava   예전엔 우리가 함께 열심히 하면 뭐든 할 수 있을 거라고 생각했거든. 이제는 모르겠어.
Theo   믿음을 가져. 어떤 문제가 닥치더라도 함께 대처하기로 약속했잖아.

TOPIC 48

face up to

직시하다, (어려운 상황을)
받아들이고 대처하다

> To confront;
> To take responsibility

You should **face up to** your
problems, or they'll be out of
control.

문제를 직시해야 합니다. 아니면 그것들은 통제 불능
상태가 될 거예요.

stay out

~을 피하다

> To avoid

Hey, son! **Stay out** of trouble when
you're given one more chance.

아들아, 한 번 더 기회를 얻었을 때는 문제 일으키지
말아라.

live with

용납하다, 받아들이다

> To accept and deal
> with something
> unpleasant

Even though this is not a best
option, I can **live with** it.

비록 이것이 최고의 선택은 아니지만, 난 받아들이고
갈 수 있어.

put up with

참다

> To tolerate or
> endure something

I'm too tired to **put up with** your
nonsense today.

내가 너무 피곤해서 오늘은 너의 헛소리를 참을 수가
없어.

SHORT DIALOGUE 3

Ethan   I heard that Harper finally **faced up to** her actions and apologized to you.

Mia   Yeah. I never thought she would actually apologize. I thought she'd just **stay out**
of my way when we're at work.

Ethan   Maybe she's trying to change. Maybe she just couldn't **live with** what she did to
you.

Mia   I doubt that, and now I will still have to **put up with** her while we wait and see if
she's actually changed or not.

Ethan   Harper가 마침내 자기가 한 행동을 직시하고 너한테 사과했다며?
Mia   응. 난 걔가 사과할 줄은 생각도 못 했어. 직장에서 날 그냥 피할 거라고 생각했는데 말이야.
Ethan   변하려고 노력하는 것일 수도 있지. 어쩌면 걔도 너에게 한 짓에 대해서 스스로 용납할 수 없었을
거야.
Mia   그렇진 않을걸. 이제 걔가 정말 변했는지 지켜보는 동안 내가 여전히 걔를 참아야 한다는 거지.

MP3 **063**

stare down

노려보다

To look at someone
intensely with the
intent to intimidate

That man in the truck over there is
staring me **down** because I cut him
off.

저기 트럭에 있는 남자가 내가 앞에 끼어들었다고
노려보네.

fight back

저항하다, 보복하다

To resist or
retaliate

If someone insults you, you
shouldn't **fight back**. Just leave.

누군가 너에게 모욕을 주면, 맞서 싸우지 말고,
그냥 떠나.

back off

물러서다, (상관하는 것을) 그만두다

To stop being involved
in a situation

Just **back off**! It's none of your
business.

상관하지 마! 네가 참견할 일이 아니야.

go away

떠나다, 점차 사라지다

To leave a situation;
To disappear
gradually

My obsession with perfection
doesn't seem to **go away**.

완벽에 대한 내 집착은 사라지지 않는 것 같아.

SHORT DIALOGUE 1

Jake   Why are you **staring** me **down** like that? What now?

Diana   You've been at the casino for the last two days!

Jake   Hey, **back off**! I'm going to win big money!

Diana   That's it. I'm going to **go away** for a while… maybe stay at my sister's. You need
         to **fight back** your gambling addiction!

    Jake   왜 날 그렇게 노려보는 거야? 또 뭐?
    Diana   당신 지난 이틀 동안 카지노에 있었잖아!
    Jake   상관하지 마! 나 큰돈을 벌 거라고!
    Diana   됐어. 그만해. 나 잠시 떠나 있을 거야. 언니네 집에서 머물 수도 있고. 당신, 정말 도박 중독에 맞서
            싸워야 한다고!

resign to

(어쩔 수 없이 체념하고) 인정하다, 받아들이다

To accept something reluctantly

I **resigned** myself **to** the fact that I would never be a doctor.
난 절대 의사가 되지 못할 거라는 사실을 인정했다.

talk through

자세히 이야기하다

To discuss something in detail

We need to **talk through** what happened last night.
우리는 어젯밤에 무슨 일이 있었는지 자세하게 이야기해야 해요.

hand over

넘겨주다, 인계하다

To give control or possession of something

I had to **hand over** all the cash when the gunman broke into my house.
총을 든 남자가 집에 침입했을 때 나는 현금을 다 줘야 했다.

be caught up

~에 빠지다, 휘말리다

To become involved in a way that cannot be controlled

Larry **was caught up** in a riot as he was walking home from work.
Larry는 직장에서 집으로 걸어오다가 폭동에 휘말렸다.

SHORT DIALOGUE 2

Sasha   It's been a hard year for me. I've almost **resigned** myself **to** giving up.

Therapist   It's good that you're starting therapy. This way, you can **talk through** your problems.

Sasha   I want to! Lately, I've felt like I'm **handing over** my life to my job! I'm so stressed.

Therapist   Let's start there. Tell me about this stress you**'re caught up** in.

Sasha   저에겐 참 힘든 한 해였어요. 거의 체념하고 포기하려고 했거든요.
Therapist   치료를 시작해서 다행입니다. 이렇게, 문제를 자세하게 이야기할 수 있으니까요.
Sasha   그러고 싶어요! 최근 들어, 내 삶을 일에다 넘겨줘 버린 느낌이 들었어요. 정말 스트레스가 심해요.
Therapist   거기서부터 시작해 보죠. 지금 겪고 있는 스트레스에 대해 말씀해 보세요.

WAR AND RIOT 전쟁과 폭동

MP3 **064**

shoot down

(비행기를) 격추하다

To cause an aircraft to crash by firing weapons

His plane was **shot down** and crashed in the ocean.

그의 비행기는 격추되었고 바다에 추락했다.

come under

경험하다, 겪다

To suddenly experience or suffer

The soldiers **came under** fire as they crossed the river.

군인들이 강을 건너는 도중에 총격을 받았다.

move in

들어가다, 안으로 이동하다

To approach or enter an area

Order the troops to **move in** to the valley!

병사들에게 계곡으로 이동하라고 명령하라!

send in

파견하다,
(군대를) 파병하다

To deploy;
To order a group
or person to respond to a situation

UN troops were **sent in** to Afghanistan.

UN군이 아프가니스탄에 파병되었다.

SHORT DIALOGUE 1

Colton   Have you heard the latest news out of Ukraine? Apparently, a Russian plane has been **shot down** in enemy territory!

Laurie   I did hear, and now another city has **come under** attack.

Colton   Yes, they say that the Russians are **moving in** but have not attacked yet.

Laurie   Why would they **send in** troops if not to attack? I hope they evacuate the town soon!

Colton   우크라이나에서 나온 최근 소식 들었어? 러시아 비행기가 적지에서 격추가 되었나 봐!
Laurie   나도 들었어. 이제는 다른 도시가 공격받고 있다고 하던데.
Colton   응, 러시아 군들이 쳐들어오는 중이지만 아직 공격은 안 했대.
Laurie   공격하지 않는다면 왜 군대를 보내겠어? 빨리 시민들이 그곳을 떠나 대피하면 좋겠다!

break out
발생하다, (전쟁이) 발발하다

To occur or happen violently

A riot **broke out** in the prison and one prison guard was killed.
감옥에서 폭동이 발생했고, 교도관 한 명이 피살됐다.

blow up
폭발하다

To explode

A car **blew up** right outside of the embassy.
대사관 바로 밖에서 차량 한 대가 폭발했다.

hold off
막다, 저항하다

To resist or defend against; To inhibit the progress of

If we can't **hold off** the enemy here, we're all captured and dead.
여기서 적을 막아 내지 못하면, 우리는 모두 잡혀서 죽는다.

pull out
철수하다, 그만두다

To retreat; To flee

The soldiers **pulled out** of the battlefield.
군인들은 전장에서 철수했다.

SHORT DIALOGUE 2

Zoe The protest last weekend turned violent. Riots **broke out** in the streets.

Blaire I didn't hear about it. What happened?

Zoe I heard there was a lot of looting, and a car **blew up**! After that, everything turned into chaos. The police had to **pull out**.

Blaire Without the police there, who protected the locals? It was their job to **hold off** the looters.

Zoe 지난 주말에 시위가 폭력적으로 변했어. 거리에서 폭동이 발생했다니까.

Blaire 난 그건 못 들었는데, 무슨 일이야?

Zoe 약탈이 많이 발생하고, 차량 한 대가 폭발했대! 그 후에, 모든 것이 아비규환으로 변했고, 경찰은 철수해야 했어.

Blaire 경찰이 없으면 누가 그 지역 주민들을 보호해? 약탈자들을 막는 게 경찰이 해야 하는 일이잖아.

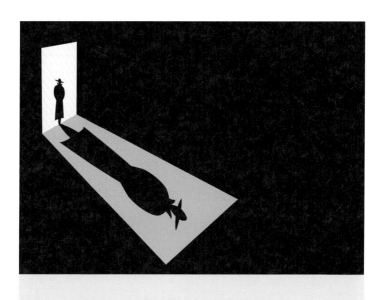

LONG DIALOGUE

Zoey: 가끔은 뉴스 보는 게 싫어.

—— **Eliot:** 뉴스가 뭐 잘못됐어?

Zoey: 뉴스는 꼭 세상이 갈등과 부정적인 것들로 가득 찬 것처럼 느끼게 만들잖아. 매번 뉴스를 켤 때 마다, 다른 사람들의 문제에 관한 이야기들이야.

—— **Eliot:** 난 어떤 문제를 겪게 된 사람들의 이야기들을 듣는 게 중요하다고 생각해. 다른 사람들이 어려운 상황을 어떻게 극복하는가를 보고 많이 배울 수 있거든.

Zoey: 하지만 뉴스는 행복한 것에 대해서는 절대 보도하지 않잖아! 죄다 전쟁이 일어났다거나 폭발 사고 같은 뉴스뿐이야!

—— **Eliot:** 나는 그런 것들에 대해서 정보를 얻는 게 좋아. 어제 뉴스에서 누가 드론을 날리면서 이웃을 염탐했다는 뉴스 봤어? 다른 이웃 중 한 명이 그것을 쏴서 떨어뜨리려고 하다가, 빗나가서 누군가의 집을 대신 쏴 버렸대.

Zoey: 거봐, 내 말이 맞지? 최악이야! 다친 사람은 없었대?

—— **Eliot:** 응, 경찰이 그 지역을 수색하고, 드론 주인을 찾기 위해서 투입되었어.

Zoey: 난 아무런 잘못 없는 무고한 사람들이 이런 일에 휘말리는 게 정말 안타까워! 그래서 내가 뉴스를 안 보는 거야.

Zoey: Sometimes I hate watching the news.

— Eliot: What's wrong with the news?

Zoey: It makes me feel like the world **is** just **riddled with** conflict and negativity. Every time I turn on the news, the stories are about other people's problems.

— Eliot: I think it's important to hear the stories of people who have **landed in** some kind of trouble. You can learn a lot from how others **work through** difficult situations.

Zoey: But they never report on anything happy! It's all about wars **breaking out** and things **blowing up**!

— Eliot: I like staying informed on those things. Did you see on the news yesterday someone was flying their drone around spying on their neighborhood? Then one of the neighbors tried to **shoot** it **down** but they missed and hit someone's house instead.

Zoey: See what I mean? That's terrible! Was anyone hurt?

— Eliot: No, but the police were **sent in** to search the area and find the owner of the drone.

Zoey: I feel so bad for the innocent people **caught up** in that! This is why I don't watch the news.

fall apart

부서지다, 무너지다

To break;
To crumble

My old car is **falling apart**. I can't even fix it.

내 낡은 차가 망가지고 있어. 더 이상 고칠 수도 없어.

break down

고장 나다

To undergo mechanical failure

My car **broke down** on the way to work.

출근 길에 내 차가 고장 났다.

take apart

분해하다, 분리하다

To separate something into all its different parts

I **took apart** my smartphone to see if I can fix it.

고칠 수 있는지 확인해 보려고 내 스마트폰을 분해했어.

pull out

제거하다, 뽑다

To remove

Technically, you can **pull out** your own teeth, but it is not a good idea.

엄밀히 따지면, 네가 직접 네 이를 뽑을 수 있지만, 좋은 생각은 아니야.

SHORT DIALOGUE 1

Theresa	Can you help me fix my motorcycle? It's **falling apart**.
Levi	I think you should just get a new one. It looks like it is about to **break down**.
Theresa	Nonsense! I just need your help **taking apart** the engine. I know how to fix it.
Levi	That's what you said three months ago. A mechanic probably needs to **pull out** the engine and look at it.

Theresa	내 오토바이 고치는 것 도와줄 수 있어? 이게 맛이 가고 있네.
Levi	그냥 새것 사는 게 낫겠다. 곧 고장 날 것 같은데.
Theresa	말도 안 돼! 엔진 분해하는 것만 도와줘. 나 어떻게 고치는지 알아.
Levi	너 석 달 전에도 그렇게 말했어. 아마 정비사가 엔진 꺼내서 직접 봐야 할 거야.

tear down

파괴하다, 허물다

To destroy;
To dismantle

The old city hall was **torn down** and a new one is being built.

오래된 시청 건물이 철거되고, 새 시청사가 지어지고 있다.

come down

무너져 내리다

To fall to the ground

Did you see that the bridge **came down** after the huge storm?

큰 폭풍 후에 다리가 무너진 거 봤어?

be made up of

~로 구성되다

To be comprised of;
To be built from

The atmosphere **is made up of** mostly oxygen and nitrogen.

대기는 주로 산소와 질소로 이루어져 있다.

build up

(건물을) 짓다, 강하게 하다

To strengthen or fortify

I **built up** the foundation of the house so that it could resist the bad weather.

악천후에도 견딜 수 있도록 나는 집의 기초 공사를 튼튼하게 했다.

SHORT DIALOGUE 2

Mason　We're going to have to **tear down** this old house. It's a shame.

Brook　Does it really have to **come down**? What's wrong?

Mason　The foundation **is made up of** rotten wood and old concrete.

Brook　I see. There would be no way to **build up** the foundation without causing too much damage.

> Mason　우리 이 낡은 집을 부숴야 할 것 같아. 아쉽네.
> Brook　이거 정말 부숴야 하는 거야? 뭐가 문제인데?
> Mason　토대가 썩은 목재랑 오래된 콘크리트로 돼 있거든.
> Brook　그렇구나. 그럼 크게 손상시키지 않고 토대를 만드는 게 불가능하겠다.

gather up

(뭔가를 준비하기 위해) 주워 모으다

To collect

Gather up all the paperwork before the meeting tomorrow.
내일 회의 전까지 모든 서류를 준비해 놔.

hunt down

찾다, 추적해서 찾아내다

To try to find a particular thing or person

I'm **hunting down** a good deal on a hotel before I can book my trip.
여행 예약하기 전에 좋은 호텔 딜을 찾는 중이야.

double up

배가하다

To use or do two times as many of something

I'm going to **double up** on my workout routine.
난 운동 루틴을 두 배로 더 강화할 것이다.

line up

정렬하다, 줄을 세우다

To organize, typically in a straight line

Line up all of the desserts on the table so that I can take a picture.
내가 사진 찍을 수 있게 식탁 위에 있는 디저트들을 모두 일렬로 정렬해 봐.

SHORT DIALOGUE 1

Eden   Not enough people are attending our sale. We need to try and **gather up** more customers.

Layla   No one seems to be interested. I'm having trouble **hunting down** anyone who wants to come.

Eden   Then we need to **double up** our efforts. I'll put up twice as many posters.

Layla   I hope it'll work out. There'll be people **lining up** out of the door when our shop opens.

Eden   우리 세일에 참여하는 사람이 별로 많지 않아. 손님을 좀 더 모아야 해.
Layla   아무도 관심이 없는 것 같은데. 오고 싶어 하는 사람들 찾기가 쉽지 않네.
Eden   그러면 우리가 노력을 두 배로 해야지. 내가 포스터를 두 배로 붙일게.
Layla   효과가 있으면 좋겠다. 우리 가게가 문을 열면, 문 밖에 사람들이 줄 서서 들어올 거야.

file into

줄 서서 들어가다

To walk there
in a line

The crowd **filed into** the movie
theater to watch the new action
film.

새로 나온 액션 영화를 보려고 사람들이 영화관에
줄 서서 들어갔다.

separate out

골라내다, 분리하다

To divide or sort
something into
different
categories

I need to **separate out** the dirty
laundry from the clean laundry.

난 깨끗한 빨랫감과 지저분한 빨랫감을 분리해야 해.

sort through

자세히 살펴보다

To scan; To observe,
sometimes in search
of something

I **sorted through** many sites and
finally found the best one.

난 여러 사이트들을 자세히 살펴봤고, 결국 최고의
사이트를 찾았다.

send away

돌려보내다, 쫓아내다

To expel; To prevent
entry

I had to **send away** the unreliable
contractor and arrange for a new
one to take over.

난 신뢰할 수 없는 하청업체를 내보내고 새로운
하청업체가 인수할 수 있게 준비해야 했어.

SHORT DIALOGUE 2

Amiri   This weekend, there will be crowds of people **filing into** this club.

Jose   I can handle it myself. I just need to **separate out** all the drunk people, right?

Amiri   There's more to being a doorman than that. You also have to **sort through** the
crowd for anyone too young to drink.

Jose   Yeah. Yeah. If they're intoxicated or underage, I have to **send** them **away**. Pretty
easy.

Amiri   이번 주말에 많은 사람이 이 클럽에 줄지어 들어올 거야.

Jose   저 혼자서도 잘 처리할 수 있어요. 술 취한 사람들만 걸러 내면 되죠?

Amiri   도어맨이 되려면 그것보다 더 많은 일을 해야 해. 나이가 너무 어려서 술 마시면 안 되는 미성년자도
잘 추려 내야 한다고.

Jose   네, 네. 술에 취했거나 미성년자면, 돌려보내야 하네요. 아주 쉬운데요.

take away

배우다, 경험에서 얻다

To learn; To gain from an experience

I didn't **take away** much from that documentary.

난 그 다큐멘터리에서 많은 것을 배우지는 못했다.

jot down

(급히) 쓰다, 적다

To write something quickly

It's very important to **jot down** your ideas.

생각을 적어 두는 것이 매우 중요하다.

ruminate on

심사숙고하다, 곰곰이 생각하다

To think carefully about something

Sometimes it hurts to **ruminate** too much **on** what happened in the past.

가끔 과거에 있었던 일을 너무 많이 생각하면 마음이 아프다.

scribble down

아무렇게나 적다, 갈겨쓰다

To write quickly or messily

I didn't have much time so I just **scribbled down** notes and handed them to her.

시간이 별로 없어서, 난 노트를 막 갈겨쓰고는 그것을 그녀한테 건넸다.

SHORT DIALOGUE 1

Ian   What did you **take away** from that seminar we went to yesterday?

Stella   You know, I was **ruminating on** what the speaker said all last night. I only wish I had **scribbled down** some notes so I could remember everything she said.

Ian   Yeah, her words were very powerful. I did **jot down** a few things. I'll give them to you.

Stella   That would be great, thanks!

Ian   어제 참석한 세미나에서 뭐 좀 배웠어?

Stella   그게 말이야. 어젯밤에 발표자가 한 말을 내가 곰곰이 생각해 봤는데 (기억이 안 나네). 아, 세미나 발표자가 말한 걸 다 기억할 수 있게 노트에 좀 적어 놨으면 좋았을 텐데.

Ian   맞아, 말들이 굉장히 강렬했어. 내가 몇 가지 좀 적었거든. 너한테 줄게.

Stella   그러면 정말 좋지. 고마워!

sum up

요약하다

To summarize; To give a brief explanation

Let me just **sum** it **up** for you.
제가 요약해 드릴게요.

occur to

(생각이) 떠오르다, 나다

To realize, often suddenly

It **occurred to** me that using flashcards is the best way to learn.
플래시카드를 이용하는 것이 가장 좋은 학습 방법이라는 생각이 들었다.

read through

꼼꼼히 읽다

To read something in its entirety

I'll **read through** this book this week.
이번 주에 내가 이 책을 꼼꼼히 읽어 볼 거야.

be interested in

~에 관심을 갖다

To be fascinated or passionate about something in particular

I'm very **interested in** Behavioral Economics.
난 행동 경제학에 매우 관심이 많다.

SHORT DIALOGUE 2

Gabriella How would you **sum up** the chapter we were supposed to read for economics class?

Alexander Did it **occur to** you that you'd get a good grade in that class if you actually read the textbook?

Gabriella It's so boring, though! I don't have the energy or the time to **read through** all of it!

Alexander If you're not **interested in** learning about economics, then why are you taking the class?

Gabriella 경제학 수업 준비용으로 읽으라고 한 챕터 말이야. 넌 어떻게 요약할 거야?
Alexander 교과서를 실제로 읽어야지 수업에서 좋은 성적을 받을 거라는 생각이 든 거야?
Gabriella 그렇지만 책이 너무 지루하단 말야! 그거 다 꼼꼼히 읽을 에너지도 없고, 시간도 없어!
Alexander 경제학을 배우는 데 관심이 없다면, 이 수업을 왜 듣는 거야?

write down

적다, 필기하다

To make a note of
something in writing

Alice **wrote down** notes in class.

Alice는 수업 중에 노트 필기를 했다.

hand out

나눠 주다

To distribute
something;
To pass it around

Can you **hand out** the syllabus to
the students?

학생들에게 강의 계획서 좀 나눠 줄래?

think up

생각해 내다

To produce a new
idea or plan

Julia is a smart girl, and I'm sure
she'll **think up** a plan.

Julia는 똑똑한 아이라서 좋은 계획을 생각해 낼
거야.

throw in

추가하다, 덤으로 주다

To include;
To add something
spontaneously

I'll **throw in** some extra practice
questions for you to work on.

네가 연습할 수 있도록 추가 문제를 줄게.

SHORT DIALOGUE 3

Professor	I need to **write down** the syllabus that I have to **hand out** to the students tomorrow.
Teaching Assistant	You're a great professor. I'm sure you'll **think** something **up**.
Professor	I'm nearly finished. I just need to add a discussion topic for the first class. These days students are so different from us, so I'm a bit at a loss as to what to do.
Teaching Assistant	Try **throwing in** something that embraces that difference and that students might be interested in, such as "philosophy of the MZ generation."

Professor	내일 학생들에게 나눠 줄 강의 계획서를 작성해야 하네.
Teaching Assistant	교수님은 훌륭하시잖아요. 분명 대단한 걸 생각해 내실 거예요.
Professor	거의 끝내긴 했어. 첫 수업에 필요한 토의 주제만 추가하면 되는데. 요즘 학생들은 우리하고 확연히 달라서, 뭘 해야 할지 좀 막막하군.
Teaching Assistant	차이를 인정하고, 학생들이 관심을 가질 만한 것을 추가해 보세요. 예를 들어서 'MZ세대의 철학' 같은 건 어떨까요?

amp up
흥분하다

To get excited

This documentary movie got me very **amped up**.
이 다큐멘터리 영화를 보고 난 매우 흥분했다.

tap into
이용하다, 활용하다

To access; To use something for your own advantage

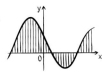

You should **tap into** your creative side for this math project.
이 수학 프로젝트에서는 네가 창의력을 발휘해야 해.

drop out
중퇴하다, 탈퇴하다

To leave an organization before completion, typically a school of some sort

Steve **dropped out** of college to pursue his dream.
Steve는 그의 꿈을 좇기 위해 대학을 중퇴했다.

read up on
많은 시간을 집중적으로 읽다, 연구하다

To spend time reading in order to find out information about something

Read up on this article before you write an essay.
에세이 쓰기 전에 이 기사를 잘 읽어 봐.

SHORT DIALOGUE 1

Teacher How do I get my kids **amped up** about learning?

Principal You have to **tap into** their curiosity. Find ways to engage them.

Teacher I want them to love learning so that they don't **drop out** of school.

Principal Maybe you should **read up on** the latest research in child psychology and education. Here I have a book you can borrow.

Teacher 어떻게 하면 아이들이 신나게 배우게 할까요?
Principal 아이들의 호기심을 이용해야 합니다. 아이들이 참여할 방법들을 찾아야죠.
Teacher 아이들이 배우는 걸 정말 좋아해서, 학교를 그만두는 일이 없으면 좋겠어요.
Principal 아동 심리학과 교육에 관한 최신 연구 자료를 자세하게 읽어 보는 건 어떨까요? 여기 책이 있으니 빌려 드릴게요.

hand in

제출하다

To deliver an
assignment for
assessment

Jay was late **handing in** his paper,
so he got a bad grade.

Jay는 과제를 늦게 제출해서 안 좋은 성적을 받았다.

spread out

펼치다, (집중적으로 하는 게 아니라) 나누어서
하다

To cover a wide area;
To divide something
evenly over a period of time

I **spread out** this course over five
days so you will have more time.

이 코스를 5일 과정으로 분산해서 여러분이 더 많은
시간을 할애할 수 있게 했어요.

look up

(정보 등을) 찾다

To search for information;
To look for information in a book or
on the Internet

Look this **up** on Google.

이거 구글에서 찾아봐.

polish up

(실력을) 갈고닦다, 다듬다

To practice a skill,
typically one that is
already possessed

I think I should **polish up** my English
before I go back to the States.

미국으로 돌아가기 전에 내 영어 실력을 다듬어야겠어.

SHORT DIALOGUE 2

Amelia   Have you **handed in** your final paper yet? It's due Friday.

Jackson   I'm still working on it. I **spread out** the work too much, so I have to rush to get it done. I think I spent too much time on the research.

Amelia   You should **look up** ways to research more efficiently. That would make your life easier.

Jackson   You're probably right. Do you recommend an article or website that would help me **polish up** on this subject?

Amelia   마지막 논문 제출했어? 금요일이 마감이잖아.
Jackson   아직도 하는 중이야. 일을 너무 벌려 놓아서, 빨리 서둘러서 끝내야 해. 리서치하는 데 시간을 너무 많이 썼나 봐.
Amelia   더 효율적으로 리서치할 방법들을 찾아봐야지. 그럼 인생이 더 수월해질 거야.
Jackson   네 말이 맞는 것 같아. 내가 이 주제를 좀 다듬는 데 도움이 될 기사나 사이트 좀 추천해 줄래?

FILE INTO

LONG DIALOGUE

Brandon: 안녕, Leah. 석사 지원은 잘 돼 가? 필요한 서류는 다 모은 거야?

— **Leah:** 실은, 그게 생각보다 더 어렵네. 필수 항목을 좀 더 주의 깊게 읽었으면, 이렇게 일을 많이 벌일 필요가 없었을 텐데.

Brandon: 그게 무슨 말이야? 지원서 제출해야 하는 때까지 얼마나 남았는데?

— **Leah:** 음, 지원서는 다 썼는데, 아직 내가 한 작업물에 대한 샘플이 두 개 필요해. 마감까지는 한 주 밖에 남지 않았고, 그냥 급하게 써서 내야 할 것 같아.

Brandon: 바보같이 굴지 말고. 너 전에 학교 과제로 했던 샘플들 이미 많잖아. 잘 살펴보고, 가장 괜찮은 것 두 개를 뽑은 다음, 잘 다듬어 봐.

— **Leah:** 그래. 네 말이 맞는 거 같아. 샘플 하나는 Robertson 교수님 강의에서 작성한 에세이에다가 내 주장을 좀 더 강화하면 될 거 같아. 그런데 두 번째 샘플은 어떤 걸 해야 할지 잘 모르겠어.

Brandon: 내가 네 작업물을 자세히 살펴보고, 의견을 주는 게 좀 도움이 될까?

— **Leah:** 제안해 줘서 정말 고마워. 내 작업물의 대부분은 짧은 과제인데, 샘플은 적어도 5페이지 이상이어야 하거든.

Brandon: 몇 개를 가지고 합칠 수도 있겠다. 괜찮을 거야. 내 도움을 받아서 다음 주에 두 배로 노력하면 할 수 있어.

— **Leah:** 다시 한번 고마워! 내가 이 상황에서 배운 교훈이 있다면, 다음에는 더 많이 준비해야겠다는 거야.

Brandon: Hi Leah, how is your master's degree application going? Have you **gathered up** all the documents you need yet?

—— Leah: Actually, it's been harder than I thought. If I had **read through** the requirements more carefully, I wouldn't have **spread** things **out** so much.

Brandon: What do you mean? How long do you have until you have to **hand in** your application?

—— Leah: Well, the application is done, but I still need two samples of my work and I only have one week until it's due. I guess I'll just have to **scribble** something **down**.

Brandon: Don't be silly. You already have many samples of your work from your previous school assignments. You just have to look through them, **pull out** the best two, and **polish** them **up**.

—— Leah: Yeah, I guess you're right. I could use an essay I wrote in Professor Robertson's class for one of them and just **build up** my argument a little bit. But I don't know what to do for the second sample.

Brandon: Would it help if I **sort through** your work and give you my opinion?

—— Leah: Thanks a lot for your offer. Most of my work **is made up of** short assignments and the samples need to be at least five pages long.

Brandon: Maybe we could combine some of them. It'll be okay, with my help you can **double up** on your efforts over the next week.

—— Leah: Thanks again! If there's anything I should **take away** from this situation, it's that I should be more prepared next time.

CHAPTER

9

PHRASAL VERBS

bring back

기억나게 하다, 상기시키다

To evoke;
To call forth

This song **brings back** good memories for me.

이 노래를 들으면 나한테 좋은 기억이 떠오른다.

take back

(옛일 등을) 떠올리게 하다

To evoke a memory intensely and suddenly

I love this song because it **takes** me **back** in my younger days.

나 이 노래 아주 좋아해. 나의 젊은 시절 기억을 떠오르게 하거든.

come back

(기억이) 돌아오다

To return to someone's memory

When Jeremy heard fireworks, memories of his horrible car crash **came back**.

Jeremy는 폭죽이 터지는 소리를 들었을 때, 끔찍한 차 사고의 기억이 돌아왔다.

go back

(그 시절로) 돌아가다

To return

Joseph wishes he could **go back** to when he was a teenager.

Joseph는 10대 때로 돌아갈 수 있으면 얼마나 좋을까 한다.

SHORT DIALOGUE 1

Bella   Doesn't walking by this park **bring back** good memories?

Aiden   It **takes** me **back** to my first year of college. That's when we first became friends!

Bella   It's all **coming back**! Remember when we went ice skating here together?

Aiden   Oh. I miss those days. I wish I could **go back** to that.

> Bella   이 공원 옆 지나니까 좋은 추억이 떠오르지 않아?
> Aiden   대학교 1학년 때가 생각나네. 그때 우리가 처음 만나서 친구가 됐잖아!
> Bella   그 시절이 전부 다 기억나! 우리 여기서 함께 스케이트 탔던 거 기억하니?
> Aiden   오, 정말 그 시절이 그립다. 그때로 돌아가면 좋겠어.

flood back

(갑자기 기억이 물밀듯이)
떠오르다, 아른거리다

To suddenly
remember very
clearly

Memories of my ex **flooded back**
to me when I saw her picture on my
phone.
전화기에 있는 전 여자 친구의 사진을 보자, 그녀에
대한 기억이 아른거렸다.

block out

(기억을) 떨쳐 버리다

To force something
out of the mind

I try to **block out** the horrible
memory but it keeps coming back.
내가 그 끔찍한 기억을 떨쳐 버리려고 하는데도 계속
생각이 나.

think back

회상하다, 돌이켜 보다

To recall

Think back to a time when you
accomblished something big.
당신이 크게 성취했을 때를 한번 회상해 보세요.

push down

억제하다

To suppress

Many people **push down** their
feeling when they should just let
them out.
많은 사람들이 감정을 표현해야 할 때, 그것을
억누르죠.

SHORT DIALOGUE 2

Luis   I found an old photo. When I looked at it, memories **flooded back** into my mind.

Clara   Were they good memories? Or were they bad memories that you **blocked out**?

Luis   Terrible memories. It made me **think back** to my childhood.

Clara   I know you didn't have an easy life back then. But it's not healthy to **push down**
those memories.

Luis   내가 오래된 사진을 하나 찾았거든. 그걸 보니까, 기억들이 되살아났어.
Clara   좋은 기억들이야? 아니면 떨쳐 버리고 싶은 안 좋은 기억들이야?
Luis   끔찍한 기억이야. 보니까 어린 시절이 생각났어.
Clara   그 당시에 네가 참 힘들었다는 것 알아. 하지만 그런 기억들을 억누르는 건 건강에 좋지 않아.

remind of

~을 생각나게 하다, 상기시키다

To evoke memories of something in particular

That movie **reminded** me **of** a book that I read about World War II.
그 영화는 내가 2차 세계 대전에 관해서 읽었던 책을 떠오르게 했다.

black out

의식을 잃다

To experience a sudden and temporary loss of consciousness

When I fell and hit my head, I **blacked out** and woke up in the hospital.
넘어져서 머리를 부딪쳤을 때, 난 의식을 잃었고 깨 보니 병원이었다.

stir up

과거의 기억을 불러일으키다

To bring up strong emotions, thoughts, or memories

The housing market crash **stirs up** bad memories for me.
주택 시장의 붕괴는 내게 안 좋은 기억을 떠올리게 한다.

dwell on

~을 깊이 생각하다, 곱씹다

To stay focused on a subject for a long time

Hmm...

Don't **dwell on** the past.
과거에 연연하지 마.

SHORT DIALOGUE 3

Michael   This song **reminds** me **of** that Halloween party we threw last year.

Eliza   I think I **blacked out** that night. I don't remember anything.

Michael   Maybe if I turn this song up, it'll **stir up** the memories.

Eliza   Please stop. Can we talk about something else? I don't want to **dwell on** this.

Michael   이 노래 들으니까 작년에 열었던 할로윈 파티가 생각난다.
Eliza   그날 밤 나 기절했던 거 같은데. 아무것도 기억이 안 나.
Michael   이 노랫소리 좀 키우면, 그 기억들이 떠오를 거야.
Eliza   그만 좀 해. 우리 다른 이야기할까? 나 이거 다시 생각하고 싶지 않아.

MP3 **072**

wind down

서서히 멈추다, 끝을 향해서 가다

To draw gradually
to a close

As the party **wound down**, the
guests said their goodbyes.
파티가 끝나가자 손님들은 작별 인사를 했다.

hold up

기다리다

To tell someone to wait
or stop

Hey, can you **hold up**? I'm not ready
yet.
잠깐만, 기다려 줄래? 나 아직 준비 안 됐어.

get over with

(나중에 안 하게) 후딱 해치우다

To do something
stressful or painful
quickly so that it doesn't
have to be done later

You've been putting it off for
months. Just do it and **get** it **over
with**.
너 몇 달 동안이나 그거 미뤄 왔잖아. 그냥 후딱
해치워!

break down

(감정이) 무너지다, 주체하지 못하다

To become
overwhelmed with
emotions

When Jack finally left me, I **broke
down** and sobbed.
결국 Jack이 나를 떠났을 때, 난 감정을 주체하지
못하고 흐느껴 울었다.

SHORT DIALOGUE 1

Lydia   I can't believe my vacation has already **wound down** to the end. I have to go to the airport in five minutes.

Alan   **Hold up**! You can't leave without saying "goodbye"!

Lydia   Oh! I'm so bad at goodbyes! We should just **get** it **over with**! Give me a hug. It was so great meeting you. I'm going to miss you.

Alan   Don't say that! You're going to make me **break down** and cry.

Lydia   벌써 휴가가 끝나다니 믿기지 않는다. 5분 후면 공항에 가야 해.
Alan   잠깐! 작별 인사는 하고 떠나야지!
Lydia   오! 나 작별에 아주 서투른데. 빨리 후딱 하자! 안아 줘. 만나서 정말 반가웠어. 보고 싶을 거야.
Alan   그런 말 하지 마! 너 내 감정을 주체 못 하게 해서 울리려는 거잖아.

go through with

(어렵지만 끝까지) 진행하다, 끝내다

To commit to or finish something that is difficult

So you're going to **go through with** the wedding even after he cheated on you?

그러니까 남자 친구가 바람을 피웠는데도 결혼을 끝까지 진행하겠다는 거야?

finish with

(~와 관련되는 것을) 끝내다, 다 쓰다

To stop being involved with; To stop using something

I can't take you lying to me anymore. I'm **finished with** you.

난 네가 나에게 거짓말하는 거 더는 참을 수 없어. 너랑은 끝이야.

result from

~로 야기되다, 결과가 ~에서 오다

To be caused by

Back pain can **result from** too much stress.

허리 통증은 지나친 스트레스에서 올 수 있다.

end up

결국 ~이 되다

To come to a conclusion that was not expected

All of the people involved in the robbery **ended up** in jail.

강도 사건과 연루된 모든 사람들은 결국 감옥에 갔다.

SHORT DIALOGUE 2

Dylan   When I first moved to New York, I wasn't sure if I could **go through with** it because I was so afraid of the crowds. But now I love it here!

Vivian   I remember that you had a rough start here. I'm glad it got better and that you are **finished with** those fears.

Dylan   It's funny. In my life, a lot of good things have **resulted from** difficult situations.

Vivian   Me too! A lot of the scariest periods of my life **ended up** leading to great things.

Dylan   내가 뉴욕에 처음 이사 왔을 때, 내가 잘 해낼지 확신이 없었어. 사람들이 너무 많아서 정말 두려웠거든. 그런데 이젠 여기가 정말 좋아!

Vivian   나도 네가 여기서 힘들게 시작한 거 기억해. 더 나아져서, 네가 두려움을 잘 극복해서 기뻐.

Dylan   재밌는 게 내 인생에서 많은 좋은 일들은 어려운 상황에서 나왔다니까.

Vivian   나도 그래! 인생에서 가장 두려웠던 시기가 결국엔 정말 멋진 일이 되더라고.

wrap up

끝내다, 마무리 짓다

To complete or finish

Before we **wrap up** this meeting, does anyone have any final questions?

이 회의를 마치기 전에, 마지막으로 질문할 사람이 있나요?

launch into

열정적으로 시작하다

To begin something with enthusiasm

When we feel attacked, we often **launch into** this counterattack.

우리는 공격을 받는다고 느낄 때 종종 반격을 시작한다.

wind up

(어떤 결과로) ~하게 되다

To arrive in a specific situation or place

My friends and I **wound up** getting food poisoning after we ate at that restaurant.

친구들과 난 그 음식점에서 식사를 하고 나서 식중독에 걸렸어.

eat up

(시간 등을) 잡아먹다

To use or take away a large part of something valuable

This won't **eat up** too much of your time.

이 일이 그렇게 시간을 많이 잡아먹지 않을 거야.

SHORT DIALOGUE 3

Zach Let's **wrap up** this meeting early. I need to pick up my kids from school.

Madeline Fine. But we need to **launch into** our project early tomorrow.

Zach What time? I don't want to **wind up** clocking in two hours earlier than usual.

Madeline We don't have much more to discuss. I won't **eat up** much of your morning.

> Zach 오늘 회의는 일찍 끝내자. 학교에서 애들 픽업해야 해.
> Madeline 그래. 그런데 우리 내일 일찍 프로젝트 시작해야 해.
> Zach 몇 시에? 평소보다 2시간 일찍 오는 건 싫은데.
> Madeline 논의할 게 그렇게 많지 않아. 아침 시간 많이 안 뺏을게.

start out

시작하다

To begin

Most of the famous musicians **started out** very poor.

대부분의 유명한 음악가들은 매우 가난하게 시작했다.

tie together

잘 마무리되다

To conclude in a fitting or satisfactory way

Her presentation **tied together** nicely.

그녀의 발표가 잘 마무리되었다.

turn out

(나중에) 알고 보니 ~다

To be the result of or the eventual conclusion of a situation

It **turned out** that Maggie was the one that stole the necklace.

알고 보니, 목걸이를 훔친 사람은 Maggie였다.

get around to

(결국에는) ~을 하다

To eventually do something; To do something that has been procrastinated

I'll **get around to** doing my laundry later.

내가 나중에 짬 내서 빨래할게.

SHORT DIALOGUE 1

Isabel   The book **started out** a bit slow, but it got so much better.

Lincoln   So did it **tie together** in the end? Wait, don't tell me. I want to read it first.

Isabel   Okay. I won't. But I'll just say that it won't **turn out** the way you might expect.

Lincoln   That makes me want to read it even more. I'll call you when I **get around to** reading it.

Isabel   책 앞부분이 살짝 지루했지만, (뒤로 갈수록) 훨씬 나아졌어.
Lincoln   결국 잘 마무리되었어? 잠깐, 말하지 마! 내가 먼저 읽고 싶어.
Isabel   알았어. 말 안 할게. 한마디만 하면, 네 예상과는 다를 거야.
Lincoln   그러니까 정말 더 읽고 싶잖아. 내가 그거 읽게 되면 전화할게.

phase out

조금씩 조금씩 없애다, 단계적으로 폐기하다

To make obsolete; To get rid of
something in favor of
something else

The hospital is **phasing out** their
old X-ray machines for more
advanced ones.

그 병원은 더 최신 기계를 들이기 위해 낡은 엑스레이
기계들을 조금씩 처분하고 있다.

burn out

기운이 소진돼 쓰러질 정도다

To be forced to stop
working because you have
become ill or very tired
from working too hard

I need to take some time off work
because I am **burnt out**.

난 기운이 다 소진돼 휴가를 내서 좀 쉬어야 해.

wear out

피곤하게 하다

To tire; To exhaust

Teaching six hours straight did really
wear me **out**.

6시간 연속해서 강의를 했더니 정말 피곤했다.

start off

시작하다

To begin a journey
or a task

We should **start off** by cutting the
vegetables if we're going to make
this soup.

이 수프를 만들려면, 먼저 채소를 써는 것으로
시작해야 해.

SHORT DIALOGUE 2

Calvin   I think Margot in Human Resources is going to quit. Apparently, she is
completely **burnt out**. Well, that's what Val said.

Maya   Really? I mean, we're all pretty **worn out** around here, but I'm surprised she's
quitting. She's worked here for so long!

Calvin   Ever since the company started to **phase out** the interns, she's had more and
more work to do.

Maya   And she already had so many responsibilities to **start off** with… I'll be sad to see
her go.

Calvin   인사팀에 있는 Margot가 그만둔다는 것 같아. 듣자 하니, 완전히 지쳐 버렸대. Val이 그렇게 말했어.
Maya   정말? 우리 다 여기서 일하는 게 아주 피곤하지. 그래도 그만둔다니까 놀랍네. 여기서 정말 오랫동안
일했잖아!
Calvin   회사가 인턴들을 조금씩 내보내면서, Margot가 해야 할 일이 훨씬 더 많아졌어.
Maya   그리고 처음부터 맡은 업무가 이미 너무 많았지. 그만두는 것 보면 슬플 것 같아.

cut off

단절되다, 끊기다

To disconnect

When the island lost power, it was **cut off** from the rest of the world.
그 섬이 정전이 되었을때, 세계와 단절이 되었다.

break into

(새로운 일을) 시작하다

To enter a new market or specialty

I started out as a car mechanic, but then I **broke into** selling cars.
난 자동차 정비공으로 시작했지만, 자동차 영업을 하게 되었다.

dry up

다 사용하다

To use up;
To expire

When all of my money had **dried up**, I knew I had to make a change.
돈을 다 썼을 때, 난 변해야 한다는 것을 알았다.

start over

다시 시작하다

To begin again;
To try once more from the beginning

I fell asleep. Can we **start** this movie **over** from the beginning?
나 졸았어. 영화 처음부터 다시 볼 수 있을까?

SHORT DIALOGUE 3

Elliot   I'm so depressed. I feel as though I've been **cut off** from my creativity. I can't draw anymore.

Brianna   Perhaps it's time for a new beginning. Maybe you need to **break into** different forms of art.

Elliot   You're not listening. I said my creativity has **dried up**. How can I make any art?

Brianna   Well then, I guess it's time to **start over** with something new.

Elliot   나 너무 우울해. 창의적인 생각으로부터 단절된 느낌이야. 더 이상 그림을 못 그리겠어.
Brianna   새로운 시작을 할 때인 것 같아. 다른 형태의 예술을 시작해 봐야 하는 거 아냐?
Elliot   내 말 제대로 안 듣는구나. 내 창의력이 고갈되었다고 했잖아. 어떻게 다른 예술을 할 수 있겠어?
Brianna   그럼, 뭔가 새로운 것으로 다시 시작할 때인 것 같은데.

MP3 **074**

go for
도전하다

To attempt

If you want to be a lawyer, **go for** it! You're very smart.
변호사가 되고 싶으면, 도전해 봐! 너 아주 똑똑하잖아.

go on
계속하다

To continue

I want to hear the rest of your story. **Go on**!
네 이야기 나머지 부분도 듣고 싶어. 계속해 봐!

wake up
정신 차리다, 꿈 깨다

To realize suddenly, typically in terms of a difficult situation

You really need to **wake up** and face the reality.
너 정말 꿈 깨고 현실을 직시해야 해!

hold out
(어려운 상황에서) 버티다, 저항하다

To continue through a difficult situation

She won't be able to **hold out** much longer if you keep attacking her.
네가 계속 그녀를 공격하면, 그녀는 더 이상 버틸 수가 없을 거야.

SHORT DIALOGUE 1

Lucia   You need to follow your dreams. If there's something you've always wanted to do, you should **go for** it.

Everett   It's not that easy. I can't **go on** following my dreams when I feel so depressed.

Lucia   I understand. But you need to **wake up** and realize that you deserve happiness.

Everett   I appreciate you saying that, but I don't think I can **hold out** much longer.

Lucia   네 꿈을 좇아야 해 항상 해 보고 싶었던 것이 있다면, 도전해 봐야지.
Everett   그게 그렇게 쉽지는 않아. 너무 우울할 때는 꿈을 계속 좇을 수가 없어.
Lucia   이해해. 하지만 빨리 정신 차리고, 너 스스로 행복할 자격이 있다는 것을 알아야 해.
Everett   그렇게 말해 줘서 정말 고마운데, 내가 더 이상 버틸 수 없을 것 같아.

settle down

진정하다

To grow calm

Hey guys! Please **settle down**! We're starting now.

얘들아, 진정하고 자리에 가서 앉아! 우리 지금 시작한다.

shut down

그만하게 하다, 닥치게 하다

To discourage intensely; To cause someone to lose enthusiasm

Jay **shut** me **down** when I was trying to explain.

내가 설명하려고 했는데, Jay가 말을 못 하게 했다.

pipe down

조용히 하다

To be quiet

Shhh...

Pipe down! I need to concentrate.

조용히 좀 해! 나 집중해야 한다고.

cut out

그만하다

To remove, exclude, or stop doing something

You're singing too loudly! **Cut it out**!

너 노래를 너무 크게 부르잖아. 그만해!

SHORT DIALOGUE 2

Mom   Hey, please **settle down** when I'm trying to work. You're too loud!

Graham   But, Mom! I'm bored! Whenever I start to have fun, you always just **shut** me **down**.

Mom   I'm not asking you to stop having fun. I just need you to **cut it out** and **pipe down** for a little.

Graham   Fine… I'll go read one of my comic books or something.

Mom   엄마가 일하려고 할 때는, 조용히 좀 있어 줄래. 너무 시끄럽잖아!

Graham   하지만 엄마! 나 심심하다고요! 재미있어지려고 할 때마다, 엄마가 맨날 못 하게 하잖아요.

Mom   재미있는 걸 그만하라는 게 아니야. 그만 시끄럽게 하고, 잠시만 조용히 하라는 거지.

Graham   알았어요…. 가서 만화책 보든지 할게요.

double down

더 세게 나가다, 전념하다

To keep doing something with even greater enthusiasm than before

I decided to **double down** on the investment for my son's education.

난 아들의 교육 투자를 더 밀어붙이기로 결정했다.

believe in

잘할 것을 믿다

To believe that someone will be successful

When everybody made fun of me, my parents always **believed in** me.

모든 사람들이 날 비웃었을 때, 부모님은 항상 내가 잘 해낼 거라고 믿었다.

cheer up

힘을 내다, 기운을 주다

To grow happier; To make someone happier

Luke, **cheer up**! You can do better next time.

Luke, 기운 내! 다음에 더 잘할 수 있잖아.

knock off

그만하다

To stop suddenly

Hey, **knock** it **off**! I'm sick and tired of you guys arguing over this.

그만해! 너희들이 이걸로 싸우는 것, 나 너무 지긋지긋해.

SHORT DIALOGUE 3

Alexander June, I know that you'll find a new job soon. You just need to **double down** your efforts.

June You're just saying that to **cheer** me **up**. You don't actually mean it.

Alexander Hmm. I suppose it doesn't matter that I **believe in** you because you don't believe in yourself.

June **Knock** it **off**! Don't you see that you're not helping? You're just bothering me.

Alexander June, 네가 새로운 일을 곧 잡게 될 거야. 지금 하는 노력에 더 몰두해 봐.
June 나 기분 좋게 하려고 그러는 거잖아. 진심으로 하는 말이 아니고.
Alexander 음. 내가 널 믿는 건 중요하지 않은 것 같아. 네가 너 자신을 믿지 않으니.
June 그만해! 날 도와주는 게 아니라는 거 모르겠어? 날 귀찮게 할 뿐이라고.

LONG DIALOGUE

Elena: 내가 이 보고서를 일주일 동안 썼어야 했는데, 지금까지 계속 미뤄 두고 있었어. 내가 더 일찍 시작했어야 했는데.

— **Cooper:** 이 얘길 들으니까 우리 어린 시절이 생각난다. 그때 넌 모든 걸 미뤘잖아. 일단 쓰기 시작하면, 문제없을 것 같아. 도전해 봐!

Elena: 결국에는 짬 내서 할 거야. 요즘 그냥 너무 에너지도 다 써 버린 것 같고 그래.

— **Cooper:** 음, 난 네가 잘 해낼 거라고 믿어. 무엇에 관한 보고서 인데?

Elena: 어린 시절 가장 좋았던 추억에 관한 거야. 예전에 좋았던 시절을 생각해야 해.

— **Cooper:** 잠깐! 좋은 생각이 떠올랐어.

Elena: 뭔데?

— **Cooper:** 우리 어린 시절의 사진을 보면서 시작하는 거야. 그럼 좋은 추억들이 생각나지 않을까?

Elena: 그래, 좋은 생각이야! 사진들 좀 볼까? 이건 예전에 우리가 축구 시합을 했던 사진이고… 이건 방학 때 한국에 갔던 때고.

— **Cooper:** 나도 많은 추억들이 떠오르네. 네가 보고서 작성하는 데 이게 도움이 되면 좋겠어.

Elena: I've had to write this paper for a week, but I've **wound up** procrastinating until now. I should've **started off** earlier.

— **Cooper:** Hearing this **brings** me **back** to our childhood when you would procrastinate everything. I think that once you start writing, you won't have a problem. Just **go for** it!

Elena: I'll **get around to** it eventually. I just feel so **burnt out** lately.

— **Cooper:** Well, I **believe in** you. What is the paper about?

Elena: It's about a favorite childhood memory. I have to **think back** to some of the good times.

— **Cooper:** **Hold up**! I have an idea.

Elena: What is it?

— **Cooper:** Well, you could **start off** by looking at some of the old photos from our childhood. Perhaps that will **stir up** some good memories.

Elena: Yeah! Good idea. Let's see some of the photos… this is one of our old football games… and here is that time we went on vacation to South Korea.

— **Cooper:** A lot of memories are **flooding back** to me, too. I hope that helps you write your paper.

reflect on
곰곰이 생각하다

To ponder; To think about something intensely

Thank you for the advice. I'll **reflect on** it and get back to you later.
충고 고마워. 곰곰이 생각해 보고, 나중에 알려 줄게.

jump out at
(갑자기) 드러나다, 눈에 띄다

To be revealed suddenly; To grab attention

Be patient! The answer to this problem won't **jump out at** you.
인내심을 가져! 이 문제에 대한 답이 바로 나오진 않을 테니까.

toy with
(막연히) 생각하다

To consider something

I'm **toying with** the idea of moving back to the States.
난 미국으로 다시 돌아가는 것에 대해서 생각하고 있다.

slip out
(나도 모르게) 튀어나오다

To be revealed accidentally or without much thought

I'm sorry but it just **slipped out**.
미안해. 나도 모르게 입에서 튀어나왔어.

SHORT DIALOGUE 1

Claire   Did you get a chance to **reflect on** who may have left you that love letter?

Parker   I did, but still the answer hasn't **jumped out at** me. I've been **toying with** the idea that it's Ariana. At least I hope it was.

Claire   You hope? Wait, do you like Ariana?

Parker   Oops, that just **slipped out**. But, yeah, I do.

Claire   혹시 누가 저 연애편지를 너한테 놓고 갔을지 곰곰이 생각해 봤어?

Parker   응, 그런데 아직도 딱히 떠오르는 사람은 없었어. 막연히 Ariana가 아닐까 생각은 하는데 말이야. 적어도 그랬으면 싶어.

Claire   그랬으면 한다고? 잠깐, 너 Ariana 좋아하니?

Parker   아… 그게… 나도 모르게 말이 튀어나왔네. 그런데 응, 맞아.

believe in

~의 가치를 믿다

To think that something is good, right, or acceptable

Do you **believe in** capital punishment?

넌 사형 제도가 가치 있다고 믿니?

zone out

멍하게 있다, 멍 때리다

To stop paying attention

Many children can't focus in school, and they **zone out**.

많은 아이들이 학교에서 집중을 못 하고, 멍하게 있는다.

drum into

(되풀이해) 주입하다

To remind frequently and forcefully

Take this piece of advice, **drum** it **into** your brain! You will thank me later.

이 충고 잘 새기고, 머릿속에 꼭 집어넣어 놔! 나중에 나한테 고마워할 거야.

go with

동의하다, 받아들이다

To agree; To concede to

Josh had a plan, I decided to **go with** it.

Josh는 계획이 있었고, 난 그것을 따르기로 했다.

SHORT DIALOGUE 2

Teacher   Sydney, next question. Which group **believed in** a strong government?

Sydney   Sorry, I was **zoning out**. What was the question?

Teacher   How many times do I have to **drum** it **into** your brain? You need to stay focused.

Sydney   What did Marsha say? I'll just **go with** her answer.

Teacher   Sydney, 다음 질문이야. 어떤 그룹이 강력한 정부의 가치를 믿었을까?

Sydney   죄송해요. 제가 잠깐 딴 생각을 했나 봐요. 질문이 뭐였죠?

Teacher   내가 얼마나 많이 반복해서 주입해야 하니? 집중해야 한다고.

Sydney   Marsha가 뭐라고 했죠? 전 그냥 Marsha의 답변을 따라갈게요.

spread around

소문내다

To be shared in the form of gossip

There's a rumor **spreading around** that big layoffs are coming.

대량 해고가 있을 거라는 소문이 돌고 있어.

walk through

(차근차근) 설명하다

To show somebody how to do something by carefully explaining

I **walked** my grandma **through** how to use her new smartphone.

나는 할머니께 새 스마트폰을 어떻게 사용하는지 차근차근 설명해 드렸다.

leave out

제외하다, 빼다

To fail to mention something; To omit

Some overqualified people sometimes **leave out** the fact that they earned Ph.D.

지나치게 고학력인 사람들 몇몇은 가끔 자신들한테 박사 학위가 있다는 사실을 숨긴다.

blurt out

불쑥 말하다, 내뱉다

To say abruptly and without consideration

Raise your hand if you know the answer. Don't just **blurt** it **out**.

답을 알면 손을 들어. 갑자기 툭 내뱉지 말고.

SHORT DIALOGUE 1

Brandon Did you **spread** it **around** the office that I was looking for another job?

Sarah I'm sorry! I was **walking** the new girl **through** our system, and then we started talking about your department…

Brandon How hard is it to just **leave** me **out** of your conversation!? Now Mr. Kingsley knows!

Sarah I know. I accidentally **blurted** it **out** when he was right behind me. Please forgive me!

Brandon 내가 구직 중이라고 네가 사무실에 소문냈어?
Sarah 미안! 신입 직원에게 우리 시스템을 설명하다 보니, 너희 부서 이야기를 꺼내게 되었어.
Brandon 네 대화에서 내 이야기를 빼고 안 하는 게 그렇게 어려운 일이야!? 이제 Kingsley 씨가 안다고!
Sarah 나도 알아. 나도 모르게 실수로 튀어나왔는데 Kingsley 씨가 바로 뒤에 있었어. 제발 용서해 줘!

leak out

누설하다, 공개하다

To spread to the public, especially involving private or secret information

Our new software was copied and **leaked out**.

우리의 새로운 소프트웨어가 복제되어서 유출되었다.

come forward

솔직하게 말하다, 증언하다

To speak up; To volunteer information

I finally **came forward** and shared my thoughts.

난 결국 솔직히 나의 생각을 말하고 공유했다.

get out

공개되다, 알려지다

To spread among a group of people, especially involving secrets

If it **gets out** that I'm dating my coworker, that could cost me my job.

내가 직장 동료와 데이트하고 있다는 것이 알려지면, 난 직업을 잃을 수도 있어.

pass on

(뉴스나 가십 내용을) 전달하다

To tell someone something; To spread news or gossip

When you get the information, please **pass** it **on** to me.

그 정보를 얻으면, 나에게 전달해 줘.

SHORT DIALOGUE 2

Victoria　We can't let the information we found **leak out** to the public.

Blake　Don't you think we should **come forward** and tell the police?

Victoria　No! If this **gets out**, we will all lose our jobs.

Blake　We just found out that our boss is embezzling! We have to **pass** this **on** to the police!

Victoria　우리가 찾은 정보를 사람들에게 누설해서는 안 돼.
Blake　우리가 나서서 경찰에 알려야 한다고 생각하지 않아?
Victoria　안 돼! 이게 공개되면, 우리는 전부 옷 벗어야 해.
Blake　사장이 돈을 횡령하는 것을 알았잖아! 우리가 이걸 경찰에 넘겨야 한다고!

pick up
듣다, 알게 되다

To overhear;
To notice;
To learn

I **picked up** a few words in Chinese when I visited Beijing.

내가 베이징을 방문했을 때 중국어 몇 마디를 알게 되었다.

expand on
~에 대해 추가로 설명하다

To give more details about something you have said or written

I'm still confused. Could you **expand on** it?

여전히 좀 헷갈리는데, 그것에 대해 추가로 설명해 주시겠어요?

hold back
비밀로 하다

To withhold information; To fail to mention something

You should be honest with me. Don't **hold** anything **back**.

너 나한테 솔직해야 해. 어떤 것도 숨기지 말고.

fill in
알려 주다, 들은 대로 말해 주다

To tell someone the details about someone or something

Fill me **in**! What happened to him?

나한테도 알려 줘! 걔 어떻게 된 거야?

SHORT DIALOGUE 3

Cecilia   I just **picked up** a tip about how to lose weight by cutting out certain foods according to your body type.

Max   Oh really? Which foods should I avoid for my body type?

Cecilia   Well, the woman in the video didn't actually **expand on** which foods.

Max   Let me guess. She **held back** that information until you subscribed and paid a fee. Once you pay, she'd **fill** you **in** on those details.

Cecilia   나 방금 체형에 따라서 특정한 음식들을 피하면서 살을 빼는 방법에 대한 정보를 알게 됐어.
Max   오, 정말? 내 체형에는 어떤 음식을 피해야 하는데?
Cecilia   음, 영상에 나오는 여자가 무슨 음식이라고 추가로 설명하진 않았어.
Max   내가 맞혀 볼까? 사람들이 구독하고, 돈을 내기 전까지 그 정보를 공개 안 한 거겠지. 일단 돈을 내면, 자세하게 말해 줄 거야.

MP3 **078**

bargain for
~을 예상하다, 대비하다

To expect or be prepared for something

I got more than I **bargained for** when the housing market boomed.
나는 주택 시장이 호황일 때 내가 기대했던 것보다 더 많은 것을 얻었다.

bring down
줄이다, 낮추다

To reduce

I won't buy this unless you **bring down** the price.
가격을 내리지 않으면 전 이거 안 살 거예요.

talk up
~을 좋게 말하다

To flatter someone or to exaggerate something

When someone is **talking** you **up** too much, it means they want something from you.
누군가 너를 지나치게 칭찬하면, 그것은 그들이 너에게 뭔가를 원한다는 의미야.

set aside
돈을 따로 떼어 두다

To budget or save a certain amount of money to spend on something

I **set aside** $2,000 to buy a new laptop.
난 새 노트북을 사기 위해서 2,000달러를 따로 모아두었다.

SHORT DIALOGUE 1

Uncle   When we go get your car, let me talk to them. Otherwise they will try to get you to pay more than you've **bargained for.**

Cynthia   Okay, uncle. I'm not sure if they'll **bring down** the price at all.

Uncle   They will once I **talk** them **up.** I've done this before.

Cynthia   Okay. But don't embarrass me. I've already **set aside** enough money to pay for the car.

Uncle   네 차 사러 갈 때, 내가 한번 말해 볼게. 안 그러면, 네가 예상한 가격보다 더 많이 내게 유도할 수도 있어.

Cynthia   알았어요, 삼촌. 가격을 깎아 줄지는 잘 모르겠어요.

Uncle   일단 내가 좋게 잘 말하면 그렇게 할 거다. 전에도 해 봤어.

Cynthia   알았어요. 그런데 저 창피하게는 하지 마세요. 그 차 살 돈은 이미 충분히 따로 모았으니까요.

turn down

거절하다

To decline

When I was offered a job, I couldn't **turn** it **down**.

일자리를 제안받았을 때, 난 거절할 수가 없었어요.

gamble away

도박으로 다 날리다

To lose something by gambling

He **gambled away** one million dollars at the casino.

그는 카지노에서 백만 달러를 날렸다.

live down

(부끄러운 일을) 잊어버리다, 극복하다

To forget something embarrassing; To live so as to wipe out the memory or effects of something

I'll never **live down** that time I farted in front of my girlfriend.

내 여자 친구 앞에서 방귀 뀐 일을 절대 잊을 수 없을 것이다.

rest on

~에 달려 있다

To depend on

Happiness **rests on** whether we have something to look forward to.

행복은 우리가 기대할 만한 것이 있느냐의 유무에 달려 있다.

SHORT DIALOGUE 2

Juliet   I wonder if Shannon will **turn down** the offer on her house. It is way too low.

Vince   I don't understand why they are selling their house anyways.

Juliet   Apparently her husband **gambled away** all their money and now they can't get by. At least that's what their neighbor told me. How will she ever **live** that **down** unless she moves?

Vince   Poor Shannon. It's a shame that this is all **resting on** her.

Juliet   Shannon이 자기 집에 대해 나온 제안을 거절할까? 정말 너무 낮잖아.

Vince   어쨌거나 난 왜 그 집을 팔려고 하는지 이해가 안 돼.

Juliet   남편이 돈을 전부 도박으로 날려서, 생활하기 힘든가 봐. 적어도 그게 주변 이웃에서 말해 준 정보야. 이사하지 않고 Shannon이 어떻게 그 부끄러운 일을 잊고 살 수 있겠어?

Vince   불쌍한 Shannon. 이 모든 것이 그녀에게 달려 있다니 안타깝네.

MP3 **079**

level with

솔직히 터놓고 말하다

> To be honest with, typically in regards to bad news

I'm going to **level with** you. I can't even remember what you said.

너한테 솔직히 말할게. 사실 나 네가 무슨 말을 했는지도 기억이 안 나.

fess up

자백하다, 진심을 이야기하다

> To tell the truth after lying

Amy **fessed up** to the fact that she stole money.

Amy는 자신이 돈을 훔친 사실을 자백했다.

make up

(없는 이야기를) 지어내다

> To fabricate; To lie about

Did you actually meet the president or are you **making** that **up**?

정말 대통령을 만났다는 거야, 아니면 그냥 지어낸 이야기야?

cover up

숨기다, 은폐하다

> To hide a mistruth, misdeed, or lie

My boss tried to **cover up** hiring illegal immigrants.

사장님은 불법 이민자를 고용한 것을 숨기려고 했다.

SHORT DIALOGUE 1

Miguel   I'm going to have to **level with** you, Hillary. I haven't been honest with you.

Hillary   You have something to **fess up** to? Go ahead. What have you been lying about?

Miguel   I wasn't out of town for your birthday. I just **made** that **up**. I went out with Mindy instead.

Hillary   I knew you were **covering** something **up**. How dare you lie to me!

> **Miguel**   너한테 터놓고 말해야 할 것 같다, Hillary. 내가 너한테 솔직하지 않았어.
> **Hillary**   털어놓을 게 있다는 거야? 말해 봐. 무슨 거짓말을 했는데?
> **Miguel**   나 네 생일날 어디 안 갔어. 그냥 지어낸 거야. 대신 Mindy하고 같이 외출했어.
> **Hillary**   네가 뭔가 숨기고 있다고 생각하기는 했어. 어떻게 네가 나한테 거짓말을 하냐!

sell out

(자기 이익을 위해) 배신하다,
신념을 저버리다

**To betray someone for
a personal benefit**

Some actors **sell out** and take roles
in stupid movies for the money.

일부 배우들은 돈을 위해서 신념을 저버리고,
바보 같은 영화에 출연하기도 한다.

tip off

(경찰에) 제보하다, 귀띔하다

**To report information
to the police
anonymously**

Jay **tipped off** the police about his
father's illegal business.

Jay는 아버지의 불법 사업에 대해 경찰에 제보했다.

vouch for

~을 보증하다, 보장하다

**To confirm that
someone is of good
character**

Charlie is a very good driver. I can
vouch for that.

Charlie는 운전을 정말 잘해. 내가 보장할 수 있어.

play along

(거짓에) 동조하다, 장단 맞추다

**To take part in a lie;
To help someone lie**

If the police pull us over, I'll talk to
them and you just **play along** with it.

경찰이 우리한테 차 세우라고 하면 내가 말할 테니까
넌 옆에서 장단 맞춰 줘.

SHORT DIALOGUE 2

Sawyer Did you **sell** me **out** to our parents? How could you do this?

Amy They said you couldn't have a party while they were out of town, so I **tipped
them off**.

Sawyer I trusted you! I thought you would **vouch for** me when they called!

Amy Sorry, I had to do it. I couldn't **play along** anymore.

Sawyer 네가 날 배신하고 우리 부모님한테 꼰질러? 어떻게 그럴 수 있어?
Amy 부모님이 어디 가셨을 때 파티 하면 안 된다고 했잖아. 그래서 귀띔해 드렸어.
Sawyer 널 믿었는데! 부모님이 전화했을 때 내가 그런 사람 아니라고 날 보증해 줄 거라고 생각했단 말야!
Amy 미안해. 그렇게 할 수밖에 없었어. 너의 일에 더 이상 동조할 수가 없었다고.

mix up

섞다

To spoil the order or arrangement of things

Jane's papers got **mixed up** after Jay bumped into her and she dropped them.

Jane이 Jay하고 부딪쳐 서류를 떨어뜨린 후 Jane의 서류가 섞여 버렸다.

seek out

찾아내다

To search for and find something or someone

I will **seek out** the best medicine for you.

내가 널 위해 최고의 약을 찾아낼 거야.

speak of

말하다

To mention

Daniel was **speaking of** you yesterday. He misses you.

어제 Daniel이 네 얘기하던데. 널 보고 싶어 해.

keep from

숨기다

To hide

How can I **keep** my pregnancy **from** my family?

어떻게 우리 가족들에게 내가 임신했다는 사실을 숨길 수 있을까?

SHORT DIALOGUE 3

Dad   Did you **mix up** your grandfather's medicines? Tell me the truth.

Annie   No. I have no idea what you're **speaking of**.

Dad   Don't lie. You're not in trouble. I'm just **seeking out** the truth because it would be very dangerous if he took the wrong ones.

Annie   Okay, I did it. I'm sorry for **keeping** it **from** you.

    Dad   너 할아버지 약을 섞어 놨니? 사실대로 말해.
    Annie   아니에요. 무슨 말씀 하시는지 잘 모르겠는데요.
    Dad   거짓말하지 마. 괜찮아. 아빠가 사실을 알려고 하는 것뿐이야. 할아버지께서 약을 잘못 드시면 아주 위험할 수 있어.
    Annie   네, 제가 그랬어요. 말씀 안 드리고 숨겨서 죄송해요.

LONG DIALOGUE

Joel: 솔직히 말할 게 있어. 나, Lola 잃어버렸어.

— Hannah: 뭐?! Maxwell의 개를 잃어버렸다고? 어떻게 그런 일이 일어나게 내버려 둔 거야? 걔가 널 믿고 개 좀 봐 주라고 맡긴 건데!

Joel: 나도 알아. Lola랑 같이 있었는데, 내가 잠깐 멍 때리는 사이에 도망갔어.

— Hannah: 그래서 Maxwell한테 말 안 했어?

Joel: 아직 말 안 했어. Maxwell이 아침에 전화했을 때, 그건 빼고 얘기했어. 걔가 알게 되면 날 가만두지 않을 거야.

— Hannah: 그런데 넌 왜 이걸 나한테 이야기하는 거야?

Joel: 제발 내 제안 거절하지 마, 알았지? Lola 찾는 데 네 도움이 필요해.

— Hannah: Maxwell이 나한테 전화하면? 난 걔한테 뭐라고 말해? 너 나한테 이것도 숨겨 달라고 부탁하는 거니?

Joel: 응, 제발! 네가 나 좀 도와줘야 해. 내가 개를 잃어버렸다고 말하지 말아 줘. 안 그럼 Maxwell이 날 다시는 안 믿을 거야!

— Hannah: 잘 모르겠다. 내가 왜 이 일을 숨기는 데 동조해야 하는데? Maxwell은 내 친구이기도 하다고!

Joel: 왜냐하면 우리는 친구잖아! 그리고 네 도움 받아서, 그 개 찾을 거라고. 걔가 물어보면, 그냥 아무 일 없다고만 해 줘.

— Hannah: 그래, 알았어. Lola 찾는 거 도와줄게. 그리고 Maxwell 한테도 말 안 할게. 그렇지만 Maxwell이 직접 물어보면, 난 비밀로 할 수 없어. 내가 솔직하게 말해야 할 거야. 너도 알겠지만 나 거짓말 정말 못해.

Joel: I have to **come forward** about something. I lost Lola.

— **Hannah:** What?! You lost Maxwell's dog? How did you let that happen? He was counting on you to watch her!

Joel: I know. I was with the dog, and then I just **zoned out** and she ran away.

— **Hannah:** And you didn't tell him?

Joel: Not yet! When he called in the morning, I just **left** it **out** of the conversation. He'd never let me **live** it **down** if he knew.

— **Hannah:** So why are you bringing this up to me?

Joel: Please don't **turn** me **down**, okay? I need your help finding her.

— **Hannah:** And what if Maxwell calls me? What do I say to him? Are you asking me to help you **cover** this **up** as well?

Joel: Yes! Please! You have to help me. You can't let it **get out** that I lost her dog or Maxwell will never trust me again!

— **Hannah:** I don't know. Why should I help you **keep** this **from** him? He's my friend, too!

Joel: Because we're friends! And with your help, we'll find the dog. I just need you to **vouch for** me if he asks about it.

— **Hannah:** Okay fine. I'll help you find Lola. And I won't tell Maxwell about it. But if he asks directly, I can't **hold back**. I'll have to **fess up** to him. You know I suck at lying.

CHAPTER

10

PHRASAL VERBS

clear out

~을 빠르게 떠나다

To evacuate
quickly

The smell was so bad that everyone
cleared out of the room.
냄새가 너무 심해서 모두 그 방을 떠났다.

put out

(불을) 끄다

To extinguish,
typically fire

Do you have a fire extinguisher in
case we need to **put out** a fire?
불을 꺼야 할 때를 대비해서 소화기가 있나요?

stay back

(위험한 사람이나 사물에서) 물러서다

To keep one's distance
from a place, often
because of some
danger

That dog looks mean. You should
stay back!
개가 사나워 보여요. 물러서세요!

order around

~에게 자꾸 이래라저래라 하다, 명령하다

To tell someone
what to do;
To boss around

The lifeguard **ordered** the children
around to keep them from running
near the pool.
안전 요원은 수영장 근처에서 뛰어다니지 못하게
아이들에게 뭐라고 주의를 주었다.

SHORT DIALOGUE 1

Firefighter Can't you hear the fire alarm? It's not safe to be in the building. Everyone needs
to **clear out**.

Wilson Don't **order** me **around**. This is my apartment, and there's no fire. I'm going in
there.

Firefighter No, **stay back**! There is a fire in the apartment above you, and my team is still
putting it **out**.

Wilson Oh, I didn't realize that.

Firefighter 화재경보 소리 안 들리세요? 건물 안에 있으면 위험합니다. 다들 얼른 나가세요.
Wilson 나한테 명령하지 마세요! 여긴 내 아파트라고요. 화재가 나지도 않았는데. 난 들어갈 거예요.
Firefighter 안 돼요. 물러서세요! 바로 위층에서 불이 나서, 우리 팀이 화재 진압을 하고 있어요.
Wilson 아, 그건 몰랐네요.

hide away

숨다, 잠복하다

To hide for
a long time

During a shooting, it's important to **hide away** in a secure location until help arrives.

총격이 발생하면 구조대가 도착할 때까지 안전한 장소에 몸을 숨기는 것이 중요해요.

come after

추적하다, 쫓다

To pursue with
bad intentions;
To hunt

I'm afraid John is **coming after** me. He was an ex-convict.

John이 날 쫓아올까 봐 무서워. 그는 전과자였어.

cover up

숨기다

To hide something

Let's **cover up** your face with this mask.

이 마스크로 네 얼굴을 가리자.

lie ahead

앞에 놓여 있다

To be going to
happen;
To be in front of

We don't know what dangers **lie ahead**, so let's make sure we're well-prepared.

앞으로 어떤 위험이 닥칠지 모르니 철저히 준비하자고.

SHORT DIALOGUE 2

Natalie This game is awesome!

Timothy Quick, get the gun and then go down the alley there. Don't worry, no more monsters are **coming after** you. But worse ones **lie ahead** in the next level.

Natalie Okay, what do I do next? Should I **cover up** my footprints, so they don't follow?

Timothy No, they disappear automatically. Just have your character **hide away** in the warehouse for now and collect coins.

Natalie 이 게임 끝내준다!
Timothy 빨리! 총 가지고 저기 골목으로 가! 더 이상 괴물들이 널 따라오지 않으니 걱정 말고. 그런데 다음 단계에서 더 악한 놈들이 기다리고 있어.
Natalie 알았어. 다음엔 뭘 하지? 괴물들이 따라오지 못하게 발자국을 없앨까?
Timothy 아냐. 발자국은 자동으로 없어져. 지금은 (게임) 캐릭터를 창고에 숨기고 코인을 모아.

lay into

강하게 비난하다,
엄청 화를 내다

**To criticize intensely
or aggressively**

The police officer **laid into** the
trucker for driving too fast.
경찰관이 과속 운전을 한 트럭 운전사를 강하게
비난했다.

put on

비난하다

To blame

You chose to leave your coat at
home, and you got a cold. Don't **put
this on** me!
네가 코트를 집에 놓고 와서 감기에 걸린 거잖아.
나한테 뭐라고 하지 매

bite back

대들다, 반격하다

**To retort; To reply
aggressively to an
insult or criticism**

I finally **bit back** at my terrible
manager and told her how I feel.
난 결국 그 못된 매니저에게 일침을 날렸고,
내 감정이 어떤지 말했다.

chew out

호되게 꾸짖다, 야단치다

**To yell at or criticize
someone intensely**

Erin **chewed out** her son for getting
into trouble at school.
Erin은 아들이 학교에서 말썽을 피워서 야단을 쳤다.

SHORT DIALOGUE 1

Charlie   Why did you have to **lay into** me about my work product at the staff meeting
yesterday?

Rachel   Don't **put** this **on** me! You're the one that has been making all the mistakes in
our department.

Charlie   Why are you **biting back**? I made a few mistakes but that's no excuse to yell at
me.

Rachel   I wouldn't be **chewing** you **out** if you just did your job right the first time.

Charlie   어제 직원 회의에서 왜 내 업무 결과물을 가지고 강하게 비난했던 거야?
Rachel   나한테 뭐라고 하지 매 우리 부서에서 일어나는 모든 실수는 네가 한 거잖아.
Charlie   왜 네가 나한테 그런 식으로 반격하는 거지? 내가 좀 실수했어. 그렇지만 그렇다고 나한테 소리 지르
는 것의 변명이 되지는 않아.
Rachel   네가 처음부터 네 일을 제대로 하면 나도 너한테 뭐라고 하지 않을 거야.

tear down

비방하다, (자존심을) 뭉개다

To make someone
feel bad;
To hurt someone's
self-esteem

I don't understand why my teacher
is always **tearing down** my work.

난 왜 선생님이 항상 내 일 가지고 깔아뭉개는지 이해가
안 돼.

put down

깎아내리다, 비난하다

To criticize

My girlfriend is always **putting
down** my ideas and that makes me
feel so small.

여자 친구는 항상 내 아이디어를 깎아내리는데, 그게
날 너무 기죽게 만들어.

come under fire

비난을 받다

To be criticized

I'll **come under fire** for saying this,
but you can't master English.

내가 이런 말을 하면 비난을 받겠지만, 너는 영어를
마스터할 수 없어.

let up

누그러지다, 약하게 하다

To grow less
intense

When is my mother going to **let up**
with her criticisms of me?

언제쯤 엄마가 나에 대한 비난을 좀 약하게 하실까?

SHORT DIALOGUE 2

Joanna   I'm trying to improve, professor, but every time I make a mistake, you **tear** me
down.

Professor   I'm not trying to **put** you **down**. I'm tough because I believe in you.

Joanna   But it's not just me. The other students are afraid to ask you questions because
they don't want to **come under fire**.

Professor   My job is to teach all of you as efficiently as possible. But if that's how you guys
feel, maybe I could try to **let up** a little more in class.

Joanna   교수님, 전 더 잘해 보려고 하는데, 제가 실수할 때마다 교수님이 자존심을 다 뭉개 버리세요.
Professor   자네를 깎아내리려는 게 아니네. 자네를 믿으니까 엄하게 하는 거지.
Joanna   하지만 저만 그렇게 느끼는 게 아니에요. 다른 학생들도 교수님께 질문하는 걸 두려워합니다.
비난받고 싶지 않으니까요.
Professor   내 일은 학생들을 최대한 효율적으로 가르치는 거야. 하지만 자네들이 그렇게 느낀다면, 강의 중
에 좀 더 살살하려고 노력해 보지.

bottle up

(감정을) 억누르다

To suppress, typically emotions

It's unhealthy to **bottle up** emotions like anger or sadness.

화나 슬픔 같은 감정을 억누르는 것은 건강에 해로워요.

weigh on

부담을 주다, 힘들게 하다

To make someone sad, stressed, or exhausted

I'm under huge pressure at work, and it's been **weighing on** me.

직장에서 큰 압박을 느끼고 있고, 이게 절 정말 힘들게 합니다.

shake off

떨쳐 버리다, 극복하다

To get over something; To get past a negative emotion

I know that meeting was horrible, but you should try to **shake** it **off**.

나도 그 회의가 최악이었던 건 알지만, 빨리 떨쳐내고 잊어버려.

hold down

힘들게 하다, (발전하는 것을) 막다

To be burdensome; To get in someone's way

I feel like I'm so **held down** by my shyness. It's hard to make friends.

난 수줍음 때문에 발전에 한계가 느껴져. 친구들을 사귀기가 어려워.

SHORT DIALOGUE 1

Margaret   I feel like my emotions are so **bottled up**. I have no one to talk to.

Counselor   You can talk to me. What's **weighing on** you?

Margaret   I have too much anxiety. I just can't seem to **shake** it **off**.

Counselor   Having that much anxiety can certainly **hold** someone **down**. Talking about it will help.

Margaret   제 감정이 너무 억눌린 것 같아요. 말할 사람이 아무도 없어요.
Counselor   저한테 얘기하세요. 어떤 것이 당신을 힘들게 하죠?
Margaret   전 불안감이 너무 심해요. 그것을 떨쳐 낼 수가 없을 것 같아요.
Counselor   그렇게 많이 불안하면 정말 힘들 수 있어요. 그것에 대해서 말하는 게 도움이 될 겁니다.

work (oneself) into

흥분해서 ~한 상태로 가게 하다

To agitate into a certain state of mind

If you're not prepared, you could **work** yourself **into** a panic during the interview.

준비가 안 돼 있으면, 인터뷰 때 매우 당황할 수 있다.

get carried away

흥분하여 통제력을 잃다

To become so excited about something that you don't control

I'm so sorry. I **got carried away** with your brilliant idea.

정말 죄송해요. 당신의 멋진 아이디어에 제가 지나치게 흥분했네요.

be tired of

지겹다, 싫증이 나다

To be bored with

Sally **is tired of** playing with her toys.

Sally는 장난감을 가지고 노는 것에 싫증을 낸다.

tear apart

마음을 찢다, 너무 (감정을) 힘들게 하다

To make someone feel extremely unhappy or upset

Seeing her suffering really **tore** me **apart**.

그녀가 괴로워하는 것을 보니 내 마음이 정말 찢어졌다.

SHORT DIALOGUE 2

Paige   I'm so busy. I think I'm going to **work** myself **into** a breakdown.

Grant   It's easy to **get carried away** with work. You need to relax every now and then.

Paige   It's hard to take time off work. My job is so important to the company, but I'm **tired of** always feeling overworked.

Grant   You need to take a break before you **tear** yourself **apart**.

Paige   나 너무 바빠. 나 이렇게 가다가는 신경쇠약에 걸릴 것 같아.
Grant   일하다 보면 일에 정신을 뺏기기 쉬워. 가끔은 좀 쉬어야지.
Paige   그런데 일을 쉬는 게 쉽지가 않아. 내 일이 회사에서는 참 중요하거든. 하지만 항상 업무 과다로 피곤한 것도 지치고 신물난다.
Grant   그렇게 힘들게 되기 전에 너 쉬어야 해.

hold back

(성공이나 진전을) 저지하다, 억제하다

To prevent from progress or success

Don't let your past **hold** you **back**.
너의 과거가 네 앞길을 막게 하지는 마!

rub in

계속해서 들먹이다

To remind someone about something they want to forget

I'm well aware that I bought my house at the worst time. You don't have to **rub** it **in**.
나도 내가 최악의 시점에서 집 산 거 잘 알아. 네가 계속 들먹일 필요 없잖아.

keep down

억누르다

To suppress

I tried to **keep down** my feelings of jealousy toward my friend, but I just can't do it.
나는 친구에 대한 질투심을 억누르려고 노력했지만 도저히 그렇게 할 수가 없다.

piss off

화나게 하다

To anger or annoy

I'm in a bad mood now, so don't **piss** me **off**.
나 지금 기분 안 좋아. 그러니 화나게 하지 마.

SHORT DIALOGUE 3

Melanie　I think you need to go to therapy, Diego. Your anger issues are **holding** you **back**.

Diego　Hey, don't tell me what to do! I've had these problems my whole life. You don't have to **rub** it **in**.

Melanie　When you try to **keep down** your emotions, they come out as anger.

Diego　Shut up! You're really **pissing** me **off**. I don't need therapy and I don't need advice!

　　Melanie　내 생각에 너 치료받으러 가야 할 것 같아, Diego. 분노 장애가 네 앞길을 막고 있다고.
　　Diego　야, 나한테 이래라저래라 하지 마! 평생 이 문제가 있었어. 네가 자꾸 들먹이지 않아도 돼.
　　Melanie　감정을 억누르려고 할 때, 그게 화로 표출이 되는 거야.
　　Diego　입 닥쳐! 너 정말 날 화나게 한다. 나 치료도 필요 없고, 네 충고도 필요 없어!

MP3 **084**

hold against

~을 안 좋게 보다

To judge someone negatively because of a particular event or action of theirs

I know I'm not perfect. But I hope you don't **hold** it **against** me.

나도 내가 완벽하지 않은 것 알아요. 하지만 그걸로 절 안 좋게 보진 않으셨으면 해요.

struggle with

힘들어하다

To have a hard time dealing with something in particular

Many Koreans are still **struggling with** speaking English after years of education.

수년간의 교육을 받은 후에도 많은 한국인들은 여전히 영어로 말하는 것을 힘들어해요.

look down on

무시하다

To think poorly of someone, typically with the belief of being better than them

Don't **look down on** me just because I'm much younger than you.

내가 당신보다 훨씬 어리다고 해서 무시하지 마세요.

not feel up to

~할 기력이 없다, ~할 에너지가 없다

To not feel empowered or willing to do something

I'm sorry, but I **don't feel up to** helping you move this weekend.

미안한데, 내가 이번 주말에 너 이사하는 거 도와줄 컨디션이 아니야.

SHORT DIALOGUE 1

Employee   You know that I'm having a hard time, but you can't **hold** it **against** me.

Boss   I don't care what you are **struggling with**. If you can't do your job, then you're fired.

Employee   Please don't fire me. I know you **look down on** me, but I can do better.

Boss   Fine, but it seems to me that you just **don't feel up to** working. Now go do your job before you lose it. This is your last warning.

Employee   제가 힘들어하고 있는 거 아시잖아요. 하지만 그것 때문에 절 나쁘게 보진 마세요.

Boss   자네가 힘든 건 상관 안 해. 일을 제대로 못 하면, 자네는 잘리는 거야.

Employee   제발 절 해고하지 마세요. 절 무시하는 거 아는데요. 저 더 잘할 수 있어요.

Boss   좋아. 그런데 내가 보기엔 자네는 일할 에너지가 없는 것 같네. 해고되기 전에 빨리 가서 일하게 나. 마지막 경고일세.

choke back

눈물을 참다

To hold back tears or sorrowful emotions

My girlfriend couldn't **choke back** her tears at the end of this movie.

내 여자 친구는 이 영화 끝부분에서 눈물을 참지 못했다.

fight against

저항하다, ~와 대항해 싸우다

To resist something

We all need to **fight against** corrpution.

우리 모두 부정부패에 맞서 싸워야 한다.

spill out

(감정이) 분출되다

To let out freely and without control

I don't know why I said that! It just **spilled out** of my mouth!

내가 왜 그렇게 말했는지 모르겠어! 그냥 입에서 튀어나왔어!

be sick of

질리다, 지긋지긋하다

To be tired, annoyed, or frustrated with something

I **am** really **sick of** hearing your complaints.

네 불평 듣는 거 정말 지긋지긋하다.

SHORT DIALOGUE 2

Ivan Each time I watch this movie, I **choke back** tears. It makes me so emotional.

Aubrey What's wrong with crying? There's no need to **fight against** your emotions.

Ivan I don't want to let them **spill out**, either. I'm a man, after all.

Aubrey Oh, please! I'm so **sick of** that excuse. Men can express their emotions too, and you'll feel better after a good cry.

Ivan 난 이 영화 볼 때마다, 눈물을 참아. 정말 감정적이 된다니까.
Aubrey 우는 게 뭐 어때서? 네 감정을 억누르려고 할 필요 없어.
Ivan 그냥 울음이 막 나오게 놔두고 싶지 않아. 어쨌든 난 남자잖아.
Aubrey 아, 좀! 너의 그런 변명 지겨워. 남자도 감정을 표현할 수 있어. 그리고 한번 실컷 울고 나면 기분이 좋아질 거야.

be hung up

집착하다, (지나치게) 신경 쓰다, 연연하다

To be worried about or affected negatively by something

Are you still **hung up** on that girl?

너 아직도 그 여자애한테 연연하는 거야?

give up

포기하다

To lose hope;
To stop doing something out of hopelessness or frustration

After three hours of trying to fix my car, I just **gave up** and took it to the auto repair shop.

세 시간 동안 차를 고치려고 했다가, 난 결국 포기하고 정비소에 가지고 갔어.

come over

엄습하다, (감정이) 영향을 미치다

To happen to;
To affect

I'm so sorry about that. I don't know what **came over** me.

그건 정말 죄송해요. 도대체 제가 뭐에 홀려서 그랬는지 모르겠어요.

shake up

(감정을) 흔들다, 힘들게 하다

To startle or scare someone to the point that they are affected for a long period of time

Hearing ghost stories can **shake** people **up** to the point that they cannot sleep.

귀신 이야기를 듣고 어떤 사람들은 힘들어져서 잠을 못 자기도 해요.

SHORT DIALOGUE 3

Zachary   Man. Today was difficult. I think I'm still **hung up** on losing Valerie.

Juliana   She moved out ten months ago. You'll find another girlfriend. You just need to start searching. Don't **give up**.

Zachary   But I loved her so much! It's so hard to cope with this terrible depression that has **come over** me.

Juliana   I understand. Getting your heart broken can really **shake** someone **up**. But you have to move on.

Zachary   아, 오늘 힘들었어. 아직도 Valerie와 깨진 것이 마음에 걸리고 신경이 쓰여.
Juliana   Valerie는 이미 10개월 전에 나갔어. 다른 여자 친구를 찾을 거야. 일단 찾기 시작해야 한다고. 포기하지 말고.
Zachary   그렇지만 난 Valerie를 정말 사랑했어! 나를 엄습하는 이 끔찍한 우울감을 어떻게 하는 게 정말 힘들어.
Juliana   이해해. 마음이 무너지는 고통은 정말 누군가를 흔들어 놓을 수 있어. 하지만 잊고 나아가야지.

LONG DIALOGUE

George: 너 뭐 하는 거야? 여기서 불 피우면 안 돼!

— Louise: 물러서! 네가 화상 입는 거 보고 싶지 않으니. 그리고 난 내가 원하는 건 뭐든 할 수 있어. 매번 나한테 화내고 비난할 필요는 없잖아.

George: 이렇게 흥분해서 이런 위험한 일을 하면 안 된다고 말하는 거야.

— Louise: 여기에 화덕이 있는 것도 아니고. 왜 그러는 건데? 이게 왜 위험하다는 거야? 내가 다 알아서 잘 한다고. 너 너무 무서워한다. 뭐가 그렇게 큰 문제야?

George: 뭐가 그렇게 큰 문제냐고? 네가 큰 산불을 낼 수도 있었어! 최근에 네가 바보 같은 행동을 많이 하고 있는데. 위험한 걸 하고 싶다는 충동이 절제가 안 되니?

— Louise: 그러면 넌 나한테 항상 뭘 하라고 말하는 충동이 절제가 안 되니? 매번 사람들한테 이래라저래라 하는 거 좋아하잖아!

George: 미안해! 널 깎아내리려는 게 아니야! 그냥 네가 걱정돼서 그러는 거지. 뭔가 힘들어서 이렇게 행동하는 거니?

— Louise: 나도 몰라! 어쩌면… 최근에 많은 것이 날 힘들게 하고 있어.

George: 네 감정을 계속 억눌러 온 것 같아. 보니까 눈물도 참으려고 하고. 나랑 같이 들어가서 얘기 좀 할래? 위험한 행동을 하는 게 네 감정을 다스리는 좋은 방법은 아니야.

George: What are you doing? You can't make a fire out here!

— **Louise: Stay back**! I don't want you to get yourself burned. And I can do whatever I want. You don't have to **lay into** me all the time.

George: I'm just saying you can't just **get carried away** and do dangerous stuff like this.

— **Louise:** We don't have a fire pit out here. What **came over** you? Why is this dangerous? I have it under control. You're so **shaken up**! What's the big deal?

George: What's the big deal? You could have started a forest fire! You know, you've been doing a lot of stupid stuff lately. Can you not **fight against** the urge to do dangerous things?

— **Louise:** And can you not **keep down** the urge to tell me what to do all the time? You just love **ordering** people **around**!

George: I'm sorry! I'm not trying to **put** you **down**! I'm just worried about you. Are you behaving like this because you're **struggling with** something?

— **Louise:** I don't know! Maybe… A lot has been **weighing on** me lately.

George: It sounds like you've been **bottling up** your emotions… and now I can see you're **choking back** tears. Why don't you come inside, and we can talk? Doing dangerous things is not a good way to deal with your emotions.

botch up

망치다

To mess up; To ruin

The surgeon **botched up** my knee surgery, and now I can't walk!

그 외과 의사가 내 무릎 수술을 망쳐 놓아서 이제 걸을 수가 없어!

slip up

실수하다

To make a mistake

Don't be afraid to **slip up**! We all make mistakes sometimes.

실수하는 것을 두려워하지 마세요! 우리 모두 가끔은 실수를 하잖아요.

screw up

실수하다, 망치다

To make a mistake;
To fail

I **screwed up** my interview yesterday. What should I do now?

나 어제 인터뷰 망쳤어. 이제 어떻게 해야 하지?

get back

복수하다, 되갚아 주다

To do something unpleasant to someone because they have done something unpleasant

I will **get** you **back** for that!

내가 너에게 그것 되갚아 줄 거야!

SHORT DIALOGUE 1

Bailey   Oh no! George is going to be so upset with me. I completely **botched up** our project.

Gavin   I'm sure it'll be okay. George **screws up** all the time, so he can't be that mad.

Bailey   No, lately I've been the one who keeps **slipping up**, and you know how vengeful he can get if you're on his bad side.

Gavin   You really think he'd try to **get** you **back** somehow? I mean he does have a temper, but surely he wouldn't overreact like that, right?

Bailey   아, 안 돼! George가 나한테 엄청 화낼 거야. 내가 우리 프로젝트 완전히 망쳐 버렸어.

Gavin   괜찮을 거야. George도 항상 망치곤 하니까, 그렇게 화낼 리 없어.

Bailey   아냐, 최근에는 계속 실수하는 건 나거든. 그리고 George의 안 좋은 점을 건드리면, 걔가 얼마나 복수심에 불탈지 너도 알잖아.

Gavin   정말 걔가 어떻게든 너한테 되갚아 주려고 할 거라고 생각하는 거야? 걔가 성깔이 있긴 하지만, 그렇게 과민 반응하지는 않을 거야. 알았어?

close off

차단하다, 고립시키다

To avoid emotional connection with others;
To isolate

Sadly, Jane **closed** herself **off** even more after the divorce.

슬프게도, Jane은 이혼 후 스스로를 더 고립시켰다.

throw out

버리다

To dispose of something

Throw out that old coat. You've been wearing for more than 10 years.

그 낡은 코트 좀 버려라. 10년 넘게 입었잖아.

brush aside

무시하다, 가볍게 여기다

To disregard something; To give something little or no importance

Even though students complained about his class, he **brushed** them **aside** and kept going.

학생들이 그의 강의에 대해서 불평을 했지만, 그는 무시하고 계속 진행했다.

fall apart

무너져 버리다

To lose one's capacity to cope

My mother **fell apart** when my father left us.

아버지가 우리를 떠났을 때 어머니는 무너져 버렸다.

SHORT DIALOGUE 2

Professor Are you okay? You're **closing** yourself **off** more in class and you haven't turned in your final essay.

Hope I'm sorry. I've been distracted with some stuff in my personal life, and I accidentally **threw out** all my notes.

Professor Personal issues are hard to **brush aside**, but we can't **fall apart** every time things get difficult. I can give you more time on your essay.

Hope Thank you. I really appreciate that.

Professor 괜찮니? 예전보다 더 수업에 참여도 안 하고, 최종 에세이도 아직 제출하지 않았네.
Hope 죄송해요. 개인적인 일로 정신이 없었어요. 그리고 실수로 노트를 다 버렸어요.
Professor 개인적인 문제는 무시하고 넘어가기가 쉽지 않지. 하지만 매번 상황이 어려울 때마다 무너질 수는 없어. 에세이 쓰는 시간을 더 주겠네.
Hope 고맙습니다. 정말 감사드려요.

disapprove of

반대하다, 못마땅해하다

To express disdain
for something in
particular; To not
accept something

I know that my father **disapproves
of** my new boyfriend, but I love him.

아빠가 내 새 남자 친구를 못마땅하게 여기는 것은
알지만, 나는 그를 사랑해.

fall for

홀랑 속아 넘어가다

To be tricked by

I pretended to be a beginner, and
you totally **fell for** it!

내가 초보자인 척했는데, 너 완전히 속았구나!

act out

못된 짓을 하다

To misbehave;
To behave
inappropriately

When children **act out**, it sometimes
means their lives are a mess.

아이들이 문제 행동을 할 때, 그것은 때때로 아이들의
가정생활에 문제가 있다는 것을 의미한다.

throw away

버리다

To discard something
as unwanted

Don't **throw away** the manual. I
need it.

그 설명서 버리지 마. 난 그것 필요해.

SHORT DIALOGUE 3

Teacher I **disapprove of** your son's behavior in my class. That's why I wanted to talk to
you.

Parent I apologize. What has he been doing?

Teacher Lately, he has been **acting out** for attention. For example, today he **threw away**
the other student's art projects. How has he been at home?

Parent I had no idea! He told me everything at school was going great. I guess I've been
falling for his act without realizing there was a problem.

Teacher 제 수업에서 아드님의 행동에 문제가 있습니다. 그래서 부모님께 말씀드리고 싶었습니다.
Parent 죄송합니다. 그 애가 어떤 행동을 했나요?
Teacher 최근에, 관심을 받기 위해서 적절하지 않은 행동을 했어요. 예를 들면, 오늘 다른 학생의 미술
프로젝트를 던져 버렸어요. 집에서는 어떤가요?
Parent 전혀 몰랐어요! 아들이 학교에서 정말 잘 지낸다고 했거든요. 문제가 있다는 것을 모르고, 세가
아무래도 아들아이에게 속은 것 같네요.

MP3 **087**

eat away at

조금씩 힘들게 하다, 괴롭게 하다

To cause persistent anxiety or distress to someone

The disease was **eating away at** Jane's body and she eventually died.

그 병은 Jane의 몸을 조금씩 쇠약하게 했고, 결국 Jane이 사망했다.

spill over

번지다, 여파를 미치다

To start to affect another situation or group of people negatively

The stress at work can sometimes **spill over** into our personal life.

직장 내 스트레스는 때때로 우리 사생활에도 영향을 미친다.

reduce to

줄어서 ~이 되다

To shrink to a smaller or weaker state

After the war, the city was **reduced to** ashes.

전쟁 후에 그 도시는 잿더미가 되었다.

mess with

(악의 없이) 놀리다, 장난하다

To tease someone, especially in a playful or good-natured way

What? I got accepted to Harvard? Stop **messing with** me!

뭐? 내가 하버드에 합격했다고? 나한테 장난 그만해!

SHORT DIALOGUE 1

Martin I have to talk to you about something. It's been **eating away at** me for a while.

Stella Let's hear it. You have been distracted lately, and it has **spilled over** into your work.

Martin Yes, and I'm sorry that our sales have been **reduced to** almost nothing lately. The truth is, our company has gone under. There's nothing left.

Stella No way! You must be **messing with** me! That can't be true!

> **Martin** 나 너한테 해야 할 말이 있어. 한동안 날 힘들게 했던 일이야.
> **Stella** 한번 들어 보자. 너 요즘 들어 정신이 없어 보였어. 그리고 그게 네 일에도 영향을 미치고 있고.
> **Martin** 응. 그리고 최근 우리 매출이 줄어들어 거의 없다시피 해서 안타깝고, 사실은 말야, 우리 회사가 파산했어. 남은 게 아무것도 없어.
> **Stella** 말도 안 돼! 너 나랑 장난하는 거지. 사실일 리가 없잖아!

miss out on

기회를 놓치다

To miss an opportunity

I **missed out on** a great opportunity to start a business.

난 사업을 시작할 수 있는 좋은 기회를 놓쳤다.

tie down

구속하다, 속박하다

To burden;
To inhibit

I'm **tied down** with too much work.

난 너무 많은 일에 얽매여 있어 옴쭉달싹 못한다.

take away

뺏다, 빼앗아 가다

To steal or confiscate

If you delay your mortgage payment for more than three months, your house will be **taken away**.

주택 담보 대출 상환을 3개월 이상 연체하면 집을 빼앗길 것이다.

fade away

조금씩 사라지다

To gradually disappear

The scar is starting to **fade away**.

흉터가 조금씩 사라지기 시작하고 있어.

SHORT DIALOGUE 2

Sandy   Since I've started working weekends, I've **missed out on** so much. I never see my friends anymore.

Fiona   I understand that. I used to have a job that **tied** me **down** every weekend.

Sandy   Maybe I should start applying for a job that doesn't **take away** so much of my time.

Fiona   I hope that works out for you. I'd like to hang out with you more often. I don't want our friendship to **fade away**.

> **Sandy**   내가 주말마다 일을 시작한 이후로, 너무 많은 것을 놓치고 있어. 이제는 친구들을 전혀 못 만나.
> **Fiona**   나도 그게 뭔지 알지. 나도 주말마다 일하느라 꼼짝도 못 하기 했으니까.
> **Sandy**   내 시간을 너무 많이 뺏지 않는 일을 구해 봐야 할 것 같아.
> **Fiona**   그렇게 되면 좋겠다. 너랑 좀 더 자주 어울리고 싶으니까. 우리의 우정이 식지 않았으면 해.

MP3 **088**

lighten up
분위기를 밝게 하다, 마음을 가볍게 하다

To make lighter;
To reduce the level
of stress

Joe made a joke to **lighten up** the
conversation.
Joe는 대화의 분위기를 띄우기 위해 농담을 했다.

live up to
기대에 부응하다, 만족시키다

To meet expectations

I didn't **live up to** my parents'
expectations.
나는 부모님의 기대에 부응하지 못했다.

hold out
기대하다, 희망을 가지다

To be hopeful or
optimistic

I don't **hold out** any hope that the
housing price will go back up again.
나는 집값이 다시 올라갈 거라고는 기대하지 않아요.

pick up
기분을 좋게 하다

To make someone
feel more energetic
and cheerful

Thanks for the gift; it really **picked
me up**.
선물 고마워요. 그것 때문에 정말 기운이 났어요.

SHORT DIALOGUE 1

Jan   I have some great news that will really **lighten up** your mood. The food festival is this weekend!

Fredrick   Last year definitely **lived up to** our expectations. I hope this year will be similar.

Jan   Well, I'm **holding out** hope that it will be even better than last year.

Fredrick   I can't wait. This will be really fun! You're right. This has really **picked** me **up**.

Jan   널 정말 기분 좋게 할 좋은 소식이 있어. 음식 축제가 이번 주말이야!
Fredrick   작년은 정말 우리 기대만큼 좋았는데. 금년도 비슷하면 좋겠다.
Jan   난 이번이 작년보다 훨씬 더 멋질 거라고 희망을 품고 있는데.
Fredrick   얼른 가 보고 싶어. 정말 재미있을 거야! 네 말이 맞네. 이 소식을 들으니까 정말 기분이 좋아졌어.

clear up

(문제, 오해 등을) 풀다, 해결하다

To mend; To settle a dispute or disagreement

I had a bad relationship with my wife until we **cleared** everything **up** after a huge fight.

크게 싸우고 나서 모든 것을 풀 때까지, 난 아내와 사이가 좋지 않았다.

move forward

(좋은 결과를 향해) 앞으로 나아가다, 진척시키다

To make something develop towards a good result

Do you have time to **move forward** with this project?

당신은 이 프로젝트를 진척시킬 시간이 있습니까?

turn into

변화하다

To transform; To change

Learning a new language sometimes **turns into** a chore.

새로운 언어를 배우는 것이 가끔은 귀찮은 일이 되기도 한다.

set up

준비하다, 계획하다

To prepare; To plan

Set yourself **up** for a productive year ahead.

생산적인 한 해를 위해서 미리 준비하세요.

SHORT DIALOGUE 2

Diane   I **cleared up** everything with my boss. I think things will be better at work now.

Dean   I'm glad it worked out well. Does this mean she will **move forward** with the plans you submitted?

Diane   I think she will. At first, she didn't take my proposal well, but then it **turned into** a good conversation.

Dean   That's great. Hopefully, having a better relationship with your boss will **set** you **up** for success.

Diane   나 상사하고 모든 걸 다 풀었어. 이제 직장 일이 훨씬 더 나아질 것 같아.
Dean   잘 해결되었다니 다행이다. 그럼 네가 제출한 기획으로 그분이 진행할 거라는 거야?
Diane   그럴 거야. 처음에는 내 제안을 잘 받아들이지 못했는데, 분위기 좋게 대화가 잘 진행됐어.
Dean   잘됐네. 상사와의 좋은 관계가 네가 성공하는 데 발판이 되면 좋겠어.

look forward to

기대하다, 고대하다

To be excited for something in the future

I'm **looking forward to** seeing my favorite band perform live!
내가 가장 좋아하는 밴드의 라이브 공연이 넘 기대돼!

cater towards

만족을 주다

To behave with care for someone's needs or desire

The book was **catered towards** children, but I enjoyed it anyway!
그 책은 아이들을 위한 거였지만, 어쨌든 전 재미있었어요!

lead up to

~에 이르다

To precede and cause

We trained very hard with a coach for months **leading up to** the performance.
우리는 공연 때까지 몇 달 동안 코치와 함께 정말 열심히 훈련했다.

cool down

차분해지다, 화를 가라앉히다

To become calm, or less stressed

I think Jane needs some time to **cool down**.
Jane이 화를 가라앉힐 시간이 좀 필요할 거야.

SHORT DIALOGUE 3

Todd   I'm really **looking forward to** Sal and Jean's wedding next Saturday. Do you think they will have Korean BBQ?

Annie   I don't know, but I doubt they are **catering** just **towards** your tastes.

Todd   You know they must be stressed. There is a lot to do in the days **leading up to** a wedding.

Annie   Luckily, they will get to **cool down** for a few days before they leave for their honeymoon.

Todd   다음 주 토요일 Sal하고 Jean의 결혼식이 정말 기대된다. 그때 한국식 바비큐가 나올까?
Annie   잘 모르겠어. 그런데 걔들이 네 취향에 맞게 음식을 준비할 거라고는 생각하지 않아.
Todd   너도 알다시피, 걔네들 스트레스 많이 받을 거야. 결혼식을 앞두고 며칠은 해야 할 일이 많거든.
Annie   다행히, 신혼여행을 떠나기 전에 며칠은 차분히 마음 가라앉힐 수 있을 거야.

shine through

빛을 발하다

> To be obvious or
> apparent, especially in
> terms of good qualities

How can I let my passion really
shine through?

어떻게 하면 제 열정이 빛을 발하게 할 수 있을까요?

get along

잘 지내다, 어울려 지내다

> To have a good
> relationship

We **got along** pretty well from the
beginning.

우리는 처음부터 꽤 잘 지냈다.

light up

(갑자기) 행복해 보이다,
빛이 나다

> To show happiness
> or excitement

His face **lights up** with joy
whenever he sees his family.

가족을 볼 때마다 그의 얼굴은 기쁨으로 밝아진다.

iron out

해결하다, 세부사항을 처리하다

> To solve problems,
> remove differences, or
> take care of details to
> complete something

We need to **iron out** a few issues, but
we're almost done with the project.

우리는 몇 가지 문제를 해결해야 하지만,
그 프로젝트를 거의 끝냈다.

SHORT DIALOGUE 1

David   I ran into Janice the other day. She seems happy. Her confidence was really
shining through.

Nancy   That's good to hear. I always **got along** well with her.

David   I know! A smile **lit up** her face when I mentioned you. On that note, she asked
if we wanted to get together with her next week.

Nancy   I'd be happy to see her. I'll call her up to **iron out** the details.

> David   나 요전 날 Janice랑 마주쳤어. 행복해 보이더라. 자신감으로 정말 빛이 나던데.
> Nancy   듣던 중 반가운 소리네. 나 항상 걔랑 잘 지냈잖아.
> David   알지! 내가 네 얘기 하니까 얼굴이 밝아지더라고. 그래서 말인데, 다음 주에 Janice가 함께 만나고
> 싶은지 물어보더라.
> Nancy   보면 너무 좋지. 내가 전화해서 자세한 거 정할게.

devote to

~에 몰두하다, 전념하다

To commit or give
a lot of energy to
a person or cause

You should **devote** at least two
hours **to** this task.

당신은 이 일에 적어도 두 시간은 전념해야 합니다.

melt away

차츰 사라지다

To disappear
gradually

When you hold my hand, all of my
fear **melts away**.

네가 내 손을 잡으면, 내 모든 두려움이 사라져.

make (it) up to

만회하다, 보답하다

To compensate
someone for
negligent or
unfair treatment

I'm sorry for yelling at you. I'll **make** it
up to you by getting you ice cream.

너한테 소리 질러서 미안해. 내가 아이스크림 사는
걸로 만회할게.

come on

자! 어서! 서둘러!

To encourage someone
to hurry up or to
follow the speaker

Come on! Let's go!
자! 어서 가자고!

SHORT DIALOGUE 2

Greeter Welcome to our retreat! Now you will be able to **devote** yourself **to** healing,
positivity, and getting back into nature.

Kendra Thanks! I'm ready for all of my stress to just **melt away**. Are there any spots left
on the sunrise hike?

Greeter I'm sorry, no. But I can **make** it **up to** you by offering this care package. **Come
on**! Follow me. I'll show you where to go.

Kendra That sounds great! After you.

> Greeter 저희 수련원에 오신 것을 환영합니다. 이제는 스스로 치유, 긍정, 그리고 자연으로 돌아가는 데
> 집중하실 수 있을 거예요.
> Kendra 고맙습니다! 제 모든 스트레스가 사라질 준비가 되었습니다. 혹시 일출 등반에 남은 자리가 있을까요?
> Greeter 죄송하지만, 없습니다. 하지만 제가 이 치료 패키지를 제공해서 보상할게요. 자, 절 따라오세요! 제가
> 어디로 가야 하는지 안내해 드리겠습니다.
> Kendra 좋습니다! 먼저 가시죠.

LONG DIALOGUE

Edward: 나 드디어 소설 집필을 끝냈어. 처음에는, 네 충고가 도움이 될 거라 생각 안 했는데, 네가 말한 것이 나를 괴롭히기 시작했어. 그러고 나서 결국 너의 충고를 따르기로 했지.

—— **Lacy:** 그래서 내가 말한 대로 해서 안 좋고, 무서운 부분은 다 스토리에서 빼 버린 거야?

Edward: 완전히 빼진 않았어. 그래도, 결국 모든 게 행복하게 결말이 나. 내가 계속 결말을 망치다 보니까 부정적인 생각이 날 옥죄고 있다는 생각이 퍼뜩 들더라고.

—— **Lacy:** 그 부정적인 생각이 완벽한 결말로 빛이 발하도록 하는 걸 가로막은 것 같네.

Edward: 이제 몇 가지 문제를 해결해야 하는데. 그러고 나면 출판을 진행할 수 있어.

—— **Lacy:** 빨리 읽어 보고 싶어. 분명히 대단할 거야.

Edward: 네 기대에 부합하면 좋겠다. 네 마음에 안 들 수도 있어!

—— **Lacy:** 정말 멋진 책일 거라는 생각을 고수할 거야. 봤지? 난 긍정적으로 생각하잖아.

Edward: 그만 좀 놀려라!

—— **Lacy:** 놀리는 거 아닌데! 그렇게 딱 차단하지 말고 장난할 때는 좀 받아들여. 나 정말로 네 책 읽게 돼서 아주 신난다고.

MP3 090

Edward: I finally finished writing my novel. At first, I didn't think your advice would help me, but then what you said started **eating away at** me. And then I decided to follow it.

— Lacy: So, you did what I said, and you **threw out** all the bad and scary parts of the story?

Edward: Not completely. But it all turns out happy in the end. Actually, I kept **botching up** the ending until I realized that my negativity was **tying** me **down**.

— Lacy: I guess that negativity was preventing you from letting the perfect ending **shine through**.

Edward: Now I just have to **iron out** a few issues, and then I can **move forward** with publishing it.

— Lacy: I'm **looking forward to** reading it. I'm sure it will be great.

Edward: I hope it **lives up to** your expectations. Maybe you won't like it!

— Lacy: I'm **holding out** hope that it'll be an amazing book. See? I'm thinking positively.

Edward: Stop **messing with** me!

— Lacy: I'm not! Stop **closing** yourself **off**. I'm actually very excited to read your book.

LONG DIALOGUE　265

INDEX

A

B

C

W